SOFTWARE DEBUGGING
FOR MICROCOMPUTERS

SOFTWARE DEBUGGING FOR MICROCOMPUTERS

Robert C. Bruce

RESTON PUBLISHING COMPANY, INC.
A Prentice-Hall Company
Reston, Virginia

Library of Congress Cataloging in Publication Data

Bruce, Robert
  Software debugging for microcomputers.

  Includes index.
  1. Microcomputers—Programming. 2. Debugging
in computer science. I. Title.
QA76.6.B776   001.6′4   79-19113
ISBN 0-8359-7021-3
ISBN 0-8359-7020-5 pbk.

© 1980 by
Reston Publishing Company, Inc.
A Prentice-Hall Company
Reston, Virginia 22090

10 9 8 7 6 5 4 3

Printed in the United States of America.

*This book is dedicated to my partner in life,
my strongest supporter and severest critic,
my wife Valerie.*

CONTENTS

Flowcharts are the best starting point for unlocking the mysteries of an unknown program prior to its debugging. This chapter examines the basic symbolism of flowcharts and illustrates their use in representing a computer program's path of execution. Many bugs are related to improper program construction; flowcharting is a technique which graphically pinpoints these errors.

Preventing errors is as much a part of debugging as correcting errors. Many bugs are caused by a programmer's incomplete or incorrect understanding of what a line of code, a block of code, or even an entire subroutine's worth of code is trying to accomplish. This is especially true if a person other than the original author of a piece of code must attempt its debugging. This chapter examines documentation, the process of labelling code with informative remarks, as an aid in bug prevention.

The most accurate method of debugging, although also the most tedious, is that of playing computer. This chapter tells how to play computer: how to go through a sequence of code step by step, following the changing status of indexes and variables, literally doing by hand with pencil and paper what a computer does electronically. The task may be difficult, but it provides a programmer with a rare closeness and insight into the minute workings of his code. The understanding thus gained often leads to a much lower error rate on the part of the programmer.

4. PRINT STATEMENTS   102

The essential aim of a programmer debugging a program is to pull information from the hidden interior of a computer out into the light of the real world where it can be examined and analyzed. Print statements admirably fill this need. There is very little that can go wrong with a print statement, making it a relatively harmless addition to a questionably functioning program. This chapter looks at print statements, their use, and their occasional misuse, and provides pointers on their capabilities and limitations.

5. FORCING   124

One object of debugging is to do the job as simply as possible. Especially when the program involves a lot of mathematical computations or conditional branches, the urge is to simplify the testing and check-out procedure. One way to simplify the check-out of a program is to reduce as many computations as possible to either zero or one, thus making it easier to predict the exact result of a program. In those instances when the actual results differ from the expected results, a bug is almost certainly to blame, and by purposely channelling the flow of execution (forcing it down certain paths to the exclusion of all others) the bug is usually smoked out with little trouble. This chapter discusses the techniques and applications of forcing.

6. BLOCK DEBUGGING   149

Programs increase in complexity from straight-line mini-programs to multiple-pathway, many-branched, many-subroutined monsters. Block debugging, the subject of this chapter, is one method particularly suited to finding and correcting errors in large, segmented programs. This technique examines each subroutine individually, out of the context of the main program, and tests it using dummy routines and special purpose supervisor programs called driver routines. A debugging method especially useful to programs written according to the rules of structured programming, block debugging is convenient and affords the programmer significant control over the program under examination.

7. SNAPSHOTS 191

Complicated programs don't necessarily contain complicated bugs, but they do provide better hiding places for the bugs that they do contain. This can often be translated into a program failure with no particular clues as to its cause. Print statements are the programmer's viewports into a program's inner workings, but if the program uses a large number of variables, or has a number of possible execution paths, covering all potential trouble spots might very well lead to a doubling of program length due just to print statements. Enter the snapshot, the subject of this chapter. The snapshot gathers together a large amount of diagnostic information, formats it for easy readability, and then displays it as a coherent whole. Snapshots give a dynamic, rather than an after-the-fact static view of program operation, while still allowing the programmer to take as much time as necessary to analyze each display, a capability not usually associated with straight print statements.

8. DESIGNING-IN 227

A program debugged for one environment and one particular set of circumstances may not work once the environment is changed. Forcing attempts to solve this by testing all possible execution paths, but as the paths become more numerous, forcing becomes less effective and applicable simply due to the effort involved. Block debugging tries to tackle the same problem by testing each subroutine separately: if the parts all work, so must the whole. But this is sometimes shaky reasoning, a false sense of security; there may be communication problems between subroutines not known and therefore not addressed by block debugging. This chapter discusses a possible remedy: designing-in. Designing-in does not cure bugs, but it makes their future discovery easier by loading a program with "sleeping" debug statements, ready to be awakened at the first sign of trouble.

9. PATCHES 279

Sometimes, despite all the best efforts of the debugger's art, a bug still escapes. Usually this is most frequently seen in simulation or game programs, in which the program structure looks more like a fishnet than a tree. In such programs, where each computation can influence the direction of the program's flow of execution, it is very difficult to apply systematic debugging methods such as forcing and block debugging and get complete success. This chapter discusses the final remedy: patches. Also known as "kluges" or "band-aids," patches heal over a rough spot of code without eliminating the bug which actually caused the problem. Far from being a cop-out, however, it takes a sure understanding of what the particular program is doing and what effect a patch will have before a programmer can safely use this last-ditch method.

Rarely can a program be debugged using exclusively one technique. More typically, various subparts of a program will react to different approaches with varying degrees of success. This chapter takes the reader through a typical debugging effort, pointing out along the way some of the most often encountered types of bugs, and illustrating how a programmer uses all the tools available to effect an accurate and solid cure in as short a time as possible.

Decimal to binary/octal conversion table

ACKNOWLEDGMENTS

I would like to acknowledge the kind and generous cooperation of Processor Technology, Inc., which provided me with a Sol/20 microcomputer with 32K of memory. I made extensive use of their product and it never once disappointed me; every program appearing in this book has been tested on the Sol, and each performed exactly as described in the various examples.

I would also like to thank the following people who, each in their own way and in their own times, have helped guide my steps when I was most in doubt: Mr. Arnold Nudell; Dr. Phillip Sheeler; and, of course, my parents.

INTRODUCTION

This is a book about debugging. Its purpose is to illustrate how, in a programming effort using a high level language such as BASIC (as opposed to the more primitive assembly language level), bugs are discovered, tracked down to their source, and eradicated. A "bug," in the context of computer programming, is a term used to describe an incorrectly functioning program. "Debugging," then, is the process of curing such errors.

Of necessity the debugging task falls to the programmer, who may or may not be the person who originally wrote the program in question. Preferably all bugs are discovered and corrected in the program development and shakedown stage, although frequently bugs are discovered by the end user once the program is put into circulation. In the past, especially in the area of microcomputers but in the realm of mini and maxi computers as well, the end user and the original programmer were one and the same, or at least both were programmers. Today this is not so much the case. Computing power is becoming ubiquitous and all-pervasive, and users of microcomputer programs are likely not programmers. Also, there is an ever-increasing number of people who are computer programmers not by virtue of professional training or educational background; rather they have purchased a microcomputer, they have quickly tired of the packaged games that came with it, and they have decided to teach themselves programming (most frequently in BASIC) so that they might write their own customized application programs. To this group of users-turned-programmers, debugging will be a hard reality to face, but a necessary skill to learn if they are to advance beyond the most simplistic programs.

Accordingly, in certain chapters, and indeed in the book as a whole, it may seem that at times the text is addressing program designers on the one hand, and program users on the other. But whether designers or users, both groups are, in the end, *programmers;* the difference is at which point in the life cycle of a program the debugging effort is begun, since that is what affects the current label that we use to describe the programmer, not the other way around.

Techniques such as flowcharting, inserting comment statements, block debugging, and designing-in are more properly the domain of the program development and shakedown stage, but they can also be put to profitable use during the active utility stage of a program's life, especially if the program to be debugged lacks a flowchart and is devoid of internal documentation.

Playing computer, forcing, using PRINT statements either alone or in groups as a snapshot, and coding in patches if necessary are all techniques generally associated with the active utility stage, although they too find wide use in the program shakedown stage.

This book assumes a certain familiarity with BASIC although, in general, commands and concepts of the language are introduced and briefly discussed before they are applied to a particular example. The concepts of the book can be applied to debugging programs written in any language, however. Flowcharts, in-program comments, forcing, and playing computer are basic and valid debugging techniques for any language running on any computer. The remaining techniques are all, in essence, variations on the same theme: the PRINT statement.

The basic requirement when debugging a program (once it has reached the state of repeated trials on a running computer) is to pull information from the binary environment of the computer out to the alphanumeric environment of the computer programmer. To accomplish this transfer of information, all languages have some provisions for I/O (input/output), and it frequently appears as some variation of the PRINT or WRITE statement. In this manner, then, so may the remaining chapters be applied to other languages.

Textually, this book is divided into two general sections and a summary. The first section, encompassing the first five chapters, deals with basic debugging techniques—the tools of the trade. The second section uses the techniques just introduced in various combinations to illustrate certain applied debugging methods. The final chapter draws from the previous material to demonstrate the progress of a typical debugging effort. We see in the final chapter that oftentimes common sense is the best debugging tool of all.

Programming pros get where they are because they have written a lot of programs. They have also debugged a lot of programs. Experience brings wisdom, but it only rarely brings perfection; oldtimers who have been programming since the days of the first UNIVAC still manage to commit errors in their programs and wind up on a bug hunt.

As we become more familiar with a particular computer language, and as we log more and more programs to our credit, the percentage of obvious mistakes drops proportionately. However, long exposure to a particular language, especially when that language is being used to implement a complicated program in a limited amount of time, often leads to a peculiar form of mental blindness. When this affliction takes hold, many people will find that not even a book that endeavors to be as complete as this one will do them much good. For such cases there is yet one more technique which is not mentioned in this book, partly because it is so powerful that it would have overshadowed all of the other techniques, and partly because it is so simple that many readers would have been offended to have seen it allocated an entire chapter.

The technique is, simply, to show the program to someone else. That second party need not invariably be another programmer. If it is a fellow programmer, this person might readily see what has been invisible to you for so long; but often a nonprogrammer is the best choice of all. Explaining a computer program to one who understands little or nothing about computers forces a certain mental discipline and clarity of thought that might not otherwise be present.

Showing a program to a fellow programmer or explaining a program to absolutely anyone will frequently catch the majority of syntax and other language-related errors. For the remaining bugs—those caused by errors in logic or program construction—this book will hopefully be a guide and inspiration.

1.

FLOWCHARTS

The first step in writing a computer program is to list on paper all those tasks the program is expected to accomplish. This helps to organize thoughts and clarify objectives, and it gives the programmer a direction and a goal.

Debugging is not always performed after the fact; time spent catching potential bugs in the preliminary stage of program development could mean hours of time saved later on during the actual testing and shake-down stage. Writing a list of specifications can point up those goals which are unrealistic, whether due to lack of time or funds to tackle such an all-encompassing request or lack of programmer proficiency. Such a list may identify goals which are so trivial that it only seems reasonable to include increased capabilities into the proposed coding.

Writing up a specification sheet helps catch what we might call conceptual bugs: bugs caused by an unclear or incomplete understanding of what the program is supposed to do.

As an example, consider the following specification: "Write a program to monitor and control the needs of a house."

Chances are that no programmer would ever be handed such a vague instruction and then be asked to write a satisfactory code, but many people would unconsciously hand themselves just such a nebulous under-taking, assuming that they knew what they wanted and therefore had no need to spell it out.

Before embarking on a programming task, always endeavor to list what inputs will be available for the program, what the output should look like, and what the body of the program is to accomplish. If nothing else, this will save time once the actual programming begins. More than that, however, by clarifying in one's mind what the job at hand will involve, we can often sidestep the more elementary bugs such as reading from the wrong input port or calculating a number using the wrong conversion factor.

FLOWCHARTING THE ORIGINAL PROGRAM

Although the flowchart of Fig. 1-1 has a number of steps, its construction is simple since it proceeds along a straight line from a single beginning to a single end.

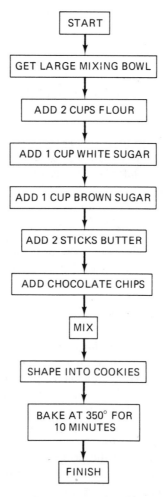

Fig. 1-1. Flowchart for the process of making cookies.

A flowchart is the intermediate step between a general description of a task and the specific step-by-step instructions required to accomplish the task.

Note the difference between the three levels of complication in the example of Fig. 1-2, in which the specification calls for a red wooden toybox about the size of a suitcase and sturdy enough for a young child to use.

Specification: Build a toybox out of wood and paint it red. The box should be about the size of a suitcase and sturdy enough for a child to use.

Flowchart:

START

↓

MARK DIMENSIONS ON WOOD

↓

CUT OUT PIECES

↓

ASSEMBLE TOYBOX

↓

PAINT THE WOOD

↓

FINISH

Program:

Step	Job
1.	Note to build a wooden toybox
2.	Make side = 18″ x 36″
3.	Make top/bottom = 24″ x 36″
4.	Make end = 24″ x 18″
5.	Get sheet of $\frac{1}{2}$″ plywood
6.	For each panel:
7.	Use a ruler
8.	Measure dimensions
9.	Mark on wood with pencil
10.	Next panel
	etc.

Fig. 1-2. Specification, flowchart, and "program" involved in making a child's toybox. Note that the program is not a computer program but a detailed sequence of steps.

The specification describes what the job will be and lists some of the qualities of the end result. The flowchart breaks the main job down into individual tasks and hooks them together in proper order. The "program" steps are the most specific of all: in Fig. 1-2, the program steps are detailed instructions as to the size of the various parts, what thickness of wood they should be, and so forth.

Because a flowchart is a graphic device, it finds wide use as a debugging aid both before and after a program is written. Drawing up a flowchart first, then using it as a guide when writing the program, catches many potential bugs before they have a chance to get written.

As an example, what if the toybox flowchart had been drawn as shown in Fig. 1-3.

This version of the toybox building program has a bug in it. The bug is not a "fatal" error, because the program would still cause a toybox to be built. But the toybox which resulted would be flawed. Since the first step had been to paint the wood, subsequent steps that called for the wood to be marked on and cut up with a saw would most likely cause the painted finish to be ruined.

If this were really a computer program, the toybox produced by following the form in Fig. 1-3 would be called "garbage output."

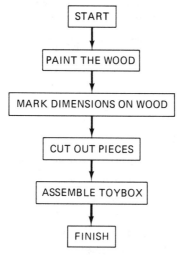

Fig. 1-3. Flowchart showing transposed sequence of events in toybox construction. This out-of-sequence flowchart introduces a bug.

Flowchart Building Blocks

So far, the flowchart examples we have seen have all been depicted as a series of linearly arranged boxes. Each box contains a description of what that step performs, and each box is connected to the box above it and below it by an arrow which symbolizes the program's order of execution.

Most programs do not, however, travel a single straight-line path from beginning to end. Programs frequently branch off into multiple paths, they use a loop to execute the same portion of code a number of times, and they leave the mainstream of program commands entirely, to execute an entire subroutine before returning.

The many options open to a programmer require more than one universal symbol if they are to be clearly depicted on a flowchart. Rectangles cannot represent everything; instead, they are reserved for command statements, such as:

CUT OUT PIECES

and

PAINT THE WOOD

A flowchart can also diagram the consequences of conditional tests. Diamonds are used to represent IF statements, as shown in Fig. 1-4.

Fig. 1-4. Conditional statements are represented on a flowchart as a diamond with two possible alternatives—a YES or a NO.

Loops are one of the most versatile concepts a programmer can make use of. Within a loop, a certain number of statements are executed as a block; the number of times the block of code is executed is governed by the value of an index variable, which increments by a specified amount each time the block is processed. When the index variable reaches a predetermined cutoff value, the block of code is skipped and the program re-

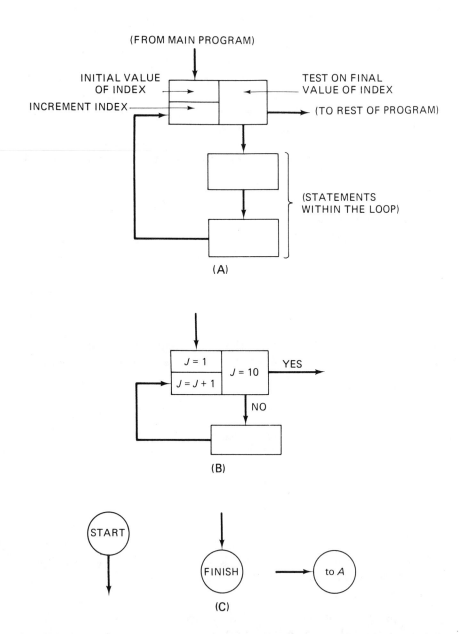

Fig. 1-5. Flowchart symbols. In (A), a flowchart loop shows that at least one set of conditions causes the program to return to a point already "visited." (B) shows the index symbol loop. The circle (C) shows "terminal" points in a program.

sumes executing with the statement immediately following the end of the block.

The general form of a flowchart loop is shown in Fig. 1-5(A). A typical index symbol is shown in Fig. 1-5(B). The final common flowchart symbol is the circle [Fig. 1-5(C)]. The third part of Fig. 1-5(C) (the encircled words "to *A*") would be used if the flowchart took up more than one piece of paper, or when diagramming a jump to a subroutine.

We can now put the three symbols—rectangle, diamond, and circle—together to form flowcharts. As we do, we will be able to see for ourselves the role that flowcharts play in the art of debugging.

Using the Flowchart Blocks

We will start by flowcharting a very simple task: obtain a series of 10 numbers from the terminal, and for each number, calculate its square, square root, cube, and cube root (Fig. 1-6).

This program will perform the same loop 10 times. Each time through the loop it reads in a number, finds the square, square root, cube, and cube root of that number, and then it will jump back up to the top of the loop, where it increments the loop counter; if the value of the index is less than the cutoff value, the loop executes again.

Or does it?

The variable *I* is being used as the index for the loop. The *I* variable

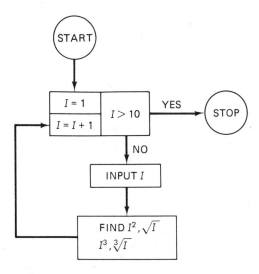

Fig. 1-6. Flowchart for obtaining 10 numbers and for calculating their squares, square roots, cubes, and cubic roots.

has an initial value of one and is incremented by one each time the loop is traversed; the loop is exited once the index becomes greater than 10—in other words, when $I = 11$. The loop is therefore executed 10 times, just as it should be.

But the value read in from the keyboard is read into the variable I. I has been previously reserved as the index variable, so this is a serious bug: the index variable must *never be changed by what goes on within the loop*. Obviously, if the first number read in was greater than 10, the program would exit the loop without having read in the correct number of values.

One way to fix the bug would be to revise the flowchart as shown in Fig. 1-7. Now at least the program will work correctly. But it still has a bug: there is no way for us to know what the various calculated quantities are because there is no output. To fix that bug, we could insert an additional command between the yes branch and the stop, as illustrated in Fig. 1-8.

Now the program goes through the loop 10 times, each time reading in a value which does not affect the contents of the index variable. And when it is all over, the program prints out the answer. Is the program all right now?

Unfortunately, since the print statement has been placed *outside* the loop, only one answer is displayed, corresponding to the last value read in. Moving the print statement into the loop (Fig. 1-9) would correct this latest bug:

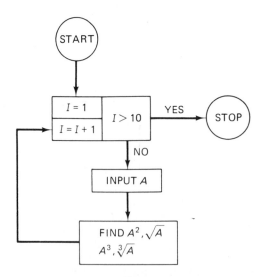

Fig. 1-7.   Revised flowchart to eliminate the bug.

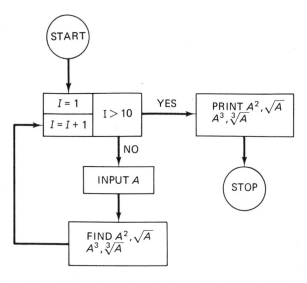

Fig. 1-8. The additional command between the YES branch and the STOP gives us the PRINT statement we need to correct our flowchart.

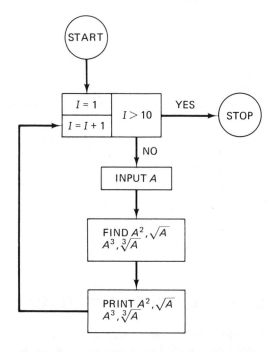

Fig. 1-9. Movement of the PRINT statement into the loop as a debug maneuver.

Finally, the program will work correctly. There is still a bug, but this one is "cosmetic" rather than fatal. The way the flowchart has the program structured, output would look something like:

```
PLEASE INPUT A NUMBER
?4
SQUARE IS 16.000
SQUARE ROOT IS 2.000
CUBE IS 64.000
CUBE ROOT IS 1.587
PLEASE INPUT A NUMBER
?2.48
SQUARE IS 6.150
SQUARE ROOT IS 1.575
CUBE IS 15.253
CUBE ROOT IS 1.354
PLEASE INPUT A NUMBER
     (etc.)
```

The output looks messy. Technically, the program is debugged (at least at the flowchart stage) because it does what it is supposed to do and it does it in the proper order. But esthetically, if the program were to be coded precisely as it is laid out in the flowchart, a conscientious programmer would still consider it to have a bug.

The final "structural" bug could be cured as in Fig. 1-10. If the program were coded exactly according to this revised flowchart, and if no syntactical or typographical errors were committed, the program would function perfectly and the output would look more presentable:

NUMBER	SQUARE	SQ. ROOT	CUBE	CUBE ROOT
4	16.000	2.000	64.000	1.587
2.48	6.150	1.575	15.253	1.354

FLOWCHARTING THE EXISTING PROGRAM

Drawing up a flowchart first—before composing any lines of code—is a good way to catch potential errors in program flow, which should be welcome news since such bugs are usually the hardest to locate.

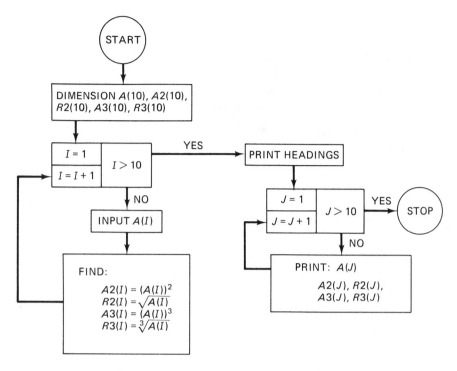

Fig. 1-10.   Curing the structural bug.

By the same token, generating a flowchart for an already written program is an excellent way to track down elusive bugs. The secret here is that since flowcharts are graphic representations of the flow of the program, bugs which can get lost in a jumble of statement numbers and conditional branches become glaringly obvious once drawn in picture form.

Take as an example the following program. Even though it is well documented, it is long enough and complicated enough that unless we resort to graphing it out, we might never discover the bug.

```
10 REM TRIP CONTROL PROGRAM FOR
20 REM GREAT CENTRAL MODEL RAILROAD
30 PRINT "WELCOME ABOARD THE GREAT CENTRAL"
40 PRINT "MODEL RAILWAY. HOW MANY"
50 PRINT "ROUND TRIPS TODAY?"
60 INPUT T
```

```
70 REM T IS THE TRIP COUNTER
80 REM LOOP TO DETERMINE TRAIN LOCATION
90 REM DATA PORTS ARE
100 REM 1=IN STATION
110 REM 2=NEARING SW 1 FROM INNER LOOP
120 REM 3=NEARING TIGHT TURN
130 REM 4=NEARING STRAIGHTAWAY
140 REM 5=NEARING SW 2
150 REM 6=NEARING X-ING
160 REM 7=ON X-ING
170 REM 8=NEARING SW 1 FROM OUTER LOOP
180 REM 9=NEARING STATION
190 REM 10=THROTTLE
200 REM 11=X-ING SIGNAL
210 REM 12=SW1
220 REM 13=SW2
225 LET N=1
230 FOR I=1 TO T
240 LET N=-N
250 LET A=INP(1)
260 IF A=255 THEN GOSUB 440
270 LET B=INP(2)
280 IF B=255 THEN GOSUB 530
290 LET C=INP(3)
300 IF C=255 THEN GOSUB 660
310 LET D=INP(4)
320 IF D=255 THEN GOSUB 750
330 LET E=INP(5)
340 IF E=255 THEN GOSUB 840
350 LET F=INP(6)
360 IF F=255 THEN GOSUB 950
370 LET G=INP(8)
380 IF G=255 THEN GOSUB 1080
390 LET H=INPUT(9)
400 IF H=255 THEN GOTO 1120
410 REM POSITION SENSOR ACTIVATED PUTS
420 REM ALL ONES (255) ON DATA LINES
```

```
430 GOTO 250
434 NEXT I
436 GOTO 1280
440 PRINT "ALL ABOARD"
450 REM WAIT FOR PASSENGERS TO BOARD
460 PAUSE 40
470 REM ACCELERATE OUT OF STATION TO SPEED 5
480 FOR J=1 TO 5
490 OUT 10, J
500 PAUSE 10
510 NEXT J
520 RETURN
530 REM NEARING SW 1
540 REM PULSE SW 1, ALL ONES
550 REM PULSES SW 1 TO INSIDE CIRCLE
560 OUT 12, 255
570 REM SLOW TRAIN ONE STEP
580 OUT 10, 4
590 REM HAVE WE CLEARED SENSOR 2 YET?
600 LET R=INP(2)
610 IF R>0 THEN GOTO 600
620 REM WAIT TO CLEAR SW 1 AND ACCEL.
630 PAUSE 10
640 OUT 10, 5
650 RETURN
660 REM NEARING RIGHT TURN
670 REM CUT TRAIN SPEED TO 2
680 FOR J=1 TO 3
690 LET S=INP(10)
700 LET S=S-1
710 OUT 10, S
720 PAUSE 10
730 NEXT J
740 RETURN
750 REM NEARING STRAIGHTAWAY
760 REM INCREASE SPEED TO 10
770 FOR J=1 TO 8
```

```
780 LET S=INP(10)
790 LET S=S+1
800 OUT 10, S
810 PAUSE 10
820 NEXT J
830 RETURN
840 REM NEARING SW 2
850 REM SET SW FOR OUTSIDE LOOP
860 IF T<0 THEN OUT 13, 0
870 REM CUT SPEED TO 5
880 FOR J=1 TO 5
890 LET S=INP(10)
900 LET S=S-1
910 OUT 10, S
920 PAUSE 10
930 NEXT J
940 RETURN
950 REM NEARING X-ING
960 REM SET WARNING FLASHER SWITCH
970 REM PORT 11 IS X-ING FLASHER
980 LET K=1
990 IF K>0 THEN GOTO 1020
1000 REM FLASHER ON
1010 OUT 11, 255
1020 PAUSE 5
1030 LET K=-K
1040 REM TEST IF WE HAVE CLEARED X-ING
1050 LET S=INP(7)
1060 IF S>0 THEN GOTO 990
1070 RETURN
1080 REM NEARING SW 1 FROM OUTSIDE
1090 REM SET SW 1 TO OUTSIDE
1100 OUT 12, 0
1110 RETURN
1120 REM NEARING STATION
1130 PRINT "NOW APPROACHING SMALLTOWN STATION"
1140 PRINT "SMALLTOWN, USA"
```

```
1150 REM SLOW TRAIN TO 1
1160 FOR J=1 TO 4
1170 LET S=INP(10)
1180 LET S=S−1
1190 OUT 10, S
1200 PAUSE 10
1210 NEXT J
1220 REM CHECK WHEN TRAIN MAKES STATION
1230 LET K=INP(1)
1240 IF K=0 THEN GOTO 1230
1250 REM STOP TRAIN
1260 OUT 10, 0
1270 GOTO 434
1280 PRINT "END OF TODAY'S RUN"
1290 END
```

At first glance, 129 lines of code may seem overpowering; but we will see that it only helps to point up the usefulness of flowcharting as a debugging tool.

Before we begin to generate our flowchart, we can learn a number of things about the program just by inspection. The program has been well documented, and we will use this documentation to our advantage as we go along.

We can tell, for instance, that the program seems to be divided into three distinct parts. The first part consists mainly of remarks explaining what the program is and what its assorted variables stand for. The second part is the main program (only about 15 lines long); and the third part consists of all those subroutines that were referenced in the main program.

Something which the program does not list, but which would be helpful to us as we try to visualize what is taking place, is a diagram of the track layout. The Great Central model railroad of the referenced program is shown schematically in Fig. 1-11.

The track has an inner route and an outer route. Both routes share a common side, the one which includes the tight turn and the straightaway. The inner loop passes by the station, where it must stop long enough for passengers to board and disembark. The outer loop carries the train through the manufacturing and business section of Smalltown.

The program was written to monitor and control the speed and location of the Great Central model railroad as it alternately traverses first the inner and then the outer loop of its right-of-way.

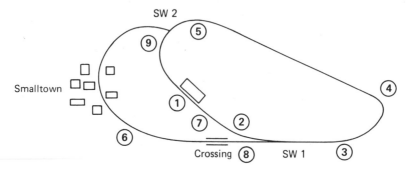

Fig. 1-11.   Layout of the Great Central model railroad.

In order to monitor the train's location, sensors have been set up at various points along the track. Actuators, which respond to a signal of 0 (all zeros) or 255 (all ones) on their data lines, have been installed on both switches and on the railroad crossing warning flashers.

We may assume that all required analog-to-digital interfacing has been properly attended to, and as a result the only bugs (there are two) are attributable to software.

We begin with the first part of the program, the explanatory section. Flowcharting this (Fig. 1-12) is trivial, since the computer does not actually perform very much.

The second part of the program, the main part, is also not difficult to graph. Each sensor in turn is interrogated; and if the sensor transmits an all-ones activated signal (numerical value equal to 255), then the program branches to the appropriate subroutine before it continues the cycling sensor interrogation.

We can draw this portion of the flowchart as shown in Fig. 1-13.

Since we were only trying to document the block of coding beginning at line 225 and ending at line 436, there were a few places that we were forced to leave blank. Specifically, we know that there is a NEXT statement to bracket the FOR statement:

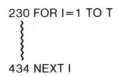

230 FOR I=1 TO T

434 NEXT I

But there is no statement in the block of coding we have just examined which sends the program down to line 434 so that the loop may be

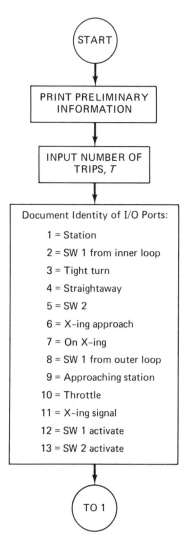

Fig. 1-12. Flowcharting the explanatory segment of the railroad program.

incremented. We assume, then, that unless this is the bug, statement 434 must be entered from some other point in the program. We signify this by having a transfer symbol feed into the incrementing section of the loop symbol.

We note that the eight conditional branches themselves form a loop. For each IF statement, if the condition is met, program flow is transferred to a subroutine. If the first condition is not met, the next one is tried, and

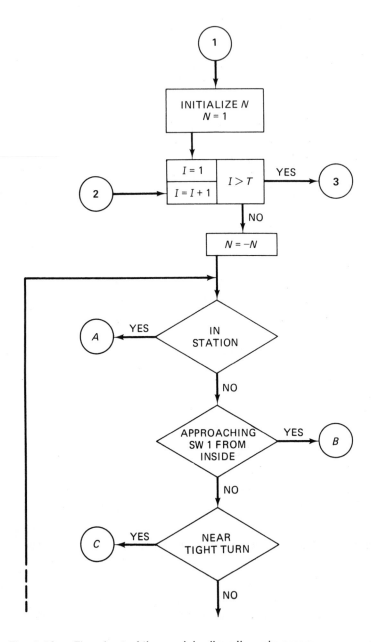

Fig. 1-13. Flowchart of the model railroad's main program.

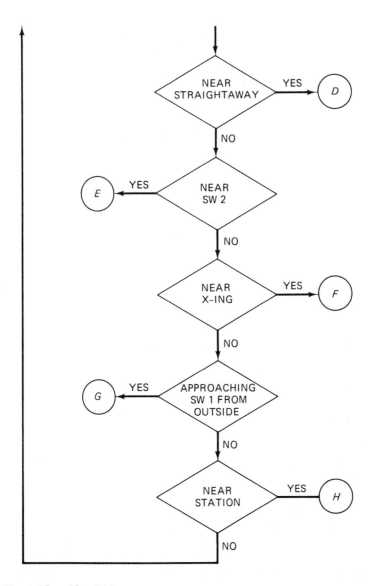

Fig. 1-13. *(Cont'd.)*

so on, apparently forever. This could be a bug: the program looks as though it is caught in an endless loop. Rather than jump to any conclusions, however, we should finish our flowcharting of the complete program.

There are seven subroutines, beginning at lines 440, 530, 660, 750, 840, 950, and 1080:

```
260 IF A=255 THEN GOSUB 440
280 IF B=255 THEN GOSUB 530
300 IF C=255 THEN GOSUB 660
320 IF D=255 THEN GOSUB 750
340 IF E=255 THEN GOSUB 840
360 IF F=255 THEN GOSUB 950
380 IF G=255 THEN GOSUB 1080
```

We will attempt to flowchart each in turn. Subroutine A, which begins at line 440, is entered if status switch 1, located in the station, reads positive:

```
440 PRINT "ALL ABOARD"
450 REM WAIT FOR PASSENGERS TO BOARD
460 PAUSE 40
470 REM ACCELERATE OUT OF STATION TO SPEED 5
480 FOR J=1 TO 5
490 OUT 10, J
500 PAUSE 10
510 NEXT J
520 RETURN
```

This subroutine prints an "all aboard" message and waits long enough for passengers to board the train. Then over a period of five seconds, the train pulls away from the station and increases its speed to 5 points (of a possible 10). We would diagram it as in Fig. 1-14.

Subroutine B, which begins at line 530 and ends at line 650, is called when the train is near switch 1, approaching from the inside curve. If the train is not to derail, the switch must be thrown up so that the tracks of the switch line up with the tracks of the inside loop. For both switch 1 and switch 2, the all-ones command (255) sets the switch to line up with the inside loop.

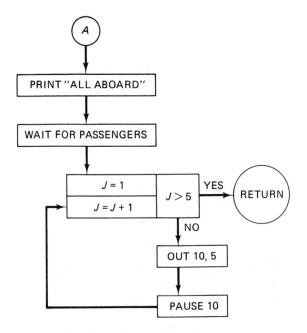

Fig. 1-14. Flowchart for "all aboard" subroutine.

The coding for subroutine B looks like this:

```
530 REM NEARING SW 1
540 REM PULSE SW 1, ALL ONES
550 REM PULSES SW 1 TO INSIDE CIRCLE
560 OUT 12, 255
570 REM SLOW TRAIN ONE STEP
580 OUT 10, 4
590 REM HAVE WE CLEARED SENSOR 2 YET?
600 LET R=INP(2)
610 IF R>0 THEN GOTO 600
620 REM WAIT TO CLEAR SW 1 AND ACCEL.
630 PAUSE 10
640 OUT 10, 5
650 RETURN
```

The flowchart for those 13 program lines that make up subroutine B has the appearance of Fig. 1-15.

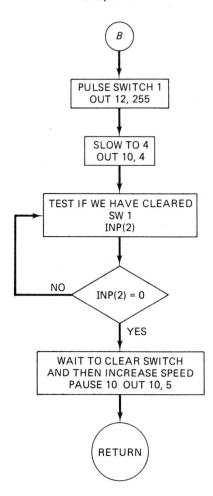

Fig. 1-15.   Flowchart for subroutine B.

The first thing that this subroutine does is to set the switch to the proper orientation so that when the train arrives at the junction it will move smoothly out onto the main loop and not become derailed.

We note that the "mini-loop" between steps three and four, where the subroutine cycles through, checks if station 2 reports all clear. Once the sensor reports clear, the train is given another second of traveling time (the argument for the PAUSE command is in tenths of a second) to allow it to clear the switch. Then the throttle is increased by a step.

Subroutine C slows the train enough to allow it to safely negotiate the tight turn just as subroutine D opens up the throttle to full power as the train enters the straightaway. The two subroutines are therefore nearly identical in construction and content, as this side-by-side comparison shows:

Subroutine C	Subroutine D
660 REM NEARING TIGHT TURN	750 REM NEARING STRAIGHTAWAY
670 REM CUT TRAIN SPEED TO 2	760 REM INCREASE SPEED TO 10
680 FOR J=1 TO 3	770 FOR J=1 TO 8
690 LET S=INP(10)	780 LET S=INP(10)
700 LET S=S−1	790 LET S=S+1
710 OUT 10, S	800 OUT 10, S
720 PAUSE 10	810 PAUSE 10
730 NEXT J	820 NEXT J
740 RETURN	830 RETURN

Each subroutine is essentially a short loop which uses the index variable to change the relative setting of the throttle (I/O PORT 10). In both cases, a supposition is made concerning the speed of the train as it enters the field of each sensor and thus as the program enters the domain of each subroutine. Subroutine C assumes the train is traveling at throttle setting 5, so that it can reduce the setting by 3 points to achieve a setting of 2. Subroutine D assumes that it will in all cases be called after C and none else, so that the throttle setting will be at 2 and will need an increase of 8 points to bring it up to full open.

For the moment, we merely take note of this information, but in the future it may help track down a bug, should the assumptions about incoming train speed prove false.

Flowcharting subroutines C and D is not difficult. The form is depicted in Fig. 1-16.

Subroutine E has two important tasks to accomplish. It must set switch 2 for the proper loop, and it must decrease the train's speed to a throttle setting of 5. No matter which fork in the track the train takes, through town or to the station, the throttle must be at 5. This is done easily enough with a block of coding nearly identical to subroutine C.

Setting the switch for the proper loop is a little harder. The program must have some way of knowing if it is on the first or the second lap of its two-lap cycle. On the first lap, the train will be coming from the station, and so we would want it to be switched to the townbound loop. On the

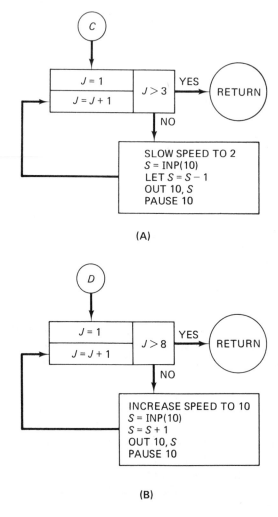

Fig. 1-16. Flowchart for (A) subroutine C and (B) subroutine D.

second lap, the train must be shunted off to the station to allow the passengers to leave and to board.

The coding is as follows, and the flowchart is shown in Fig. 1-17.

```
840 REM NEARING SW 2
850 REM SET SW FOR OUTSIDE LOOP
860 IF T<0 THEN OUT 13, 0
```

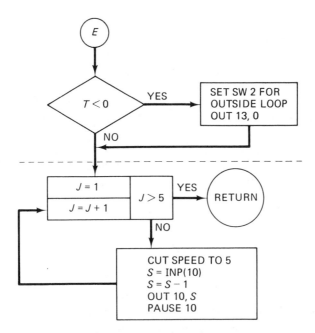

Fig. 1-17. Flowchart for setting the switch for proper loops.

```
870 REM CUT SPEED TO 5
880 FOR J=1 TO 5
890 LET S=INP(10)
900 LET S=S−1
910 OUT 10, S
920 PAUSE 10
930 NEXT J
940 RETURN
```

We can divide subroutine E into two parts. The part below the dotted line in Fig. 1-17 is very similar to subroutine C, just as we said it would be. The section of subroutine E above the dotted line, however, has problems. We see that the program tests on T, and if T is less than zero it pulses switch 2 and causes the track to line up with the outside loop. But T is the variable used to index the number of round trips. Recall:

```
60 INPUT T
70 REM T IS THE TRIP COUNTER
```

Also, T is never made negative anywhere in the program. This being true, the test of subroutine E would never be met, and SW 2 would never be set properly. Depending upon how switch 2 was set when power was applied, the train would either run in perpetual circles through town or through the station.

We can guess that the program is trying to test which lap it is on, and that it is trying to use that information to decide whether or not to pulse the switch.

If T is not the correct variable, what is? The variable N is initialized to a positive 1; and then once inside the trip loop, it flips back and forth between positive and negative:

```
225 LET N=1
230 FOR I=1 TO T
240 LET N=-N
```

If we were to key on N, what would be the outcome? The first time through, N would be less than zero, and the test would be met. As a result, SW 2 would be set to the outside loop, and the train would go into Smalltown.

The subroutine would then return control to the main program. But, as we learned when we flowcharted the main program, there is no provision for getting the code down to line 434, where the loop is incremented:

```
430 GOTO 250
434 NEXT I
```

As a result, N would remain forever negative and the train would continue to follow the outer loop, never returning to the station.

Line 250 begins the loop which queries each sensor in turn to determine the train's location. We might try moving the sign-change coding for N inside of this loop:

```
250 LET A=INP(1)
255 LET N=-N
```

Then every time the main program jumps back to line 250 to begin another status search, the sign of N is changed. Unfortunately, this loop is executed many times each second, since the computer can process instructions far faster than the train can travel from sensor to sensor (which explains why so many PAUSE statements have been included). Consequently, the status of N would be merely a matter of chance and would not be a reliable index for switch 2.

We can make an assumption, however, which should be true in all cases. Each time the train leaves the station it pulses switch 1 to the inside circle. It does this without asking the status of switch 1 beforehand. Switch 1 is also unconditionally set to the outer loop whenever the train reaches the crossing. It would appear, then, that by checking the status of switch 1, we may determine what the status of switch 2 ought to be. This is reflected in the revised flowchart portion depicted in Fig. 1-18.

Recoding of that section of the subroutine might look something like:

```
840 REM NEARING SW 2
845 REM TEST STATUS OF SW 1
850 LET L=INP(12)
852 REM DEFAULT SW 2 TO OUTSIDE
854 OUT 13, 0
860 IF L=0 THEN OUT 13, 255
```

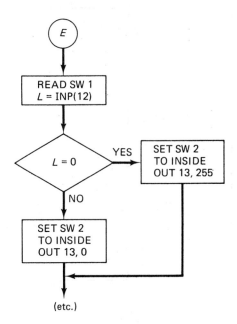

(etc.)

Fig. 1-18. Flowchart to determine the status of switch 1, which tells us what switch 2 should be.

Subroutine F is concerned with activating the warning signal at the train crossing. For this task the program must flash a warning light as long as the train is in the crossing. The flowchart for subroutine F is shown in Fig. 1-19; it is coded as follows:

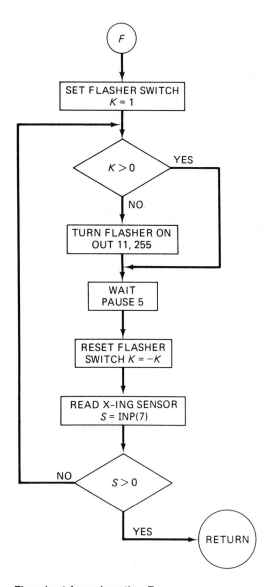

Fig. 1-19.   Flowchart for subroutine F.

```
950 REM NEARING X—ING
960 REM SET WARNING FLASHER SWITCH
970 REM PORT 11 IS X—ING FLASHER
980 LET K=1
990 IF K>0 THEN GOTO 1020
1000 REM FLASHER ON
1010 OUT 11, 255
1020 PAUSE 5
1030 LET K=−K
1040 REM TEST IF WE HAVE CLEARED X—ING
1050 LET S=INP(7)
1060 IF S>0 THEN GOTO 990
1070 RETURN
```

Using words to describe what the flowchart tells us in pictures, let's see what we have. The program enters subroutine F, and a switch variable K is initialized to 1. K is then tested to see if it is greater than zero. It is, so the program pauses, changes the sign of K to negative, and interrogates sensor 7 to see if the train has left the crossing yet. The train has not, so the program jumps back to the test of K. This time, K is negative, and consequently the warning light is turned on. Again the pause, change of sign, interrogation of sensor 7, and jump back to the test of K. Now the sign of K is back to positive, so the program . . . a bug! The second one we discovered using this technique. The warning light never gets turned off. It is supposed to flash on and off, but as we can see using the flowchart, nothing of the sort takes place.

A logical fix for this bug would be to modify the flowchart as shown in Fig. 1-20.

Subroutine G is trivial in that it need only pulse switch 1 to line up with the outer circle whenever sensor 8 is activated:

```
1080 REM NEARING SW 1 FROM OUTSIDE
1090 REM SET SW 1 TO OUTSIDE
1100 OUT 12, 0
1110 RETURN
```

Its flowchart, equally simple, is shown in Fig. 1-21.

The coding which begins at line 1120 and ends at line 1270—what we

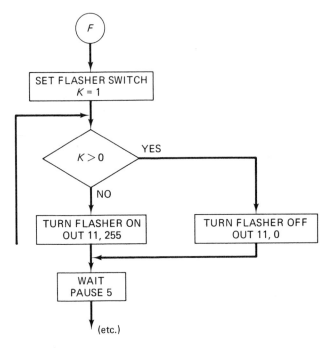

Fig. 1-20. Flowchart modification to generate flashing model light.

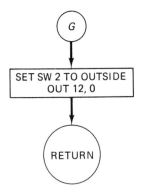

Fig. 1-21. Flowchart for subroutine G.

call subroutine H—is not technically a subroutine in that it does not end
with a RETURN statement; rather, it terminates with a GOTO:

```
1270 GOTO 434
```

At least we have found how the program closes the main loop. As the
train approaches the station, it is slowed down; the structure of this part
of subroutine H is similar to all of the other speed-change subroutines,
and so it should be familiar to us by now. Once the train reaches the station (as reported by sensor 1), it is brought to a dead stop and the main
program loop is incremented. The coding is as follows:

```
1120 REM NEARING STATION
1130 PRINT "NOW APPROACHING SMALLTOWN STATION"
1140 PRINT "SMALLTOWN, USA"
1150 REM SLOW TRAIN TO 1
1160 FOR J=1 TO 4
1170 LET S=INP(10)
1180 LET S=S-1
1190 OUT 10, S
1200 PAUSE 10
1210 NEXT J
1220 REM CHECK WHEN TRAIN MAKES STATION
1230 LET K=INP(I)
1240 IF K=0 THEN GOTO 1230
1250 REM STOP TRAIN
1260 OUT 10, 0
1270 GOTO 434
```

The flowchart derived from that coding is shown in Fig. 1-22.

There do not appear to be any bugs in this last block of coding. On
paper, at least, the program is debugged. Once the program is put into
use, other bugs might very well appear. For instance, perhaps the train
accelerates or decelerates too quickly. Or perhaps because of the relative
placement of the position sensors, the switches do not react quickly
enough. Both bugs would be related to the same problem: an incorrectly
specified PAUSE statement. Unfortunately, the program is full of PAUSE
statements. The program *is* well documented, however, and this is a real

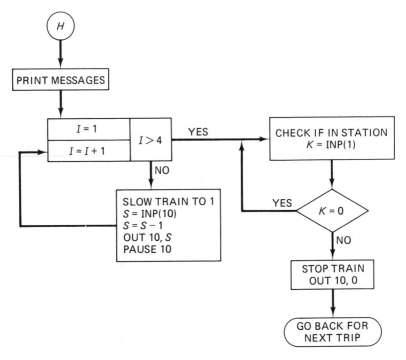

Fig. 1-22.   Flowchart for subroutine H.

help when trying to debug, as we shall see in the next chapter. But the availability of flowcharts would help make the solution for such bugs apparent at a glance.

2.

COMMENT STATEMENTS

The practice of sprinkling lots of comments throughout a computer program, known as *internal documentation,* helps to clarify what is taking place in the program, both for the person who wrote it and for those who must come along later and read the program.

PLANTING COMMENTS IN PROGRAMS

It is never wise to assume that just because a program was understood when it was written, it will always remain so. Computer code is just that—code. In order for a program to be solved by a computer, it must be broken down into small computer-manageable pieces and then structured to fit into the very rigid form of whatever programming language is to be used.

Take, for example, this short undocumented program:

```
10 LET R1 = −1000
20 LET R2 = 1000
30 INPUT R
40 PRINT R
50 IF R>R1 THEN GOTO 70
60 IF R<R2 THEN GOTO 90
70 GOTO 100
80 LET R1 = R
90 GOTO 50
```

```
100 LET R2=R
110 GOTO 30
120 PRINT "MAX="; R1; "MIN="; R2
130 END
```

Apparently, judging from line 120, this program finds the minimum and maximum values of a list of numbers. If we were to load the program into our SOL microcomputer, however, we would not get any error messages, but we would also not get a printout telling us the minimum and maximum.

There are several problems with the above example. Upon typing a RUN command, we would see nothing on our video monitor; there is no prompting information to be sent to the person running the program. If we dismissed that problem by assuming that we would be the only one using the program, and hence prompts were unnecessary, we would soon discover, after entering as many values as we wished, that there is no way to stop the program and make it print the answer.

Suppose we put the program away and leave it for a couple of months, then come back to it and try to fix it up and make it useful. Where do we start? The program has no comments, no helpful hints to unlock the code of how it is put together. How much better off we would be if, when we had originally written the program, we had had the sense to insert explanatory remarks between lines of code. If we had, we might have come up with the following:

```
10 REM PROGRAM TO FIND THE MINIMUM
20 REM AND MAXIMUM OF A LIST OF NUMBERS
30 REM INITIALIZE MIN AND MAX VARIABLES
40 REM R1 IS MAX, R2 IS MIN
50 LET R1=-1000
60 LET R2=1000
70 REM INPUT VALUE AND ECHO IT BACK
80 INPUT R
90 PRINT R
100 REM TEST IF VALUE IS GREATER THAN OLD MAX
110 IF R>R1 THEN GOTO 160
120 REM TEST IF VALUE IS LESS THAN OLD MIN
130 IF R<R2 THEN GOTO 200
140 GOTO 220
```

```
150 REM SET MAX EQ TO VALUE
160 LET R1=R
170 REM VALUE MAY ALSO BE THE MIN
180 GOTO 130
190 REM SET MIN EQ TO VALUE
200 LET R2=R
210 REM GO BACK FOR ANOTHER VALUE
220 GOTO 80
230 REM PRINT OUT THE ANSWER
240 PRINT "MAX="; R1; "MIN="; R2
250 END
```

Commenting the program made it roughly twice as long, but it also made it more than twice as easy to follow. Not all programs need to be this heavily commented; as a person gains experience as a programmer, certain programming patterns become familiar and do not have to be spelled out in intimate detail each time they occur.

Now that we have a documented program to work with, debugging becomes much easier. The first bug had to do with the fact that there was no prompt given to tell us when to input a value. We see by the documentation that the input process takes place at line 80. (Program lines in BASIC must be numbered, but they do not have to be numbered in increments of 10. The increase-by-10 method is usually chosen, however, because of its convenience at times like this, when a bug has been discovered and it looks as though additional coding may have to be inserted. BASIC will accept program lines numbered consecutively and incremented by one each time, but BASIC will not accept fractional-value line numbers.)

Since the monitor program which came with our SOL microcomputer has editing capability (as does most every other manufacturer's monitor routine), we can easily type in an additional line of code, prefacing it with a line number which lies between the two existing lines of code that bracket the chosen position of the new line. The SOL editor will then insert the line right where it should be in the program.

So, in the case of the prompt, we might write the following line of code:

```
75 PRINT "PLEASE INPUT A VALUE"
```

Having learned the value of documenting what we do, however, we might want to flesh out that line of code with a short comment:

```
73 REM DISPLAY PROMPTING MESSAGE
75 PRINT "PLEASE INPUT A VALUE"
```

That takes care of the prompting message, but what about the bug that keeps the program in a continuous loop so that the answer never gets printed out?

If we look closely at the documented version of the program, we see that there is no way for the computer to ever get down to line 230. Every time the computer works its way down to line 220 it is immediately bounced back up to line 80 to read in another value. This is known as a loop. Of course, we want the program to keep looping and accepting new values, because we want to input more than one number.

However, we do not want to read values indefinitely; we need some way to stop the program and get the answer. There are several methods we might use to accomplish this. One approach would be to put an upper limit on the number of times the loop is executed. To do this would require some sort of indexing arrangement, in which the index variable was initialized at the beginning of the program and then updated (increased in value by one) each time the program was executed.

Another method would be to jump to the end of the program and print the answer if the number we read in is equal to some predetermined cutoff value, such as 999.

Choosing the second method, we might write:

```
84 REM TEST IF THIS IS LAST VALUE
86 IF R=999 THEN GOTO 240
```

The program now looks like this:

```
10 REM PROGRAM TO FIND THE MINIMUM
20 REM AND MAXIMUM OF A LIST OF NUMBERS
30 REM INITIALIZE MIN AND MAX VARIABLES
40 REM R1 IS MAX, R2 IS MIN
50 LET R1=-1000
60 LET R2=1000
70 REM INPUT VALUE AND ECHO IT BACK
73 REM DISPLAY PROMPTING MESSAGE
75 PRINT "PLEASE INPUT A VALUE"
80 INPUT R
```

```
84 REM TEST IF THIS IS LAST VALUE
86 IF R=999 THEN GOTO 240
90 PRINT R
100 REM TEST IF VALUE IS GREATER THAN OLD MAX
110 IF R>R1 THEN GOTO 160
120 REM TEST IF VALUE IS LESS THAN OLD MIN
130 IF R<R2 THEN GOTO 200
140 GOTO 220
150 REM SET MAX EQ TO VALUE
160 LET R1=R
170 REM VALUE MAY ALSO BE THE MIN
180 GOTO 130
190 REM SET MIN EQ TO VALUE
200 LET R2=R
210 REM GO BACK FOR ANOTHER VALUE
220 GOTO 80
230 REM PRINT OUT THE ANSWER
240 PRINT "MAX="; R1; "MIN="; R2
250 END
```

The program should work now. A prompting message will be printed out, and once the value 999 is read in from the keyboard, the program will branch to the part that prints out the answer and then stop.

We give the computer a RUN command. Immediately, the message

```
PLEASE INPUT A VALUE
```

appears. So far, so good. We type in a number:

```
PLEASE INPUT A VALUE
?12
```

The computer echoes our entry:

```
PLEASE INPUT A VALUE
?12
12
```

Nothing else. The computer should prompt again for another entry, but it does not. Either we missed a bug the first time around, or we included a new bug in those few lines we added to the program. If the latter turns out to be the case, it would not be the first time that an improvement to an existing program results in its own bugs.

Fortunately, the program is now clearly documented, and tracking down the bug is no great problem. Our best clue is that the prompting message is only printed out once. This suggests that for some reason either the program is not performing the loop, or, if it *is* looping, it is not going back up far enough to include the line of code which prints out the prompt.

Examining the program, we find that the second possibility is the correct one: the program, when it reaches the end of the loop at statement line 220, is not being sent back far enough. It is being sent to line 80, which is the statement that reads in fresh data; but it should instead be sent to line 75, the prompting statement just above where the program is currently being sent.

The corrected line would read:

220 GOTO 75

Using SOL's editing routine, we delete the old line 220 and replace it with the correct new line 220. We rewind the program and type in a RUN. We are rewarded with:

PLEASE INPUT A VALUE

We do as asked, and the computer echoes our entry:

PLEASE INPUT A VALUE
?20
20
PLEASE INPUT A VALUE

Perhaps the program is fixed. We decide to give the program a good work-out, and so continue to enter numbers.

PLEASE INPUT A VALUE
?20

```
20
PLEASE INPUT A VALUE
?14
14
PLEASE INPUT A VALUE
?2
2
PLEASE INPUT A VALUE
?75
75
PLEASE INPUT A VALUE
?999
999
MAX=75, MIN=2
```

Is the program debugged? From the looks of our test run results, the program works. Certainly the minimum value of the group of numbers 20, 14, 2, and 75, is 2, and the maximum value is 75. But what about negative numbers, or fractional numbers? How would they affect the program? And what about numbers greater than 999, or less than −999? To answer these questions, we would really have to test every possible situation, and then if necessary, make provisions in the code for unusual circumstances.

However, in the case of positive whole numbers less than 999.0, we can say with a fair amount of certainty that our program to find the minimum and maximum values of an arbitrarily long list of numbers is debugged.

"COMMENTING" GUIDELINES

The purpose of internal documentation is to clarify, in plain English, what is taking place in not-so-plain computer code. Good documentation will help us, as we have seen. Bad documentation, documentation that is too long or wordy or too short and cryptic, can often be more confusing to us than clarifying.

The first guideline might therefore be "Don't overdo it." The documentation exists to complement the coding, not the other way around. As an example, look at this heavily overdocumented program:

```
10 REM "AVRG", A PROGRAM TO FIND
20 REM THE NUMERICAL AVERAGE OF TWO
30 REM CONSECUTIVE VALUES
40 PRINT "NUMBER AVERAGING ROUTINE"
50 REM THIS PROGRAM WORKS BY ASKING THE
60 REM OPERATOR TO TYPE IN TWO DIFFERENT
70 REM NUMBERS FROM THE KEYBOARD
80 REM THE PROGRAM CALCULATES THE SUM
90 REM OF THESE TWO NUMBERS, AND THEN
100 REM DIVIDES THAT QUANTITY BY N, THE
110 REM NUMBER OF VALUES READ IN
120 REM THE RESULTING QUOTIENT IS DISPLAYED
130 REM ON THE VIDEO SCREEN, AND
140 REM THE PROGRAM TERMINATES
150 REM WE BEGIN BY READING IN THE
160 REM TWO VALUES
170 INPUT X, Y
180 REM X IS THE FIRST VALUE
190 REM Y IS THE SECOND VALUE
200 REM NOW WE MUST CALCULATE THE SUM
210 LET Z=X+Y
220 REM BEFORE WE CAN USE N WE MUST
230 REM INITIALIZE IT
240 LET N=2
250 REM FINALLY WE CAN CALCULATE THE AVERAGE
260 LET A=Z/N
270 REM PRINT OUT THE ANSWER
280 PRINT "THE AVERAGE OF"; X; "AND";
290 PRINT Y; "IS="; A
300 END
```

What a mess! In 30 lines of program, there are only eight valid lines of
code, and two of those lines are unnecessary.

The program could easily be trimmed down to less than 10 lines,
comments included, with no loss in completeness but with a large resul-
tant increase in clarity, as follows:

```
10 REM PROGRAM "AVRG"
20 PRINT "NUMBER AVERAGING ROUTINE"
30 REM OPERATES ON TWO NUMBERS AT A TIME
40 INPUT X, Y
50 LET Z=(X+Y)/2
60 PRINT "THE AVERAGE OF"; X; "AND";
70 PRINT Y; "IS"; Z
80 END
```

The program is now much easier to take in at one glance and understand. A point worth remembering is that documentation can backfire if used to excess. Besides burying the working part of the program in non-executable text, it also eats up large amounts of your machine's memory. Text must be stored as a "literal," a character at a time, in memory. For ASCII-encoded text, this means roughly one computer word per *letter*. In the case of the overcommented example, this translates into approximately 600 *words* of memory. It would take just 12 or 13 short programs or subroutines, written in the same wasteful manner, to fully occupy 8 kilobytes of memory, which is all the memory many people's computers have available for everything, including monitors, loaders, translators, and the program itself.

Identify Variables

Computers do not generally accept arbitrarily long words to be used as variable names. This can often become a problem. Computer programs are written to answer a specific need: balance a checkbook, keep inventory for a business, analyze trends in the stock market, graph the results of students' test scores, and so forth.

In all these uses, real-world events must be reduced to the artificial environment of the computer. Items such as names of merchandise, accounts, parts, and people must (for the computer) become simple, short variables. It is not uncommon to find a restriction of seven characters, or four characters, or even one character, being placed on the maximum permissible length of a variable name.

The difficulty caused by having short, cryptic variable names to represent their longer real-world counterparts is that it does not take long to forget just what the variables stand for.

Consider this short program:

```
10 REM PAYROLL COMPUTATION
20 INPUT R, T, T1, T2, E, S, C
30 LET G=R*T
40 LET F=G*T1
50 LET S1=G*T2
60 LET D=G*.01
70 LET N=G-F-S1-D-E-S-C
80 PRINT "PAY IS"; N
90 END
```

This program is not very sophisticated; each line of calculations uses only the simplest of mathematical structures, but without documentation to tell what the different variables stand for, the program may as well be written in some foreign language.

See the difference that comments make:

```
10 REM PAYROLL COMPUTATION
20 REM R=HOURLY RATE
30 REM T=HOURS WORKED
40 REM T1=FEDERAL TAX RATE
50 REM T2=STATE TAX RATE
60 REM E=EMPLOYEE INSURANCE PLAN
70 REM S=SAVINGS PLAN
80 REM C=CHRISTMAS CLUB
90 INPUT R, T, T1, T2, E, S, C
100 REM G=GROSS PAY
110 REM F=FEDERAL TAX
120 REM S1=STATE TAX
130 REM D=STATE DISABILITY INSURANCE
140 REM N=NET PAY
150 LET G=R*T
160 LET F=G*T1
170 LET S1=G*T
180 LET D=G*.01
190 LET N=G-F-S1-D-E-S-C
200 PRINT "PAY IS"; N
210 END
```

While it is true that in the above example the comment lines outnumber the lines of code, each line of documentation is, at least, relevant.

The above program has a bug. Why? Certainly we are not attempting anything very difficult. Thanks to the comments, we know what all of the input variables are, and we also know what we are trying to calculate. The employee's net take-home pay is going to be equal to his gross pay less deductions for state and federal tax, for state disability insurance, for employee work insurance, and for contributions to a company savings plan and a Christmas club.

We know that his gross pay is a result of the number of hours worked times the hourly wage he earns (line 150). The federal tax is equal to his gross pay times the federal tax rate for his bracket (line 160); likewise the state tax is equal to his gross pay times the state's percentage (line 170). The state disability insurance is a flat rate times his gross earnings (line 180).

Since we know what the program is supposed to do, and since we know what the variables stand for, then it should be a simple matter to debug this particular program.

Sure enough, the bug is in line 170.

```
170     LET S1=G*T
```

We are multiplying the employee's gross pay times the hours worked to get his state tax. According to the program the way it is now, the employee is going into debt to the state at the rate of his hourly wage times his number of hours worked, squared. At the end of only one week, he would owe 40 times his weekly salary! The T in line 170 should be T2. A minor typographical error, but with major consequences.

The bug may have been caught without such extensive documentation; the working portion of the program is only seven lines long. Most programs are not so short, however. It would be very easy to forget the meanings of variables used in a longer computer program, and as a result spend unnecessary time searching for a simple typographical error.

Label Default Values

Default values are those values which a variable will assume if it is not modified by a computation or by the input of replacement data. Default data often takes the form of constants—quantities which have no reason to be changed, but which are used in calculating other variables.

The next example is a program to convert centimeters into either inches or feet, depending upon the value of a variable S, which is used as a switch: if it equals one or greater, the program converts to feet. If S equals zero or less, it converts the input value to inches.

```
10 REM PROGRAM "CNVRT"
20 REM CONVERTS CM TO IN OR FT
30 REM DEPENDING UPON S
40 REM I1=DIV FACTOR FOR IN
50 REM F1=DIV FACTOR FOR FT
60 LET I1=2.45
70 LET F1=30.48
80 PRINT "PLEASE ENTER VALUE IN CM"
90 INPUT C
100 PRINT "ENTER 1 FOR FT, 0 FOR IN"
110 INPUT S
120 IF S>=1 THEN GOTO 170
130 REM CONVERT TO INCHES
140 LET X=C/I1
150 PRINT C; "CM="; X; "IN"
160 GOTO 200
170 REM CONVERT TO FEET
180 LET X=C/F1
190 PRINT C; "CM="; X; "FT"
200 END
```

The above program has a bug. If we were to load the program into our computer and type RUN we would get

PLEASE ENTER VALUE IN CM

Suppose we then choose some random value and enter it as we have been asked. We would get

PLEASE ENTER VALUE IN CM
?41
ENTER 1 FOR FT, 0 FOR IN

We decide to choose the foot conversion option:

PLEASE ENTER VALUE IN CM
?41
ENTER 1 FOR FT, 0 FOR IN
?1
41 CM=1.345 FT

Suppose we try the branch of the program which converts to inches. The sequence would be:

PLEASE ENTER VALUE IN CM
?41
ENTER 1 FOR FT, 0 FOR IN
?0
41 CM=16.735 IN

There does not seem to be a bug; the program ran to completion both times. Both times, the correct prompting information was displayed, and both times the answer printed out just the way it was supposed to. But the printout reflects an incorrect answer.

Not all bugs cause a program to bomb, though. It is entirely possible for a program to execute successfully, yet deliver false information at its end. Never assume that just because a program ran that it is correct. If at all possible, numerical results provided by a program should be independently verified. In the case of a long and involved program with many conditional branches (IF statements), the verification process may be unmanageably difficult, unless first a number of simplifying assumptions are made. In the present case, however, independent verification will not be a problem.

We can discover, using a table of conversion factors, that there are approximately 30.48 centimeters in one foot, and 2.54 centimeters in one inch. Doing a bit of long division, we find:

$$41 \div 30.48 = 1.345$$

and

$$41 \div 2.54 = 16.142$$

Checking back with the output from the program, we see that the conversion to feet is correct, while the conversion to inches is not.

According to the documentation we placed in our program, centimeters are converted to inches at line 140.

```
130 REM CONVERT TO INCHES
140 LET X=C/I1
```

In this particular example, we could deduce with little trouble what the variable *I1* stands for. We know that the program is supposed to convert centimeters to either feet or inches, and the remark statement clearly marks line 140 as the line which converts centimeters to inches. *I1* is therefore the centimeter-to-inch conversion factor.

Fortunately, we documented the constants and default values in this program (lines 40 and 50). *I1* is indeed supposed to be the division factor to convert centimeters to inches. The program lists it as:

```
60 LET I1=2.45
```

We have found the bug. The conversion factor is 2.54, not 2.45. Apparently the last two digits were interchanged when we entered the program.

Again, we find that once the nature of the bug is discovered, it is not at all difficult to correct, nor hard to understand how it occurred. Most program bugs are like that: simple misspellings or transpositions, an add instead of a subtract, a multiplying scale factor used as a divisor, etc. The longer a program becomes, the easier it is for the meanings of the variables to get lost in the shuffle. Clearly, labelling the identity of constants can be a significant aid to keeping track of such quantities, and it is particularly helpful in debugging program statements of which those quantities are a part.

Identify Loops

One reason people buy microcomputers is that they are so well suited to performing monotonous, repetitive tasks. Usually, when the same operation is to be applied to each member of a long list, the operation is written into the program at only one place. Then, by means of an indexing arrangement, the various members to be operated on are accessed and brought into the single block of code. Such a structure is called a *loop*, and any program that performs the same task more than two or three times is almost sure to contain at least one loop.

Consider the following example:

Universal Consolidated Widgits uses a microcomputer in its sales department to keep track of pricing information. UCW carries 10 styles of widgits; each style comes in four different colors, and each color has three different sizes. Thus, there are 10 × 4 × 3, or 120 possible combinations of style, color, and size.

Every month UCW prints out a new price list for its distributors. The program they use is:

```
10 REM UCW PRICE COMPUTATION PROGRAM
20 REM B=BASE PRICE
30 REM S1=STYLE COST FACTOR MULTIPLIER (CFM)
40 REM C=COLOR CFM
50 REM S2=SIZE CFM
60 DIM S1(10), C(4), S2(3)
70 REM INPUT VARIABLES
80 INPUT B
90 PRINT "ENTER STYLE CFM"
100 FOR I=1 TO 10
110 INPUT S1 (I)
120 NEXT I
130 PRINT "ENTER COLOR CFM"
140 FOR J=1 TO 4
150 INPUT C(J)
160 NEXT J
170 PRINT "ENTER SIZE CFM"
180 FOR K=1 TO 3
190 INPUT S2(K)
200 NEXT K
210 FOR L=1 TO 10
220 REM T=STYLE MARKUP
230 LET T=B*S1(I)
240 FOR M=1 TO 4
250 REM C2=COLOR MARKUP
260 LET C2=B*C(J)
270 FOR N=1 TO 3
280 REM Z=SIZE MARKUP
290 LET Z=B*S2(K)
300 REM P1=SALES PRICE
310 LET P1=B+T+C2+Z
320 PRINT "PRICE FOR STYLE"; L; "COLOR"; M;
330 PRINT "SIZE"; N; "="; P1
340 NEXT N
350 NEXT M
360 NEXT L
370 END
```

In this example, the variables are all identified, but the program is still difficult to follow. The mathematical operations are not complicated, but the number of loops and the way in which they are interconnected can be confusing.

We can make things a little clearer by indenting lines of code which are bracketed by a FOR . . . NEXT pair, and by inserting blank comments. This will set the various loops apart from each other, as follows:

```
10    REM  UCW PRICE COMPUTATION PROGRAM
20    REM  B=BASE PRICE
30    REM  S1=STYLE COST FACTOR MULTIPLIER (CFM)
40    REM  C=COLOR CFM
50    REM  S2=SIZE CFM
60         DIM S1(10), C(4), S2(3)
70    REM  INPUT VARIABLES
80         INPUT B
90    REM
100        PRINT "ENTER STYLE CFM"
110        FOR I=1 TO 10
120        INPUT S1(I)
130        NEXT I
140 REM
150        PRINT "ENTER COLOR CFM"
160        FOR J=1 TO 4
170        INPUT C(J)
180        NEXT J
190 REM
200        PRINT "ENTER SIZE CFM"
210        FOR K=1 TO 3
220        INPUT S2(K)
230        NEXT K
240 REM
250        FOR L=1 TO 10
260 REM        T=STYLE MARKUP
270            LET T=B*S1(I)
280 REM
290            FOR M=1 TO 4
300 REM        C2=COLOR MARKUP
```

```
310              LET C2=B*C(J)
320 REM
330              FOR N=1 TO 3
340 REM             Z=SIZE MARKUP
350              LET Z=B*S2(K)
360 REM             P1=SALES PRICE
370              LET P1=B+T+C2+Z
380              PRINT "PRICE FOR STYLE"
390              PRINT L; "COLOR"; M; "SIZE"
400              PRINT N; "="; P1
410           NEXT N
420        NEXT M
430     NEXT L
440     END
```

The program is now much easier to read. The three initialization loops are distinctly set apart at the top of the program. The purpose of the program is also clear. The first half is data accumulation; the various factors which affect the price of a finished widgit are read into the memory. Note the variables used as index pointers I, J, and K. There is nothing special about these variables, except that they should not be involved in any computation to alter their value. I increases from 1 to 10 because there are 10 styles of widgits. J increases from 1 to 4, which corresponds to the four different colors of widgits. And K increases from 1 to 3 in relation to the three sizes of widgits.

The second part of the program computes the exact sales price for each of the 120 possible combinations. In this portion of code the loops are *nested*. The innermost loop is for the size variable, and concludes its three cycles before the index pointer on the color loop is incremented. The color loop, in turn, must complete its four cycles before the outermost loop, for style variables, can be incremented.

Note that the second half of the program uses a new set of indexes— L, M, and N. This is perfectly allowable; any integer-valued (as opposed to real-valued) variable may be used as an index variable.

When the program is run, however, the same number is printed out 120 times, as below:

```
PRICE FOR STYLE 1 COLOR 1 SIZE 1=23.14
PRICE FOR STYLE 1 COLOR 1 SIZE 2=23.14
PRICE FOR STYLE 1 COLOR 1 SIZE 3=23.14
```

PRICE FOR STYLE 1 COLOR 2 SIZE 1=23.14
PRICE FOR STYLE 1 COLOR 2 SIZE 2=23.14
PRICE FOR STYLE 1 COLOR 2 SIZE 3=23.14

and so on up to

PRICE FOR STYLE 10 COLOR 3 SIZE 3=23.14

Obviously, there is a bug in the program. But what could it be? The loop indexes are working correctly, as indicated by the properly incrementing style, color, and size information. If this is so, how could the same price be printed out for every combination?

First, by performing a few hand calculations we find that, for example, the true price for style 1 color 1 size 1 is $12.02, and for style 1 color 2 size 1 the price is $14.20.

Turning to the listing of the program, we decide to begin at the end of the program and work our way up to the beginning—a common debugging practice.

We start with the PRINT statement. Perhaps we are not printing out what we think. The final variable listed in the print statement is $P1$ (line 400).

If $P1$ were a constant instead of a variable, it would explain the occurrence of 120 lines of the same number. But according to the remark on line 360, and the coding on line 370, $P1$ is indeed the sales price, a constantly recomputed value:

```
360 REM        P1=SALES PRICE
370            LET P1=B+T+C2+Z
```

B is the basic price, a constant. It is read into the program at line 80 and is never updated.

Therefore, the variability in the sales price must be governed by the values of T, $C2$, and Z. Values for these variables are initially stored one right after the other on the three loops indexed by I, J, and K, at the top of the program. These stored values should then be sequentially recalled from memory in the lower part of the program, during the execution of the loops indexed by L, M, and N.

Look at the innermost loop, the one that updates Z. It begins on line 330 and ends at line 410:

```
330                    FOR N=1 TO 3
340  REM               Z=SIZE MARKUP
350                    LET Z=B*S2(K)
360  REM               P1=SALES PRICE
370                    LET P1=B+T+C2+Z
380                    PRINT "PRICE FOR STYLE",
390                    PRINT L; "COLOR"; M; "SIZE"
400                    PRINT N; "="; P1
410                NEXT N
```

The beginning and ending values for N, the index for this loop, are correct; there are three different sizes of widgits. For each time through the loop, then, they should get the corresponding size cost-factor multiplier, multiply that times the base price, and arrive at the markup for size.

But the size CFM is indexed on K. K was used as the index for the size loop at the top of the program, but it should not be used here. S2(K) will always be the same value: the last value it assumed during the loop from line 200 to line 230. K left that loop equal to 3, and it was never updated. Therefore, S2(K) will always be S2(3). The coding should be changed to read:

```
350                    LET Z=B*S2(N)
```

since in this loop, N is the index.

The same holds true for T and C2. In each case, the old indexes were used. The coding for them should be changed to read:

```
270                    LET T=B*S1(L)
```

for the style loop index, and

```
310                    LET C2=B*C(M)
```

for the color loop index.

Once the indexes are changed to reflect the new variable identities, the program works perfectly.

In the previous example, the bugs are all related and were found rather easily. But if the loops had been clearly labelled and the index variables identified as to purpose earlier, the bugs might have been caught while the program was being written, saving valuable time.

Identify Blocks of Code

Often, especially after a programmer has gained some experience, certain programming patterns develop which become familiar. Such blocks of code do not have to be explained one line at a time with detailed comments, but they should still be identified. The familiarity one gains is with the form of the coding, but not with the specific computational job which the block of code is performing.

A very simple example of an easily recognizable block of code is:

```
410      FOR I=1 TO 100
420      LET A1 (I)=0.0
430      NEXT I
```

This is just a simple way to zero out a list of numbers. As a preliminary step to performing other calculations somewhere down the line, it would not hurt to reintroduce the variable just before it is used in the block, as:

```
405 REM  ZERO OUT ALTITUDE ARRAY
410      FOR I=1 TO 10
420      LET A1(I)=0.0
430      NEXT I
```

For a more complicated example, suppose we want to program our own video game. Any program that outputs graphic information is going to make heavy use of simple geometry equations, such as the one which finds the distance along a line drawn between two points. The general form of the equation is:

$$D = \sqrt{(X_2 - X_1)^2 + (Y_2 - Y_1)^2}$$

We might decide to code the equation in an equally general way:

```
230      LET A=X2-X1
240      LET B=Y2-Y1
250      LET A2=A*A
```

```
260     LET B2=B*B
270     LET D=SQR (A2+B2)
```

We could go on to use those same five lines of code, changing the variables as necessary, in any number of graphics programs. Each time we ran across that pattern we would know that when we had written that particular program, we had wanted to find the straight-line distance between two points. Without any more information, however, we would be hard put to use our familiarity with the pattern to help us debug the program.

Consider this usage of that pattern:

```
1670    LET X=E2-E1
1680    LET Y=R2-R1
1690    LET X2=X*X
1700    LET Y2=Y*Y
1710    LET Z=SQR (X2+Y2)
```

The example looks correct. At least, it fits the pattern with which we are familiar. But, this block of code has a bug; and judging by the statement line numbers, it is probably buried so far in the main program that determining what the variables stand for and then getting an idea of what they should be equal to at this point in the program would be a very difficult task at best.

A few lines of documentation can clear things up considerably:

```
1664 REM  FIND DISTANCE BETWEEN
1666 REM  STARSHIP ENTERPRISE (E1, E2)
1668 REM  AND ROMULAN WARSHIP (R1, R2)
1670 REM  LET X=E2-E1
1680 REM  LET Y=R2-R1
1690 REM  LET X2=X*X
1700 REM  LET Y2=Y*Y
1710 REM  LET Z=SQR (X2+Y2)
```

Now at least we know the identity of the variables, and we can debug the code. The form of the block is correct; it matches in computer code the English-language definition of the distance formula: the distance between two points, lying in the same plane, is equal to the square root of

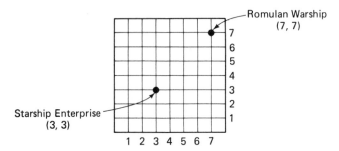

Fig. 2-1. Graph showing the galactic coordinates and positions of ships.

the sum of the squares of the differences in the X and Y values for each point. Or, in the graph shown in Fig. 2-1, Starship Enterprise is at galactic coordinates (3,3), and Romulan Warship is at coordinates (7,7). The distance between the two ships is 5.6569 star units, as follows:

$$D = \sqrt{(X_2 - X_1)^2 + (Y_2 - Y_1)^2}$$

or

$$D = \sqrt{(7 - 3)^2 + (7 - 3)^2}$$

or

$$D = \sqrt{4^2 + 4^2}$$

or

$$D = \sqrt{16 + 16}$$

or

$$D = \sqrt{32}$$

or

$$D = 5.6569$$

However, the coding, as written, tells quite a different story. The simple hand calculation we've just seen shows that even though the outline of the block of code is correct (the 8 program lines from 1664 to

1710)—which is to say that the proper things are done in the proper order—the results of that block are incorrect, because the wrong values are being subtracted from each other. The way the variables have been set up, the distance formula is being executed as follows:

$$D = \sqrt{Y_1 - X_1)^2 + (Y_2 - X_2)^2}$$

or

$$D = \sqrt{(3-3)^2 + (7 - 7)^2}$$

or

$$D = \sqrt{0^2 - 0^2}$$

or

$$D = 0$$

The difference in execution is significant. To correct the bug, lines 1670 and 1680 should be changed to read:

```
1670      LET X=R1−E1
1680      LET Y=R2−E2
```

The block of coding would now produce the correct results.

Without documentation, the bug might have persisted for some time, eluding debugging attempts to find it simply because it is such a familiar-looking code block. With the documentation in place, however, the error becomes immediately visible. In fact, as before, if documentation had been included as the program was being written, in all probability the bug would never have occurred.

Explain Conditional Branches

One of the easiest ways to get hopelessly lost in a program is to have to attempt to wade through a series of IF statements (conditional branches) without benefit of documentation to explain what the importance and consequence of the various conditions are. The problem is not an idle one, since there are few programs of any versatility that do not make heavy use of IF statements.

The following example is of a very simple program written to play tic-tac-toe. This program makes no attempt to win, as each move is taken at random and the only conditional branch is a test to see if a space on the playing field has already been taken. The playing field is laid out as shown in Fig. 2-2. The program reads:

```
1 | 2 | 3
4 | 5 | 6
7 | 8 | 9
```

Fig. 2-2. Playing field for simplified tic-tac-toe game.

```
10 REM "TIC-TAC"
20 REM PROGRAM TO PLAY TIC-TAC-TOE
30 DIM S(9)
40 REM ZERO OUT SPACE ARRAY
50 FOR J=1 TO 9
60 LET S(J)=0
70 NEXT J
80 REM CLEAR MOVE COUNTER
90 LET L=0
100 PRINT "PLEASE INPUT YOUR SPACE NUMBER"
110 INPUT I
120 REM INCREMENT MOVE COUNTER
130 LET L=L+1
140 IF L>=9 THEN GOTO 260
150 LET S(I)=1
160 REM RND RETURNS A RANDOM NUMBER
170 REM BETWEEN 0 AND 1
175 LET R=(L*I)/(L+I)
180 LET K=INT(10*RND(R))
190 REM TEST IF THIS SPACE IS TAKEN
200 IF S(K)=1 THEN GOTO 180
210 LET S(K)=1
220 LET L=L+1
230 PRINT "I CHOOSE SPACE"; K
240 REM GO BACK FOR MORE INPUT
```

```
250 GOTO 100
260 PRINT "FIELD IS FULL, MUST END GAME"
270 END
```

The bug in this program is that the program is so limited. It makes no internal distinction between moves made by the operator and those made by the computer. It merely allows choices to continue until the playing field is full.

Or does it? Output from the program looks like this:

```
RUN
PLEASE INPUT YOUR SPACE NUMBER
?2
I CHOOSE SPACE 4
PLEASE INPUT YOUR SPACE NUMBER
?2
I CHOOSE SPACE 7
PLEASE INPUT YOUR SPACE NUMBER
?2
I CHOOSE SPACE 1
PLEASE INPUT YOUR SPACE NUMBER
?2
I CHOOSE SPACE 6
PLEASE INPUT YOUR SPACE NUMBER
?2
FIELD IS FULL, MUST END GAME
```

We cheated, but the program did not catch it. The program tested only on *its* choice of space to see if the space was already occupied. Not only that, the program won the game on its third move (1, 4, and 7 makes for a win down the first column) but was unable to recognize it. In addition, the program determined that the playing field was full by counting the number of entries made by it and the player, even though we entered the same number five times: five of our moves plus four of the computer's moves adds up to nine moves, and that is all the field will hold.

Obviously, the program has bugs. But they are not bugs of faulty programming; the program did not bomb in midexecution because of a bad instruction. Nor are the bugs caused by nonexistent or useless documentation. Rather, the bugs are related to insufficient programming: the code will only work under a very limited set of conditions.

If the operator was honest enough to only choose an open space, and good enough to always play a tied game, the two bugs which we just demonstrated would never be discovered. But placing those kinds of constraints on a program limits its application almost to the point of uselessness. We will now see how a few IF statements applied to a program can determine its success or failure:

```
10 REM "TIC-TAC"
20 REM PROGRAM TO PLAY TIC-TAC-TOE
30 DIM S(9), B(4)
40 REM ZERO OUT SPACE ARRAY
50 FOR J=1 TO 9
60      LET S(J)=0
70 NEXT J
80 REM CLEAR MOVE COUNTER
90 LET L=0
100 PRINT "PLEASE INPUT YOUR SPACE NUMBER"
110 INPUT I
120 IF S(I)>0 THEN GOTO 160
130 IF S(I)<0 THEN GOTO 180
140 LET L=L+1
150 GOTO 200
160 PRINT "YOU ARE ALREADY ON THAT SPACE!"
170 GOTO 100
180 PRINT "THAT'S MY SPACE!"
190 GOTO 100
200 LET S(I)=1
210 LET K=1
220 REM TEST FOR WINNING COMBINATION
230 FOR J=1 TO 3
240      LET A=(J-1)*3+1
250      LET B(1)=S(A)+S(A+2)+S(A+3)
260      LET B(2)=S(J)+S(J+1)+S(J+2)
270      IF ABS (B(1) )=3 THEN GOTO 350
280      IF ABS (B(2) )=3 THEN GOTO 350
290 NEXT J
300 LET B(3)=S(3)+S(5)+S(7)
310 LET B(4)=S(1)+S(5)+S(9)
```

```
320 IF ABS (B(3) )=3 THEN GOTO 350
330 IF ABS (B(4) )=3 THEN GOTO 350
340 GOTO 420
350 FOR J=1 TO 4
360      IF B(J)>0 THEN GOTO 400
365      IF B(J)<0 THEN GOTO 380
370 NEXT J
380 PRINT "YOU LOSE, TOO BAD"
390 GOTO 570
400 PRINT "YOU WIN"
410 GOTO 570
420 IF L>=9 THEN GOTO 560
430 IF K=0 THEN GOTO 100
440 LET K=0
450 REM RND RETURNS A RANDOM NUMBER
460 LET R=(L*I)/(L+I)
470 LET N=INT(10*RND(R))
475 IF N<1 THEN GOTO 495
480 REM TEST IF THIS SPACE IS TAKEN
490 IF S(N)=0 THEN GOTO 510
495 LET I=I+1
500 GOTO 470
510 LET S(N)=-1
520 LET L=L+1
530 PRINT "I CHOOSE SPACE"; N
540 REM TEST IF WE ARE THE WINNER
550 GOTO 220
560 PRINT "FIELD IS FULL"
570 PRINT "GAME IS OVER"
580 END
```

Essentially, the program is the same as before, with the exception that now it has been given the ability to do a little "creative thinking" on its own.

Output for this revised version of the program looks like this:

RUN
PLEASE INPUT YOUR SPACE NUMBER

?2
I CHOOSE SPACE 4
PLEASE INPUT YOUR SPACE NUMBER
?2
YOU ARE ALREADY ON THAT SPACE!

The new program will not allow us to cheat; that bug has been eliminated. Playing fair now, we continue the game trying for a win in the cen-
ter column.

PLEASE INPUT YOUR SPACE NUMBER
?8
I CHOOSE SPACE 7
PLEASE INPUT YOUR SPACE NUMBER
?5
I CHOOSE SPACE 6
YOU LOSE
GAME IS OVER

Wait! Now who is cheating? We had a win down the middle column.
Obviously, there must be a bug. We recall that the program is basically
the same as originally written, with the addition of some simple deci-
sion-making capabilities, in the form of a few IF statements.

It follows, then, that this new bug is related to the additional coding,
especially the conditional branches. But the program is 58 lines long, and
with a program this lengthy containing so many undocumented conditional branches, there is no simple way to determine what the code is
doing. Instead of being like a straight road running directly from beginning to end, the code has become a large treelike structure, with branches
splitting into more branches. Each IF statement increases the number of
potential paths by a power of two. In other words, if there are 10 separate
conditional branches in a program, as there are in *tic-tac,* there could be
as many as 2^{10}, or 1024 *different* paths. However, with our program for
tic-tac-toe, many of the alternatives merge and fold back on each other,
reducing the actual number of paths considerably.

A common way to learn how a program works (and to discover why
it does not work correctly), is to play computer—read through the program beginning at the top and work down.

To use this technique properly, we will have to make certain assumptions as we go along, and we will also have to remember that the
various quantities are equal to. For a program the length of *tic-tac* we can

probably do all of this in our head, although longer programs might require pencil and paper as a memory aid.

The first test we run across is at line 120:

```
120 IF S(I)>0 THEN GOTO 160
```

We know that S is the space array, corresponding to the nine playing spaces of the tic-tac-toe figure. We also know that the preceding line

```
110 INPUT I
```

refers to the space number that the player wants to take. S(I) then, refers to some quantity associated with space I.

However, we do not know the significance of the test. Assuming that S(I) is greater than zero, what does this imply? If the test is true, and S(I) is greater than zero, we must jump to line 160:

```
160 PRINT "YOU ARE ALREADY ON THAT SPACE!"
170 GOTO 100
```

Then we jump back up to line 100 where the player is requested to input a new value.

If we make the opposite assumption, that I is not greater than zero, but instead less than zero, we would not meet the test at line 120. We would then not be transferred to line 160, but would instead continue on to the following line. Once there, we would be shunted to line 180.

```
120 IF S (I)>0 THEN GOTO 160
130 IF S (I)<0 THEN GOTO 180
:
:
180 PRINT "THAT'S MY SPACE!"
190 GOTO 100
```

Now we know what happens if the space selected by the player already contains either a positive or a negative value: a warning message is printed and the player is asked to select a different space.

What if the space selected does not have a positive or a negative value associated with it?

```
100 PRINT "PLEASE INPUT YOUR SPACE NUMBER"
110 INPUT I
120 IF S(I)>0 THEN GOTO 160
130 IF S(I)<0 THEN GOTO 180
140 LET L=L+1
150 GOTO 200
160 PRINT "YOU ARE ALREADY ON THAT SPACE!"
170 GOTO 100
180 PRINT "THAT'S MY SPACE!"
190 GOTO 100
200 LET S(I)=1
```

If the value of the space chosen is zero, we jump down to line 200 and set the value of that space to 1.

We now know enough about the functioning of the two conditional tests at lines 120 and 130 to document them in the program.

The program tests to see if a space chosen by the player is already occupied; and further, if the space is already taken by the player himself. The program makes the distinction by assigning a +1 value to a space occupied by the player, and a −1 value to a space occupied by the computer (line 510).

We might therefore insert the following documentation immediately before the first IF statement at line 120:

```
112 REM TEST IF SPACE IS TAKEN
114 REM IF SO, WARN AND TRY AGAIN
116 REM S(I)>0 MEANS PLAYER ALREADY HAS SPACE
118 REM S(I)<0 MEANS COMPUTER ALREADY DOES
```

The most extensive modification in the program is contained in the 14 lines of code beginning with line 230, and prefaced by the statement:

```
220 REM TEST FOR WINNING COMBINATION
```

Most of the conditional branches contained in the program appear in this block of code, so chances are good that the bug is also in this block. As always, the challenge is in trying to find it. Still playing the part of the computer, we attempt to execute the code.

```
230 FOR  J=1 TO 3
240       LET A=(J−1)*3+1
250       LET B(1)=S(A)+S(A+2)+S(A+3)
260       LET B(2)=S(J)+S(J+1)+S(J+2)
270       IF ABS (B(1) )=3 THEN GOTO 350
280       IF ABS (B(2) )=3 THEN GOTO 350
290 NEXT J
300 LET B(3)=S(3)+S(5)+S(7)
310 LET B(4)=S(1)+S(5)+S(9)
320 IF ABS (B(3) )=3 THEN GOTO 350
330 IF ABS (B(4) )=3 THEN GOTO 350
340 GOTO 410
350 FOR J=1 TO 4
360       IF B(J)>0 THEN GOTO 400
365       IF B(J)<0 THEN GOTO 380
370 NEXT J
```

First, we enter a loop indexed by the variable J. We set up a secondary index variable A and then proceed to find two sums, keyed to the indexes of A and J. If either of these two sums is equal to 3, we branch out of the loop to line 350. After three times through the loop, if we have still not found a sum equal to 3, we calculate two more sums, $B(3)$ and $B(4)$, and test if they are equal to three. If either sum meets the test, we again branch to line 350. If none of the eight sums we have calculated is equal to 3, we jump to line 420, and then eventually to where either the player or the computer makes the next move.

What is the significance of the eight sums, and of testing them to see if their absolute value is equal to 3? The program calculates eight sums because there are eight ways to win at tic-tac-toe: three horizontal, three vertical, and two more along the diagonals. Also, each winning combination would have to contain either three +1s (if the player wins), or three −1s (if the computer wins).

We may therefore conclude that the sums calculated in the loop (lines 230 to 290), $B(1)$ being calculated three times, as is $B(2)$, relate to the horizontal and vertical winning combinations. $B(3)$ and $B(4)$ must therefore relate to the diagonal combinations, and indeed their subscripts lend strong support to this idea.

The eight possible winning combinations are:

HORIZONTAL: 1, 2, 3
              4, 5, 6
              7, 8, 9
VERTICAL: 1, 4, 7
              2, 5, 8
              3, 6, 9
DIAGONAL: 1, 5, 9
              3, 5, 7

Since the horizontal and vertical combinations are calculated in the loop beginning at line 230, the bug is most likely there.

As mentioned before, A and J are the two independent indexes used to specify the S-array subscripts. By writing the equations for B(1) and B(2) only once, and then placing them inside a loop, we have saved between 6 and 10 lines of repetitive coding. But we have also made things more difficult to follow than if it had all been written out in full.

We note that A, a variable being used as an index, is itself being keyed to the value of J, the master loop index. Suppose we were to write out the values of A, B(1), B(2), etc., as J increments through the loop:

First time: J = 1
               A = (J−1)*3+1 = (1−1)*3+1 = 1
               B(1) = S(1)+S(3)+S(4)
               B(2) = S(1)+S(2)+S(3)
Second time: J = 2
               A = (2−1)*3+1 = 4
               B(1) = S(4)+S(6)+S(7)
               B(2) = S(2)+S(3)+S(4)
Third time: J = 3
               A = (3−1)*3+1 = 7
               B(1) = S(7)+S(9)+S(11)
               B(2) = S(3)+S(4)+S(5)

We have found the bug. The indexing method is completely messed up: only one combination out of the six, the first calculation of B(2), is correct. The rest are nonsense. We can see now why the computer won: its "winning combination" of 4, 6, 7 is the second calculation of B(1).

The correct indexing, along with proper documentation, would look like this:

```
220 REM TEST FOR WINNING COMBINATION
222 REM FIRST LOOK FOR WINS ALONG
224 REM ROWS OR COLUMNS
230 FOR J=1 TO 3
232 REM A IS INDEX FOR ROWS
240      LET A=(J-1)*3+1
250      LET B(1)=S(A)+S(A+1)+S(A+2)
260      LET B(2)=S(J)+S(J+3)+S(J+6)
262 REM IF SUM IS ALL + OR -1
264 REM WE HAVE A WINNER
270      IF ABS(B(1) )=3 THEN GOTO 350
280      IF ABS(B(2) )=3 THEN GOTO 350
290 NEXT J
292 REM CALCULATE DIAGONAL SUMS
300 LET B(3)=S(3)+S(5)+S(7)
310 LET B(4)=S(1)+S(5)+S(9)
320 IF ABS (B(3) )=3 THEN GOTO 350
330 IF ABS (B(4) )=3 THEN GOTO 350
332 REM NO WIN CONTINUE GAME
340 GOTO 420
342 REM IS PLAYER THE WINNER?
350 FOR J=1 TO 4
360      IF B(J)>0 THEN GOTO 400
365      IF B(J)<0 THEN GOTO 380
370 NEXT J
```

Tic-tac is not a very aggressive program, since all of its moves are random while those of the player are deliberate. Other, more sophisticated processes could be built in to make the program actively seek winning combinations. But as each refinement is coded in, we should always remember to document our steps, lest they rise up to haunt us with bugs later on.

Explain Condensed Coding

As mentioned previously, the experienced programmer learns to recognize certain commonly used sequences of code. This is a labor-saving device as much as anything else, since it means not having to reinvent the wheel every time the job calls for something round!

Another programming labor-saving device is condensed coding. With growing experience and confidence, many programmers find it unnecessary to break up operations into many small steps, as they did when they were beginners. Rather than having one operation for each line of code, they let a single line do many jobs.

Condensing code saves space on paper because there are fewer lines of code to write; and it saves space in the machine, since there are fewer variables in need of a memory location. But condensed coding also has the potential of making a program very cryptic and hard to follow.

Consider the following piece of condensed code:

```
100 LET P1=B*(1+S1(L)+C(M)+S2(N) )
```

This example might not be too hard to recognize as the sales price computation equation we used earlier for Universal Consolidated Widgits. In this case, three lines of code have been condensed into one. Even though the variables *S1*, *C*, and *S2* have already been identified earlier in this program, some documentation should still be included preceding line 100:

```
70 REM COMPUTE SALES PRICE A SUM OF
80 REM BASE PRICE AND B TIMES
90 REM STYLE, COLOR, AND SIZE CFM'S
100 LET P1=B*(1+S1(L)+C(M)+S2(N) )
```

Jumps to Subroutines

Blocks of code which are used over and over again within the same program are usually given the status of subroutines. A subroutine is a block of code which usually performs only one or two basic functions and is written into a program only once. But a subroutine is referred to many times within a program from many different locations in the program. Since it is written only once, the chances for error are minimized; and since the subroutine can be referenced from anywhere in the main program, it amounts to having been written out in full whenever it is requested.

A subroutine is invoked as follows:

```
210 GOSUB 1570
```

In this example, line 210 causes the flow of the program to jump to the subroutine beginning at line 1570. When the subroutine has finished its task, the program flow then jumps back to the line immediately following line 210, and the program continues to execute.

As we see in the example, the call to a subroutine and the subroutine itself can be separated by a considerable distance, even though such separation complicates matters and makes debugging difficult. There may be a number of subroutines in a program, and unless the function of each subroutine is known intimately, we would have to be constantly flipping back and forth between the line that calls the subroutine and the subroutine itself, checking which variables are changed and what they stand for.

Happily, most of this confusion can be erased through the use of proper documentation. Just before each call to a subroutine, a few remarks are inserted to explain what the subroutine will do and what important variables will be changed as a result of its actions. Still using the above example:

```
204 REM FIND DISTANCE BETWEEN (X1,Y1)
206 REM AND (X2,Y2)
210 GOSUB 1570
```

Warn About Potential Bugs

There are times when a programmer might write a section of code knowing full well that it has a bug in it. Such action is usually taken when the programmer is running out of time and does not want to spend the time and effort required to write bug-free code, assuming that the specific set of circumstances which cause the bug to manifest itself will never happen.

Such an assumption is never really valid. The programmer who wrote the shaky coding might likely forget the qualification in a few weeks. Equally likely, the circumstances which the programmer thought would never happen will undoubtedly arise.

The only way to prevent a bug is to write it out of the code. If a situation comes up that makes it truly impossible to write sturdy code, then a warning message stating the existence of a possible bug should be inserted into the code. This will insure against the certain-to-occur debugging task to come at a later date.

As an example:

```
740 LET R=43+8*LOG(X2*A)
```

For the purposes of this discussion, it makes no difference what the significance of the above line of code is, nor does it matter what job is performed by the program of which it is a part. What *is* important is that should the quantity X2*A ever become less than or equal to zero, the program would bomb when it tried to take the logarithm of such a number.

The most proper and complete solution to such a bug would be to test on the quantity X2*A, and if it should ever fail to be greater than zero, print a message and perform some alternate computation. If it is not possible to code the bug out, then a remark similar to the following ought to be inserted immediately preceding the offending line of code to warn others using the program:

```
734 REM THIS SECTION ONLY VALID
736 REM FOR (X2*A)>0
740 LET R=43+8*LOG(X2*A)
```

3.

PLAYING COMPUTER

One of the best ways to debug a program is to play computer. This method often takes more time than others, and is not as easy as tracing program execution with print statements, but the attention to detail that playing computer requires of the programmer forces a clear understanding of what a particular piece of code is doing.

As an example, we will try to debug the following program, the flow-chart for which is shown in Fig. 3-1.

```
10 REM PROGRAM IPOWR
20 REM FINDS THE VALUE OF A TO THE B
30 REM POWER WHERE A AND B ARE BOTH
40 REM INTEGERS AND THE RESULT IS
50 REM ACCURATE TO 100 PLACES
60 REM SET UP BUFFERS
70 DIM A1(100), B1(100), A2(100)
80 DIM C1(10), B2(100)
90 LET J=0
100 REM J=ROOT DIGIT COUNTER
110 REM CLEAR BUFFERS
120 FOR I=1 TO 100
130 LET A1(I)=0
140 LET B1(I)=0
150 LET A2(I)=0
160 LET B2(I)=0
```

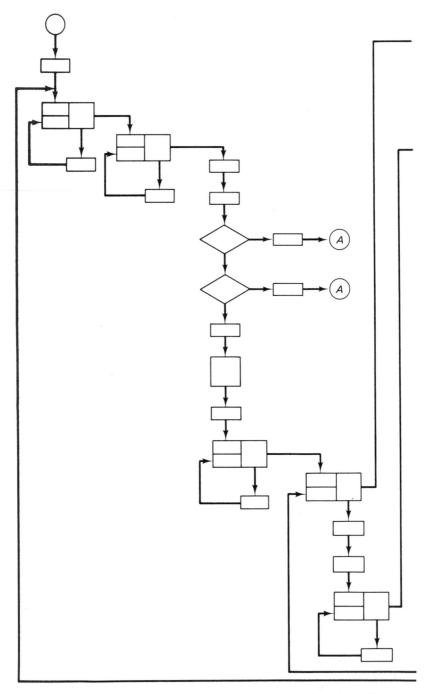

Fig. 3-1. Flowchart from program IPOWR, general overview. The individual blocks are identified in subsequent illustrations.

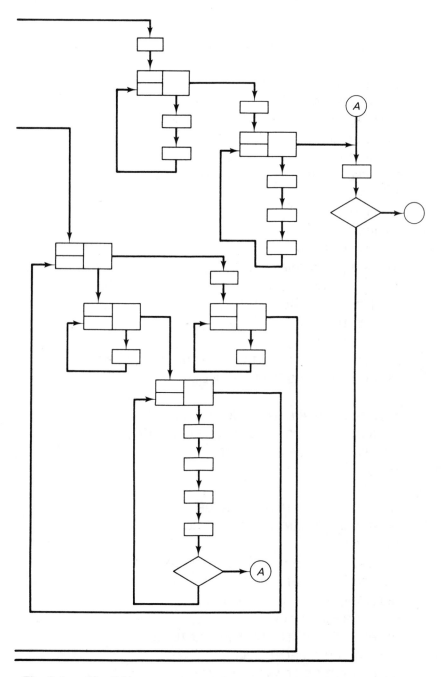

Fig. 3-1. *(Cont'd.)*

```
170 NEXT I
180 REM A1=ROOT STORAGE BY DIGIT
190 REM B1=CARRY ARRAY
200 REM A2=PRINT ARRAY
210 REM B2=TEMP RESULT ARRAY
220 FOR I=1 TO 10
230 LET C1(I)=0
240 NEXT I
250 REM C1=MULTIPLIER DIGIT STORAGE
260 INPUT R, E
270 PRINT "& K"
280 PRINT "WORKING . . ."
290 REM R=ROOT
300 REM E=EXPONENT
310 IF R=0 THEN GOTO 1290
320 IF E=0 THEN GOTO 1310
330 LET R1=R
340 LET R2=R
350 REM R1=INCREMENTAL FLOATING POINT RESULT
360 REM R2=CONSTANT MULTIPLIER
370 REM
380 REM REDUCE E BY 1 SINCE NO. OF
390 REM MULTIPLICATIONS IS ONE LESS THAN
400 REM VALUE OF EXPONENT
410 LET E=E-1
420 LET J2=E
430 REM J2=EXPONENT STORAGE
440 REM INCREMENT ROOT DIGIT COUNTER
450 LET J=J+1
460 REM TRANSFER ROOT TO A1 ARRAY
470 REM A DIGIT AT A TIME
480 LET A1(J)=R-(10*INT(R/10))
490 LET R=INT(R/10)
500 REM TEST IF ALL DIGITS ARE ENTERED
510 IF R>0 THEN GOTO 450
520 REM SET ROOT AND MULT. ARRAYS EQUAL
530 FOR I2=1 TO J
540 LET C1(I2)=A1(I2)
```

```
550 NEXT I2
560 REM BEGIN LOOP ON EXPONENT
570 FOR I=1 TO E
580 REM MULT. INCREASING RESULT BY ROOT
590 LET R1=R1*R2
600 REM HOW MANY DIGITS IN RESULT?
610 LET P=INT(LOG10(R1))+1
620 REM P=NUMBER OF PLACES
630 REM CLEAR TEMP RESULT ARRAY
640 FOR J1=1 TO 100
650 LET B2(J1)=0
660 NEXT J1
670 REM BEGIN LOOP ON MULTIPLIER DIGIT COUNT
680 FOR M1=1 TO J
690 REM CLEAR CARRY ARRAY
700 FOR N=1 TO 100
710 LET B1(N)=0
720 NEXT N
730 REM BEGIN LOOP ON MULTIPLICAND DIGIT COUNT
740 FOR M2=1 TO P
770 REM DO ONE DIGIT MULTIPLY, MULTIPLIER*
780 REM MULTIPLICAND+CARRY
790 LET T1=A1(M2)*C1(M1)+B1(M2)
800 REM T1=TEMPORARY RESULT
810 REM WHAT IS OUR DIGIT POSITION?
820 LET D=M1-1+M2
830 REM ADD RESULT OF THIS MULTIPLICATION
840 REM TO PREVIOUS RESULT
850 REM (T1-10*(INT(T1/10)))=UNITS DIGIT OF RESULT
860 REM B2=PREVIOUS RESULT DIGIT
870 LET T2=(T1-10*(INT(T1/10)))+B2(D)
880 REM BREAK THIS RESULT INTO UNITS AND TENS
890 REM FOR THE UNITS;
900 LET B2(D)=T2-10*(INT(T2/10))
910 REM FOR THE TENS;
920 LET B2(D+1)-INT(T2/10)
930 REM HAVE WE RUN OUT OF ROOM?
940 IF D+1=100 THEN GOTO 1270
```

```
950 REM FIND NEW CARRY DIGIT
960 LET B1(M2+1)=INT(T1/10)
970 NEXT M2
980 NEXT M1
990 REM UPDATE MULTIPLICAND ARRAY
1000 FOR N=1 TO 100
1010 LET A1(N)=B2(N)
1020 NEXT N
1060 NEXT I
1070 REM REVERSE ORDER OF RESULT ARRAY TO PRINT
1080 FOR N=1 TO P
1090 LET C=(P+1)−N
1100 LET A2(N)=A1(C)
1110 NEXT N
1120 REM PREPARE TO DISPLAY ANSWER
1130 REM RESTORE EXPONENT
1140 LET E=E+1
1150 CURSOR 6, 0
1160 PRINT "FOR THE EXPRESSION"; R2; "TO THE";
1165 PRINT E; "POWER, THE ANSWER IS"
1170 FOR N=1 TO P
1180 CURSOR 8, N
1190 IF N>60 THEN CURSOR 9, N−60
1200 LET Z=A2(N)+48
1210 SET DB=Z
1220 NEXT N
1250 PRINT
1260 GOTO 1320
1270 PRINT "NUMBER TOO BIG, OVERFLOW"
1280 GOTO 1320
1290 PRINT "ZERO TO ANY POWER IS ZERO"
1300 GOTO 1320
1310 PRINT "ANY NUMBER TO THE ZERO POWER IS ONE"
1320 PRINT "TYPE 1 FOR MORE, 0 TO STOP"
1330 INPUT S
1340 IF S=1 THEN GOTO 90
1350 END
```

Program IPOWR has been nicely documented—nearly every operation is prefaced by a short explanatory statement, and nearly every variable is defined. Still, the mechanics of IPOWR are not easily understood without study. This program displays many traits referred to in earlier discussions: there are numerous loops and loops-within-loops, and condensed coding such as the following is common:

```
870 LET T2=(T1−10*(INT(T1/10)))+B2(D)
```

The remarks at the beginning of IPOWR state that the program "finds the value of A to the B power where A and B are both integers and the result is accurate to 100 places."

What is so special about that? Raising one number to the power of another number is no great task; we merely need write:

```
LET C=A∧B
```

Suppose we were to do precisely that. Suppose further that we were to choose:

```
A=14
B=23
```

The result would be printed out:

```
C=2.2958579E+26
```

The SOL BASIC compiler will let us specify output formats as either integer, floating-point, or exponential notation. If we want greater accuracy, we might try to print the result out in integer format as in the following example. After all, a whole number multiplied by itself n times will still yield a whole number.

```
PRINT %26I;C
```

Unfortunately, the largest field we may specify on the SOL (and this is similar to most other machines) is a field 26 digits wide. The result of our effort in the above example, then, is:

FO ERROR IN LINE_____

The term *FO* means *field overflow;* we have tried to display a number larger than the specified format will allow. We should have seen that the number would not fit a 26I field: E+26 implies 26 digits to the right of the decimal point, not including the digit 2 on the left of the decimal point. The upper limit on field size is 26 digits only, not 27, so our number is too large for the format.

What if we were to try an exponential representation, with the maximum number of decimal places displayed? Again, the upper limit on total number of characters is 26, and after taking into account plus and minus signs and room for the exponent, the maximum number of digits to the right of the decimal point is 19, as follows:

PRINT %26E19;C
C=2.2958579000000000000E+26

It does not look as though we gained any accuracy: we now have the number represented by 20 digits, but 12 of those digits are zeros. If we do some long multiplication by hand, we discover that those trailing zeros are purely an artifact of the way our computer handles its internal representation of numbers.

As an example, raising 14 only to the eighth power instead of the twenty-third as in previous examples, long multiplication results in:

$14^8 = 1475789056$

Already we have two digits of greater accuracy than the computer can provide. The computer's problem is that it cannot keep track of more than 8 digits at a time. What we need (if we are to have answers accurate to more than 8 digits) is a program that mimics hand multiplication, a program which (1) takes first the *units* digit of the multiplier and multiplies it by all of the digits in the multiplicand, then (2) takes the *tens* digit and does the same, then (3) moves on to the *hundreds* digit, (4) the *thousands* digit, and so on as required, until all digits of the multiplier have been multiplied against all digits of the multiplicand, and the many intermediate results have been added up to produce the final result:

```
    4572
×    326
```

27432 ← ——————— result of 4572 × 6

9144 ← ——————— result of 4572 × 2

13716 ← ——————— result of 4572 × 3

1490472 ← ——————— total

Apparently, IPOWR is supposed to do just that: digit-by-digit multiplications between numbers to arrive at an answer accurate to 100 places. Considering that the unaided computer is accurate only to 8 places, the program IPOWR, if it works, represents a considerable improvement.

In order to test IPOWR, we must first provide an accurate standard of reference. We can do this by performing a hand multiplication on some number raised to a conveniently low power. For this first trial, the answer need not exceed 8 digits, although that aspect of the program will have to be tested eventually.

Suppose we try 5 × 5. We write:

```
    5
×   5
───
   25
```

Using the computer, we would have:

```
? 5, 2
WORKING. . .
FOR THE NUMBER 5 TO THE 2 POWER, THE
ANSWER IS 25
```

No problem there. Let's try a two-digit number, something easy:

```
   10
×  10
───
  100
```

and, using IPOWR:

```
? 10, 2
WORKING . . .
```

FOR THE NUMBER 10 TO THE 2 POWER, THE
ANSWER IS 100

Everything appears to be working correctly, but 10 is a special-case
number, one which does not test those parts of the program involved
with carrying over partial results, etc. We decide to choose a more representative number:

```
      46
  ×   46
  ------
     276
     184
  ------
    2116
```

and:

```
  ? 46, 2
  WORKING . . .
  FOR THE NUMBER 46 TO THE 2 POWER, THE
  ANSWER IS 1916
```

A bug! The answer is incorrect by 200. We try another set of values, first
by hand:

```
      24
  ×   24
  ------
      96
      48
  ------
     576
  ×   24
  ------
    2304
   1152
  -------
   13824
```

then using the program:

```
  ? 24, 3
  WORKING . . .
```

FOR THE NUMBER 24 TO THE 3 POWER, THE
ANSWER IS 11524

This time the computer's answer is off by 2300. The magnitude of the two errors can perhaps give us some clue as to the origin of the bug, but 2300 does not seem related in any simple way to the first error we observed of 200. If we study the second level of the hand multiplication, however, something very interesting presents itself.

$$
\begin{array}{r}
576 \\
\times\ 24 \\
\hline
\end{array}
$$

Group A ⟶ 2304 ⟵ Group B
(1152)

13824

If we take the digits circled in group B, we have 11524, the same as the incorrect value given by the computer. In addition, the digits in group A (after allowing for the digit 4 which was used to occupy the *units* place) equal 2300, the magnitude of the error.

It would seem we have found the bug. IPOWR is not correctly summing the temporary results. Is this true? If it is, we should observe the same bug for all other calculations involving two intermediate sums.

We can check our hypothesis by looking at the previous example:

$$
\begin{array}{r}
46 \\
\times\ 46 \\
\hline
\end{array}
$$

Group A ⟶ 276 ⟵ Group B
(184)

2116

Applying the same logic to this example, we could predict that the answer would be 1846, with a resulting error of 270. As we saw, however, in this case the program gave an answer of 1916, and an error of 200. Our method does not work in this case. Consequently, we must say that our explanation for the bug, while it looks good for the case of 24^3, did so only by a fortunate set of circumstances, and no more.

We are going to have to look much deeper to find the cause of this bug.

IPOWR is much longer than any of the programs we've looked at so far; but by using techniques already familiar to us we can break the program down into workable blocks.

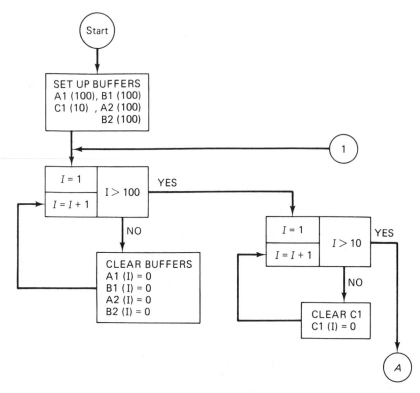

Fig. 3-2.   Flowchart, program IPOWR—initialization and clearing of the buffers.

We begin with the flowchart representation of the IPOWR initialization sequence (Fig. 3-2). The flowchart will give us the structural outline of this phase of IPOWR, while the program listing will tell us precisely what is taking place.

We are now playing computer. We will do whatever we are commanded to do by the lines of code. As we execute the program we will use a pad of paper and a pencil as our memory. In the interest of saving time, however, we will not find it necessary to list the entire contents of a 100-element array, for instance.

The first thing we must do is allocate room in our memory for five different arrays, as in Fig. 3-3. We cannot correctly say that the arrays, since they are newly created, contain nothing, and that "nothing" is logically and mathematically equivalent to zero. If we want each memory location of each array to contain a zero, we must actively load it with a zero. After

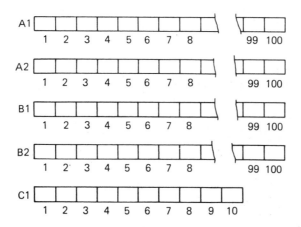

Fig. 3-3. Representation of the arrays in memory, after creation by DIM statement.

Fig. 3-4. Array A1 cleared and initialized with all zeros. Arrays A2, B1, B2, and C1 would look similar.

we were to so load array A1 it would look like Fig. 3-4. Arrays A2, B1, B2, and C1 would be similar.

Now we can proceed to the next flowchart segment, illustrated in Fig. 3-5. (Remember, these segments are taken from the master flowchart of Fig. 3-1.) We are now told to get the variables R and E from the keyboard. We already know that 46^2 gave an incorrect answer of 1916 when it should have been 2116, so since there is only one level of multiplication involved (simplifying our manual trace), we decide to use those same numbers:

$$\underline{R} = 46$$
$$\underline{E} = 2$$

Exponentiating a number, or raising a number to the power n, means that we will multiply that number times itself $n-1$ times. We will therefore be using E as an index variable for a master loop over the total number of multiplications. But in order to do so correctly we must first decrease the value of E by 1:

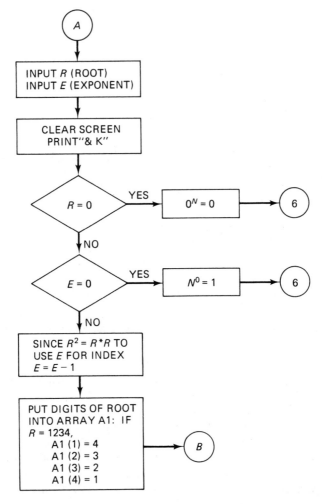

Fig. 3-5. Flowchart, program IPOWR—input of variables, test for zero values, load root array.

$$E = E - 1 = 2 - 1 = 1$$

Since we will be performing a digit-by-digit multiplication we must break up the root value R, one digit at a time, and store those digits in array A1. The algorithm (the pattern) we use to do this is:

480 LET A1($\underline{J}$)=$\underline{R}$−(10*INT($\underline{R}$/10))

The computer's operational hierarchy begins with the innermost set of parenthesis and works out, each time performing mathematical operations according to the rules:

Priority	Operation
1	- (unary negate)
2	^ (exponentiate)
3	* , / (multiply, divide)
4	+ , − (add, subtract)

We, as computer, must do the same. Using $R = 46$, we would have:

1. $(\underline{R}/10) = 46/10$
   $\qquad\quad = 4.6$
2. $INT(\underline{R}/10) = INT(4.6)$
   $\qquad\qquad\quad = 4$
3. $10*INT(\underline{R}/10) = 10*4$
   $\qquad\qquad\qquad\quad = 40$
4. $\underline{R}\text{-}(10*INT(\underline{R}/10)) = 46\text{-}40$
   $\qquad\qquad\qquad\qquad = 6$

$A1(1) = 6$

The first time through the loop J would equal 1, so array A1 would look like Fig. 3-6.

Fig. 3-6. Array A1 with units digit of the multiplicand loaded into the first element.

The next command:

490 LET $\underline{R}$ = $INT(\underline{R}/10)$

replaces R with a new value. The phrase on the right side of the equal sign looks familiar from before. R still equals 46 going into this line of code:

$\underline{R}=46$
1. $\underline{R}/10 = 46/10$
   $\qquad\quad = 4.6$

2. $INT(\underline{R}/10) = INT(4.6)$
$$= 4$$

3. $\underline{R}=4$

We now loop back up to line 450 where we increment the value of J:

$\underline{J}=\underline{J}+1$
$=1+1$
$=2$

and begin again. This time:

$\underline{R}=4$
$\underline{J}=2$
$A1(\underline{J})=\underline{R}-(10*INT(\underline{R}/10))$

1. $\underline{R}/10 = 4/10$
$$= .4$$

2. $INT(\underline{R}/10) = INT(.4)$
$$= 0$$

3. $10*INT(\underline{R}/10) = 10*0$
$$= 0$$

4. $\underline{R}-10*INT(\underline{R}/10) = 4-0$
$$= 4$$

$A1(2) = 4$

Array A1 now looks like Fig. 3-7.
Again we find a new value for R:

$\underline{R}=INT(\underline{R}/10)$
$=INT(4/10)$
$=0$

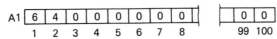

Fig. 3-7. Array A1 with both digits of the multiplicand loaded into the first two elements.

Since R=0, the test at line 510 fails:

```
510 IF R>0 THEN GOTO 450
```

and we proceed in the execution of the program.

Since we want to multiply R times itself E number of times, we must first set the multiplier and the multiplicand equal to each other. We do this with a simple loop, after which arrays A1 (multiplicand) and C1 (multiplier) look like Fig. 3-8.

A1	6	4	0	0	0	0	0	0	0	…	0	0
	1	2	3	4	5	6	7	8	9	…	99	100

C1	6	4	0	0	0	0	0	0	0	0
	1	2	3	4	5	6	7	8	9	10

Fig. 3-8. Equating of arrays A1 (multiplicand) and C1 (multiplier).

We now begin the master loop over the number of multiplications, indexed by E:

```
570 FOR I=1 TO E
```

Indexing is always a good source of bugs, so we will want to pay close attention to how the index values are used and updated. To make the task a little easier we will start a special table where we can keep track of index variable values, as in Fig. 3-9. We're working in that segment of the flowchart depicted in Fig. 3-10.

IPOWR spends the bulk of its time looping over 100-element arrays like A1, A2, etc. We can speed up program execution if we only concern

Index	Function	Value
I	EXPONENT	1

Fig. 3-9. Index variable status for first loop, at line 570.

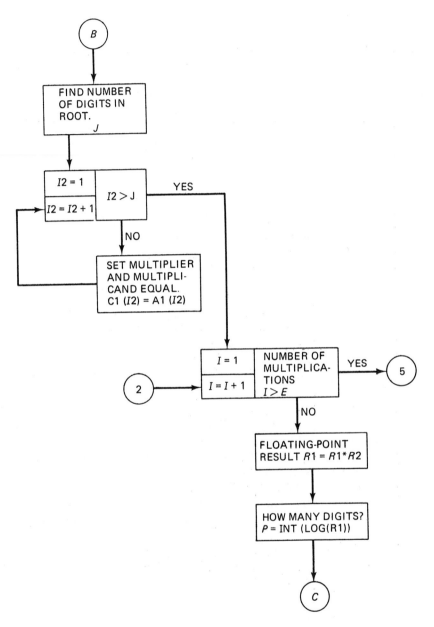

Fig. 3-10. Flowchart, program IPOWR—equate multiplier and multiplicand, begin loop over total number of multiplications, and calculate number
of digits in current temporary result.

ourselves with those elements which are active. One way to do this is to do a floating-point multiplication operation and find out from it how many active digits are required to represent the answer.

```
590 LET R1=R1*R2
600 REM HOW MANY DIGITS IN RESULT?
610 LET P=INT(LOG10(R1))+1
620 REM P=NUMBER OF PLACES
```

In our role as computer, we would do the following:

1. $\underline{R}$=R1*R2
    =46 × 46
    =2116.0
2. LOG10(R1)=LOG(2116)
    =3.3255
3. INT(LOG10(R1))=INT(3.3255)
    =3
4. INT(LOG10(R1))+1=3+1
    =4

$\underline{P}$=4

There are in fact four digits which make up the number 2116.

We now enter the many loops-within-loops of program IPOWR. A general outline of the program's structure in this regard is shown in Fig. 3-11.

The asterisk in Fig. 3-11 identifies our current position, while the loops are all marked with their function and the name of their index variable.

We note that loop 2 clears the temporary result storage array, B2. This array was already cleared and loaded with zeros at the top of the program, but we do it again here. Why? Because after every transit through the main loop, the temporary array will contain data from the previous calculation, which must be cleared away if the current calculation is going to be correct.

We use loop 4 to clear the carry array for the same reason.

Arriving at line 790, we are inside the innermost loop and at the meat of the calculation. We check the status of our index variables in Fig. 3-12, and we execute line 790. The flowchart segment now being processed is illustrated in Fig. 3-13. Our index table gives us the current values of M1

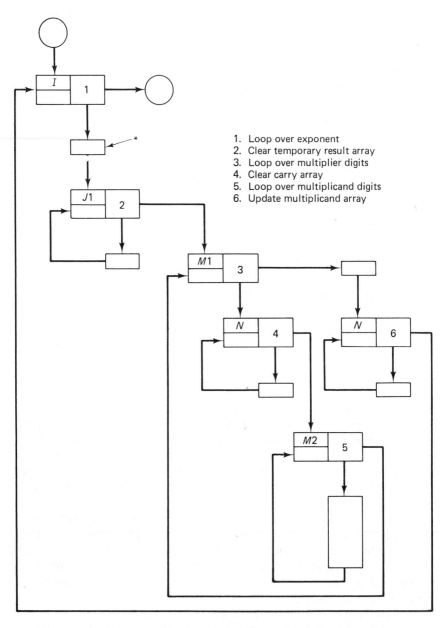

1. Loop over exponent
2. Clear temporary result array
3. Loop over multiplier digits
4. Clear carry array
5. Loop over multiplicand digits
6. Update multiplicand array

Fig. 3-11. Flowchart of program IPOWR showing those loops directly concerned with digit-by-digit multiplication.

Index	Function	Value
I	EXPONENT	1
$M1$	MULTIPLIER	1
$M2$	MULTIPLICAND	1

Fig. 3-12. Index variable status for first loop, at line 790.

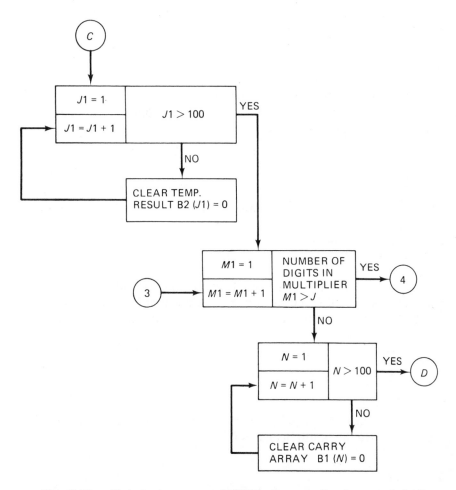

Fig. 3-13. Flowchart, program IPOWR—temporarily clear result buffer, begin loop on number of digits in multiplier, and clear carry array.

and M2, and we can check our arrays to see what values are being pointed to. We find:

```
A1(M2)=A1(1)=6
C1(M1)=C1(1)=6
B1(M2)=B1(1)=0
```

so we may decode line 790 to read as follows:

```
LET T1=A1(1)*C1(1)+B1(1)
    T1=6*6+0
    T1=36
```

It might help if we had stopped to relate these events to the steps which one must go through to accomplish multiplication by hand. Our object is to multiply 46 by 46:

```
   46
× 46
```

We may identify the two participants in the multiplication as follows:

```
   46 multiplicand
× 46 multiplier
```

Perhaps now it is easier to understand why we loaded the arrays A1 and C1 in apparent reverse order; in multiplication we first multiply the units digit of the multiplier times the units digit of the multiplicand:

```
× 4
───
36
```

But the 3 of 36 does not go below the line; it is a carry-over number and is written above the multiplicand as follows:

```
   3
   46
× 46
───
    6
```

Program IPOWR accomplishes this by first determining where to place the units digit of the temporary result (Fig. 3-14).

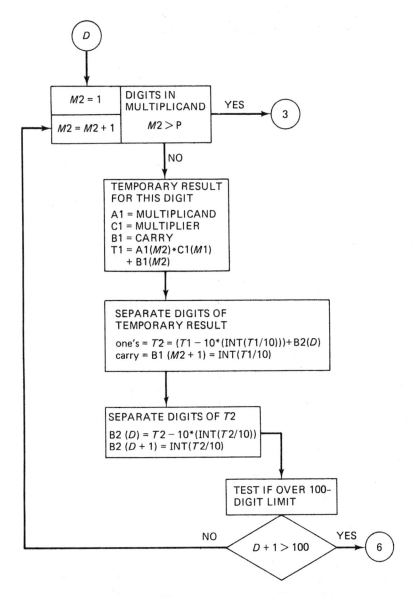

Fig. 3-14. Flowchart, program IPOWR—loop over digits in multiplicand, find temporary results for each digit, add the units, carry the tens, and check for overflow.

```
810 REM WHAT IS OUR DIGIT POSITION?
820 LET D=M1−1+M2
```

Referring back to our table of index values, we know that:

$M1 = 1$

$M2 = 1$

therefore

$$D = M1 - 1 + M2$$
$$= 1 - 1 + 1$$
$$= 1$$
$$D = 1$$

The 6 of 36 therefore belongs in the first digit place. We cannot, however, simply assign it to that space and continue. This same block of code must be correct for any number in any position, which means that there may be occasions in which the units digit of the just-calculated temporary result must be added to a digit already occupying that space to yield the final result. Line 870 does this:

```
870 LET T2=(T1−10*(INT(T1/10)))+B2(D)
```

We know that D is the pointer to the current digit position, and the coding underlined is also familiar to us as a pattern which replaces the rightmost digit of a number with zero. We have, therefore:

$$T2 = 36 - 30 + B2(1)$$
$$= 6 + B2(1)$$
$$= 6 + 0$$
$$= 6$$
$$T2 = 6$$

The quantity $B2(1)$ is the digit from a previous calculation referred to earlier. But why couldn't we have performed the following?

```
B2(D)=(T1−10*(INT(T1/10)))+B2(D)
```

The reason we cannot perform the above calculation is that T2 might very well be a two-digit number, and each of the arrays—A1, A2, B1, B2, and C1—may only hold one digit per element. Lines 900 and 920 take care of this task by breaking T2 up into its two component digits and assigning them to neighboring positions in array B2:

900 LET B2(D)=T2−10*(INT(T2/10))
920 LET B2(D+1)=INT(T2/10)

Updating the carry array, B1, is accomplished at line 960:

960 LET B1(M2+1)=INT(T1/10)

Now is a good time to review the index values and the contents of the various arrays, as in Fig. 3-15.

Index	Function	Value
I	EXPONENT	1
$M1$	MULTIPLIER	1
$M2$	MULTIPLICAND	1
D	DIGIT POINTER	1

(A)

| A1 | 6 | 4 | 0 | 0 | 0 | 0 | 0 | 0 | 0 | | 0 | 0 | (Multiplicand) |

| A2 | 0 | 0 | 0 | 0 | 0 | 0 | 0 | 0 | 0 | | 0 | 0 | (Printout) |

| B1 | 0 | 3 | 0 | 0 | 0 | 0 | 0 | 0 | 0 | | 0 | 0 | (Carry) |

| B2 | 6 | 0 | 0 | 0 | 0 | 0 | 0 | 0 | 0 | | 0 | 0 | (Temporary result) |

　　1　2　3　4　5　6　7　8　9　　　99　100

(B)

Fig. 3-15. In (A), index variable status (first traverse through each loop, at line 900); (B) shows array contents at end of first digit multiplication. Note that the 3 was carried into element B1(2).

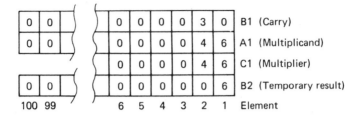

Fig. 3-16. Array grid overlaid on conventional representation of hand multiplication to show relationship to various elements.

If we were to lay a grid on top of our hand calculation, and label it to correspond to the various arrays being used in IPOWR, we would find results as in Fig. 3-16. The similarity to our hand method is obvious.

We have finished our first traverse through loop 5, so we must now go back up to statement 740, increment the index variable M2, and go through the loop again.

As before, we execute line 790:

790 LET T1 = A1(M2)*C1(M1)+B1(M2)

The index values are found in Fig. 3-17 so we interpret line 790 to be:

$$T1 = A1(2)*C1(1)+B1(2)$$
$$= 4*6+3$$
$$= 24+3$$
$$= 27$$
$$T1 = 27$$

Index	Function	Value
I	EXPONENT	1
$M1$	MULTIPLIER	1
$M2$	MULTIPLICAND	2

Fig. 3-17. Index value status—units digit of multiplier times tens digit of multiplicand, at line 790.

We find an updated digit position pointer:

820 LET D=M1−1+M2
    D=1−1+2
    D=2

And as before, the units digit (7) is chopped off of the temporary result T1, and added to the digit already occupying that position:

870 LET T2=(T1−10*(INT(T1/10)))+B2(D)
    T2=7+0
      =7

In order to be general we must allow for the possibility that T2 is a two-digit number (although in this case it is only one digit long). We go through the coding at lines 900 and 920 to split T2 into its units-digit and tens-digit components, and assign them respectively to spaces B2(D) and B2(D+1) of the temporary result array.

Also as before, the tens digit of the first temporary result, T1, is chopped off and installed as the new carry digit in array B1:

950 REM FIND NEW CARRY DIGIT
960 LET B1(M2+1)=INT(T1/10)

Using the display method of Fig. 3-16, we may check our progress as in Fig. 3-18.

We know that loop 5 (Fig. 3-11) is set up to multiply each digit from

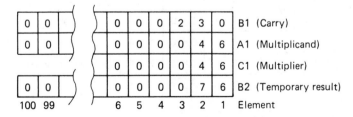

Fig. 3-18. Array contents—unit digit of multiplier times tens digit of multiplicand, showing updating of array B2 and digit carry in array B1.

array C1 (as currently specified by the index variable M1 from loop 3) times a total of P number of elements from array A1:

740 FOR M2 = 1 TO P

Loop 5 could have been indexed from 1 to 100, which would cause each digit of the multiplier to operate on all 100 elements of the multiplicand array, regardless of whether or not all of those elements were important. By finding out beforehand how many digits comprise the answer, as we did when we calculated P, we save ourselves the considerable extra time involved in looping through all 100 elements, while still insuring that all required digits are operated on.

Loop 5 therefore executes four times in this example, since $P=4$. Our index array tables now have the appearance of the elements shown in Fig. 3-19.

We can check that $46 \times 6 = 276$, so this part of the program works correctly. We have not yet found the bug, but if we continue to follow and execute the program just as the computer must, we will eventually find it.

Index	Function	Value
I	EXPONENT	1
$M1$	MULTIPLIER	1
$M2$	MULTIPLICAND	4

(A)

0	0			0	0	0	2	3	0	B1 (Carry)
0	0			0	0	0	0	4	6	A1 (Multiplicand)
				0	0	0	0	4	6	C1 (Multiplier)
0	0			0	0	0	2	7	6	B2 (Temporary result)
100	99			6	5	4	3	2	1	Element

(B)

Fig. 3-19. In (A), index variable status (units digit of multiplier cycling through first four elements of multiplicand, as required by variable P); (B) shows array status at the end of units-digit multiplication—the intermediate result.

Having completed our final transit through loop 5 we find ourselves also at the end of loop 3:

970 NEXT M2

980 NEXT M1

We now go back to line 680 where we increment M1, the loop 3 index, cycle through loop 4 to clear the carry array B1, then increment the loop 5 index M2, in order to begin the this-time multiplication of the multiplicand by the *tens* digit of the multiplier.

We check our index and array status, as in Fig. 3-20. We may list the contents of loop 5, without the intervening comments, in only a few lines:

LET T1 = A1(M2)*C1(M1)+B1(M2)

LET D=M1−1+M2

LET T2=(T1−10*(INT(T1/10)))+B2(D)

LET B2(D)=T2−10*(INT(T2/10))

LET B2(D+1)=INT(T2/10)

LET B1(M2+1)=INT(T1/10)

Index	Function	Value
I	EXPONENT	1
*M*1	MULTIPLIER	2
*M*2	MULTIPLICAND	1

(A)

0	0		0	0	0	0	0	0	B1 (Carry)
0	0		0	0	0	0	4	6	A1 (Multiplicand)
			0	0	0	0	4	6	C1 (Multiplier)
0	0		0	0	0	2	7	6	B2 (Temporary result)
100	99		6	5	4	3	2	1	Element

(B)

Fig. 3-20. In (A), index variable status at beginning of loop over second digit of multiplier; (B) is array status, with cleared carry array in preparation of cycle over tens digit of multiplier.

Since we are playing computer, we must supply the proper index values and do the computations ourselves:

T1 = A1(1)*C1(2)+B1(1)
   = 6*4+0
T1 = 24

D̲ = M1−1+M2
  = 2−1+1
D̲ = 2

T2 = (TI−10*(INT(T1/10)))+B2(D̲)
   = (24−10*(INT(24/10)))+7
   = (24−20)+7
   = 4+7
T2 = 11

B2(D̲) = T2−10*(INT(T2/10))
       = (11−10)
B2(2) = 1

B2(D̲+1) = INT(T2/10)
         = INT(11/10)
B2(3)   = 1

B1(M2+1) = INT(T1/10)
         = INT(24/10)
B1(2)   = 2

We may now use these values to update our arrays, as in Fig. 3-21. (The flowchart segment is shown in Fig. 3-22.)

But something is obviously incorrect. This new temporary result is less than the previous temporary result. We have in all probability found the bug. The problem now is to analyze the symptoms and, if possible, determine the cause.

The final expression, B2(1), equals 6, as it did at the end of the first pass through loop 3. This is as it should be, since D pointed to the second element. The program correctly multiplied 4 times 6 to give 24; it carried

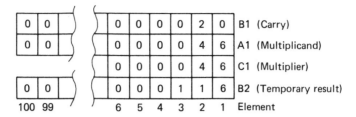

Fig. 3-21.   Array contents—tens digit of multiplier times units digit of multiplicand. Note the incorrect temporary sum in array B2.

the 2, added the 4 to the 7 already present at location B2(2), to yield 11, and then it placed the units digit in B2(2) and the tens digit in B2(3).

But what about the 2 already occupying B2(3)? Instead of replacing the 2 of B2(3) with a 1 from the tens digit of 11, we should instead have added 2 and 1 to give 3.

The offending line of code is 920:

```
920 LET B2(D+1)=INT(T2/10)
```

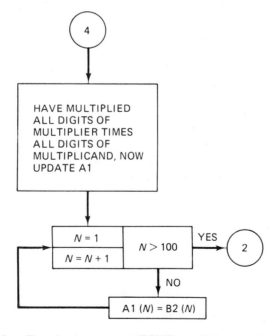

Fig. 3-22.   Flowchart, program IPOWR—exit from main loop, at which point all digits of multiplier have been multiplied by all digits of multiplicand. Update array A1 with results of this multiplication to prepare for next cycle.

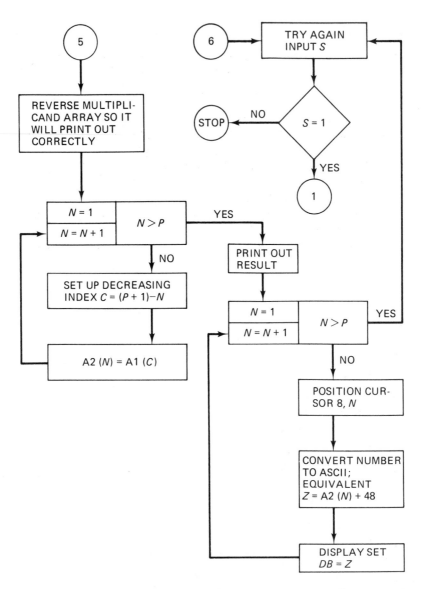

Fig. 3-23. Flowchart, program IPOWR—have finished R^E, transfer final answer to print array in reverse order. Display result one digit at a time. Then test if program is to be repeated. If not, stop.

It should be modified as follows:

    920 LET B2(D+1)=INT(T2/10)+B2(D+1)

We can easily use the SOL's editing capability to modify line 920, and then rerun the program to see if we did the right thing:

    RUN
    ? 46,2
    WORKING . . .
    FOR THE NUMBER 46 TO THE 2 POWER, THE
    ANSWER IS 2116

We could continue to trace through the balance of the program (Fig. 3-23) on paper, playing computer as we have been doing, for an exercise. But we seem to have found and corrected the bug so it is not necessary that we do so.

Since the SOL is only accurate to eight digits, a restraint shared by other easily available tools such as pocket calculators, there really is no way to check the upper-accuracy limit of IPOWR save through long and involved hand calculations. But by using examples that fall within those limits, it is possible to test IPOWR and convince ourselves that the bug has indeed been stamped out and that IPOWR is now a correctly functioning program.

Trying IPOWR again on the original example of 14^{23}, we have:

    RUN
    ? 14, 23
    WORKING . . .
    FOR THE NUMBER 14 TO THE 23 POWER, THE
    ANSWER IS 2291807325125827717 29260544

The method of debugging we used for this program is long and involved, but it is thorough. By playing computer we put the program under a microscope, examining each step and calculation in detail. And bugs, once discovered, are then obvious and easily fixed.

PRINT STATEMENTS

Print statements are among the easiest to use and the most often used debugging tools available to the computer programmer: They are straightforward to construct, are simple to insert into existing blocks of code, and have the potential of yielding large amounts of information. The challenge, when using print statements to debug a program is in determining which variable quantities to display and at what point in the program to do so.

Consider the following example: The specifications call for a program that will sort, in descending order, an arbitrarily long list of numbers and then display the result. The value −1 will signal that the last number has been input and that the sorting process is to begin.

Suppose we generate the flowchart shown in Fig. 4-1 to describe the sorting algorithm. Tracing through the diagram we can see that the first step is to set up storage space for two arrays, A and B. We then initialize an index variable I and read in our first value, storing it in the first element of array A. If the value just read in equals −1, the termination value, we branch over to the sorting routine. If A(I) does not equal −1, we increment the index I and read in another variable.

Once all of the values have been accumulated, we enter the actual number-sorting phase of the program. Two concentric loops perform the sorting operation; the outer loop indexes the B array for the result, and the inner loop indexes the A array, which contains the unsorted data. If the current value from the A array is greater than that from the B array against which it is being compared, the B array element is set equal to it. If the A value is less than the B value, the next A value is fetched and the testing begins again.

When all of the comparisons are done, we branch to a final loop to print out the answer as it appears in array B.

The program which results from the flowchart is:

```
5 REM PROGRAM TO SORT NUMBERS
10 REM SET UP ARRAYS
20 DIM A(100), B(100)
30 PRINT "YOU MAY ENTER UP TO 100 NOS, −1 ENDS LIST"
40 REM INITIALIZE INDEX
50 LET I=1
60 REM READ DATA, STOP IF = −1
70 INPUT A(I)
80 IF A(I)=−1 THEN GOTO 110
90 LET I=I+1
100 GOTO 70
110 REM SORT LIST OF NUMBERS
120 FOR J=1 TO I
130 FOR K=J TO I
140 IF B(J)>=A(K) THEN GOTO 170
150 LET B(J)=A(K)
160 GOTO 130
170 NEXT K
180 NEXT J
190 REM PRINT OUT ANSWER
200 FOR L=1 TO I
210 PRINT B(L)
220 NEXT L
230 END
```

Apparently the largest numbers are sorted out first, so in order to keep a test run as simple as possible it would be permissible to use a sequence of values such as 1, 2, and 3, with results as follows:

```
RUN
YOU MAY ENTER UP TO 100 NOS, −1 ENDS LIST
? 1
? 2
? 3
? −1
3
```

3

3

0

READY

The results are obviously not correct. The program printed out four numbers instead of the three we read in (−1 does not count as a valid number), and of those numbers which *should* have been valid, all appeared as equal to 3.

We can make a preliminary guess at the bug and say that it might either be an indexing problem, since all three values are identical; or the logic of the sorting routine itself is in error.

To successfully make use of a print statement, we must first answer these two questions: What variables would we like to see displayed? Where in the program is the best (most informative) place to grab these values?

Based upon our initial hunch as to what might be causing the bug in the sorting program, we would probably want to take a look at the index variables J and K, since they are the variables related to arrays B and A, respectively. And, since the values contained in arrays A and B are essentially at the heart of the sorting program, we will also want to examine them during program execution.

The best place to print out the index values is at the beginning of the innermost loop:

```
120 FOR J=1 TO I
130 FOR K=J TO I
→ INSERT PRINT STATEMENT HERE ←
140 IF B(J)>=A(K) THEN GOTO 170
150 LET B(J)=A(K)
160 GOTO 130
170 NEXT K
180 NEXT J
```

The innermost loop encompasses only three lines of code, none of which appear to affect the value of either index variable J or K. Therefore, printing out the values of J and K right after line 130 will most likely yield reliable results.

Where to print out the A and B array values and how many values from each array to print each time require careful consideration. We could, for instance, print out every element of both arrays each time the program made a transit through loop 3 (see Fig. 4-1). This is certainly the most complete approach, but it may also be the most inefficient: both arrays A and B contain 100 elements each. It would be very difficult, if not impossible, to fit all 100 elements of one of the arrays on to the CRT screen at one time, and it would definitely be impossible to do so for all elements of both arrays for more than one cycle.

Instead, we elect to display the current values of the index variables and the elements which these variables point to in arrays A and B. This reduces our output to only four values per loop and brings down the total volume of output to a manageable level, assuming we continue to test the program with a small sampling of input variables.

As for the placement of the array element print statement, we could try making it line 165, immediately before the ending statement of the innermost loop. By putting the print statement at the end of the loop we may be able to follow the progress of how values are loaded into array B from array A.

If we insert the following two statements:

```
135 PRINT "J,K"; J; K
165 PRINT "B(J), A(K)"; B(J); A(K)
```

and then run the program, we would get:

```
RUN
? 1
? 2
? 3
? −1
J,K 1 1
J,K 1 2
J,K 1 3
J,K 1 4
J,K 2 2
J,K 2 3
J,K 2 4
J,K 3 3
J,K 3 4
J,K 4 4
3
```

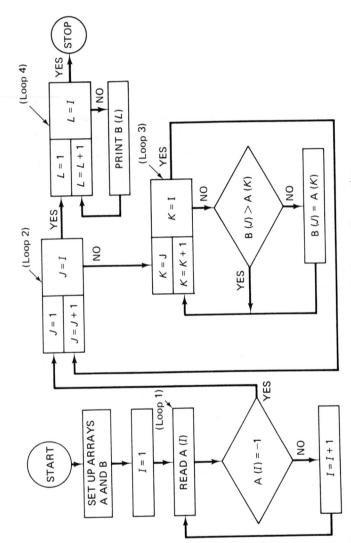

Fig. 4-1. The original flowchart for the number-sorting routine.

3
3
0
READY

Apparently one of our print statements did not get executed. A listing of the sorting section of the code reveals why:

```
120 FOR J=1 TO I
130 FOR K=J TO I
135 PRINT "J,K"; J; K
140 IF B(J)>=A(K) THEN GOTO 170
150 LET B(K)=A(K)
160 GOTO 130
165 PRINT "B(J),A(K)"; B(J); A(K)
170 NEXT K
180 NEXT J
```

The program never reaches line 165. It is directed to either skip over it:

```
140 IF B(J)>=A(K) THEN GOTO 170
```

or branch back to the beginning of the loop before ever reaching line 165:

```
160 GOTO 130
```

This illustrates one of the main considerations when using print statements: Correct placement is very important, and making such a determination is not always an automatic procedure.

Referring to the flowchart in Fig. 4-1, it looks as though a print statement would be successful placed anywhere along the return line leading into the index increment box of the loop symbol. Such is not the case, however, as we found out in the previous examples. This would not be the first time the structure of a coded program did not perform exactly as the corresponding flowchart would indicate. Rather than being a curious anomaly, this is a sign of sloppy programming and should be corrected.

For the moment, however, rather than modify the existing code before being entirely sure of what exactly it is doing, we decide to move the A(K) and B(J) print statement to another location.

We might move the array printout up to join with the index variable printout at line 135, but we should first convince ourselves that the printout is working correctly. Looking at our diagnostic print, we have:

```
J,K 1 1
J,K 1 2
J,K 1 3
J,K 1 4
J,K 2 2
J,K 2 3
J,K 2 4
J,K 3 3
J,K 3 4
J,K 4 4
```

When J equals 1, K ranges from 1 to 4; when J equals 2, K ranges from 2 to 4; for J equal to 3, K equals 3 and 4; and for J equal to 4, K equals 4. This seems to be in accord with the ranges of the two index variables as specified in the program:

```
120 FOR J=1 TO I
130 FOR K=J TO I
```

We might note in passing and for future reference that the index variable for the innermost loop, K, is itself indexed upon the index variable of the outermost loop, J. This may be intentional or it may be a bug. Hopefully, our print statement debugging method will tell us which it is.

Aside from our question about the specific choice of end points for the J and K index variables, we may assume that the print statement which is supposed to display those values does in fact work. Therefore, moving the array printouts to the same point in the code would probably work correctly also.

Deleting line 165 and modifying line 135 results in:

```
135 PRINT "J,K,B(J),A(K)"; J;K;B(J);A(K)
```

Running the program with this modification yields:

```
RUN
YOU MAY ENTER UP TO 100 NOS, −1 ENDS LIST
? 1
? 2
? 3
? −1
J,K,B(J),A(K) 1 1 0 1
J,K,B(J),A(K) 1 2 1 2
J,K,B(J),A(K) 1 3 2 3
J,K,B(J),A(K) 1 4 3 −1
J,K,B(J),A(K) 2 2 0 2
J,K,B(J),A(K) 2 3 2 3
J,K,B(J),A(K) 2 4 3 −1
J,K,B(J),A(K) 3 3 0 3
J,K,B(J),A(K) 3 4 3 −1
J,K,B(J),A(K) 4 4 0 −1
3
3
3
0
READY
```

The index values are as before, and at last we are able to see what is contained in the A and B arrays.

If we now take the time to analyze the short table of printout that we have just generated, we will realize that one simple print statement has yielded much useful information. For example, we can follow each element of the B array as it is filled. Suppose we arrange the data a little differently. Consider the case when the outermost loop index is equal to 1, and we are cycling through the innermost loop as it increments from the starting value of J (in this case, 1) to the terminal value of I (always equal to 4), as in Fig. 4-2.

We can see that for the first loop the code is performing as it should. Initially, B(1) is equal to 0 and A(1) is equal to 1. The code falls through the inside loop; and when it makes its way back to the beginning of the loop, B(1) has been assigned the value of A(1)—which is as it should be, since 1 is greater than 0.

J	K	B (J)	A (K)
1	1	0	1
1	2	1	2
1	3	2	3
1	4	3	−1

Fig. 4-2. PRINT statement data for sorting routine, first traverse through outermost loop.

After every subsequent traverse through the inner loop, B(1) either retains its old value or takes on the value of the current element from array A (A(I)), depending upon which is the greater. Since at the end of the last time through the inner loop, 3 is greater than −1, B(1) finished the inner loop equal to 3.

Figure 4-3 shows what happens during the second cycle through the outer loop, when J is equal to 2. In this instance K ranges from 2 to 4, since it begins with the value of J, which is 2. Whereas in the first iteration over J the element from B was compared against all four elements of A, this time the new element from B is only being tested against three members from A.

The logic of the method makes sense: if during the first iteration the largest of N numbers contained in array A was discovered and placed into the first element of B, then during the second iteration we need only concern ourselves with N-1 numbers in array A. Likewise, in each subsequent iteration we can shorten the search by ignoring those numbers already sorted out and concentrating on the ever decreasing list of unsorted numbers.

J	K	B (J)	A (K)
2	2	0	2
2	3	2	3
2	4	3	−1

Fig. 4-3. PRINT statement data for sorting routine, second traverse through outermost loop.

Unfortunately, the actual coding does not coincide with the suggested logic. The way the code is structured, a correct answer will only result if the numbers are already in a sorted sequence, as follows:

```
RUN
YOU MAY ENTER UP TO 100 NOS, −1 ENDS LIST
? 3
? 2
? 1
? −1
J,K,B(J),A(K) 1 1 0 3
J,K,B(J),A(K) 1 2 3 2
J,K,B(J),A(K) 1 3 3 1
J,K,B(J),A(K) 1 4 3 −1
J,K,B(J),A(K) 2 2 0 2
J,K,B(J),A(K) 2 3 2 1
J,K,B(J),A(K) 2 4 2 −1
J,K,B(J),A(K) 3 3 0 1
J,K,B(J),A(K) 3 4 1 −1
J,K,B(J),A(K) 4 4 0 −1
3
2
1
0
READY
```

We must do two things if we are to debug the sorting program: (1) Since the numbers in array A are in an arbitrary order (which is the whole point of having a sorting routine), we must compare every value of A against the current value from B. The way to fix this is to have K range from 1 to I:

```
130 FOR K=1 TO I
```

(2) We require some method of eliminating from consideration those values from array A which have already been sorted out and transferred to array B. This could be as simple as making those values zero, but we

first need a way of identifying which elements of A are to be zeroed out. Line 140 has some of the qualities we seek:

140 IF B(J)>=A(K) THEN GOTO 170

This line of code says that if the maximum has already been found, then we are to pass over the particular number under consideration and move on to the next. Note, however, that line 140 is testing for two different properties of the number from array A. Line 140 asks if that number is either greater than or equal to the current number from array B. We can use this line of code to our advantage by breaking it up into two separate statements:

140 IF B(J)>A(K) THEN GOTO 170
145 IF B(J)=A(K) THEN LET A(K)=0

Clearly, if B(J) is greater than A(K), A(K) is not a new maximum, and we must move on to the next value. However, if B(J) equals A(K) then we have found the maximum value. It should be zeroed out in array A so as not to cause bugs later on.

Also, we should delete line 160:

160 GOTO 130

This line, in effect, is circumventing the termination statement of a FOR-NEXT loop, and while no serious bugs seem to have resulted, it is very poor programming practice and should be avoided.

A complete listing of the program as currently modified is as follows:

```
5 REM PROGRAM TO SORT NUMBERS
10 REM SET UP ARRAYS
20 DIM A(100), B(100)
30 PRINT "YOU MAY ENTER UP TO 100 NOS, −1 ENDS LIST
40 REM INITIALIZE INDEX
50 LET I=1
60 REM READ DATA, STOP IF = −1
70 INPUT A(I)
```

```
80 IF A(I)=1 THEN GOTO 110
90 LET I=I+1
100 GOTO 70
110 REM SORT LIST OF NUMBERS
120 FOR J=1 TO I
130 FOR K=1 TO I
140 IF B(J)>A(K) THEN GOTO 170
145 IF B(J)=A(K) THEN LET A(K)=0
150 LET B(J)=A(K)
170 NEXT K
180 NEXT J
190 REM PRINT OUT ANSWER
200 FOR L=1 TO I
210 PRINT B(L)
220 NEXT L
230 END
```

Running the program this time results in:

```
RUN
YOU MAY ENTER UP TO 100 NOS, −1 ENDS LIST
? 1
? 2
? 3
? −1
J,K,B(J),A(K) 1 1 0 1
J,K,B(J),A(K) 1 2 1 2
J,K,B(J),A(K) 1 3 2 3
J,K,B(J),A(K) 1 4 3 −1
J,K,B(J),A(K) 2 1 0 1
J,K,B(J),A(K) 2 2 1 2
J,K,B(J),A(K) 2 3 2 3
J,K,B(J),A(K) 2 4 3 −1
J,K,B(J),A(K) 3 1 0 1
J,K,B(J),A(K) 3 2 1 2
J,K,B(J),A(K) 3 3 2 3
```

```
J,K,B(J),A(K) 3 4 3 −1
J,K,B(J),A(K) 4 1 0 1
J,K,B(J),A(K) 4 2 1 2
J,K,B(J),A(K) 4 3 2 3
J,K,B(J),A(K) 4 4 3 −1
3
3
3
3
READY
```

By changing the limits of index variable K to range from 1 to I instead of from J to I, we have caused a 60% increase in the length of the diagnostic printout.

But by splitting the "greater than or equal to" test of line 140 into two separate tests, we do not seem to have accomplished anything at all. Why? The diagnostic printout, as reproduced in Fig. 4-4, tells the story.

The innermost loop is now comparing each element of array A against the current value from array B and the greatest value from A is being fed to B, just as it should be. The bug which we see manifested in the "answer" printout and which is made glaringly visible in the diagnostic print statement, is that array A remains unaffected through the entire sorting process. We should see the contents of array A being replaced with zeros as the numbers are pulled out in decreasing order.

Referring to the listing, we see why:

```
120 FOR J=1 TO I
130 FOR K=1 TO I
135 PRINT "J,K,B(J),A(K)"; J; K; B(J); A(K)
140 IF B(J)>A(K) THEN GOTO 170
145 IF B(J)=A(K) THEN LET A(K)=0
150 LET B(J)=A(K)
170 NEXT K
180 NEXT J
```

Line 145 will zero out the element in array A if it is equal to the current maximum as represented by the element from array B. However, as we can see from the diagnostic printout, at any particular combination of J and K values, B(J) and A(K) are never equal.

J	K	B (J)	A (K)
1	1	0	1
1	2	1	2
1	3	2	3
1	4	3	−1
2	1	0	1
2	2	1	2
2	3	2	3
2	4	3	−1
3	1	0	1
3	2	1	2
3	3	2	3
3	4	3	−1
4	1	0	1
4	2	1	2
4	3	2	3
4	4	3	−1

Fig. 4-4. Diagnostic printout for sorting program, after first round of modifications.

What if we were to move line 145 down to line 155? Certainly B(J) would then equal A(K), because they were just made equal at line 150. The error in this reasoning should be obvious, but it is easily demonstrated by making the change and running the program:

```
155 IF B(J)=A(K) THEN LET A(K)=0
DELETE 145
RUN
```

YOU MAY ENTER UP TO 100 NOS, −1 ENDS LIST
? 1
? 2
? 3
? −1
J,K,B(J),A(K) 1 1 0 1
J,K,B(J),A(K) 1 2 1 2
J,K,B(J),A(K) 1 3 2 3
J,K,B(J),A(K) 1 4 3 −1
J,K,B(J),A(K) 2 1 0 0
J,K,B(J),A(K) 2 2 0 0
J,K,B(J),A(K) 2 3 0 0
J,K,B(J),A(K) 2 4 0 −1
J,K,B(J),A(K) 3 1 0 0
J,K,B(J),A(K) 3 2 0 0
J,K,B(J),A(K) 3 3 0 0
J,K,B(J),A(K) 3 4 0 −1
J,K,B(J),A(K) 4 1 0 0
J,K,B(J),A(K) 4 2 0 0
J,K,B(J),A(K) 4 3 0 0
J,K,B(J),A(K) 4 4 0 −1
3
0
0
0
READY

For J equal to 1 (the first time through the outermost loop), K ranged from 1 to 4. The first transit through the inside loop, $J=1$ and $K=1$; also, $B(1)=0$ and $A(1)=1$. Since 1 is greater than 0, the test at line 140 failed:

140 IF B(J)>A(K) THEN GOTO 170

A(1) was therefore assumed to be the new maximum, and B(1) was set equal to it at line 150.

150 LET B(J)=A(K)

Immediately thereafter, line 155, the line which we shuffled around, promptly replaced A(1) with a 0.

155 IF B(J)=A(K) THEN LET A(K)=0

This process repeated itself for all the numbers in array A, one after the other, except for the last value, −1. The value −1, being less than all the other numbers, including 0, would be the only value to pass the test at line 140.

We note that if the list of numbers read into the program had *not* been in strictly ascending order, a significantly different outcome would have resulted, as for example (minus the diagnostic printout):

RUN
? 4
? 10
? 5
? 1
? 6
? −1
10
6
1
0
0
0
READY

Judging by the output just generated we might come to a completely different (and incorrect) conclusion about the nature of the bug. At the very least, we would waste a greater amount of time in general head-scratching. This points up another technique, to be discussed in the next chapter, called *forcing*. When debugging a program, the guiding principle should be to simplify as much as possible; try to get the maximum amount of *useful* information out of every technique employed.

We are now nearing the point of final resolution for this particular problem. As we pointed out earlier, we need a way of unambiguously es-tablishing which element of array A, for any given iteration over the in-

nermost loop, is the current maximum. Once identified, we will also want
to remove that element from further consideration.

We were correct in believing that the test at line 140 was a strong clue
towards resolving our dilemma:

```
140 IF B(J)>=A(K) THEN GOTO 170
150 LET B(J)=A(K)
```

If B(J) already contains the maximum value to be found during the
current iteration, then whatever quantity is represented by A(K) will be
less than B(J). The test will be true and the program will move on to the
next value in array A. However, if B(J) is less than the value of A(K), then
B(J) will be updated to be equal to A(K), the new current maximum.

We cannot zero out any A array values within the innermost loop
since, as we learned previously, unpredictable results will occur unless
the data already exists in order of decreasing value. The only safe place
to perform such "zeroing out" is outside the bounds of the innermost loop
but before the next transit of the outermost loop, as in Fig. 4-5.

In terms of coding, this would be expressed as:

```
175 LET A(T)=O
```

The only thing left to resolve is the identity of the index variable T. T
must point to that element of array A which has been identified as the
current maximum value sorted out during the last cycle of iteration
through the innermost loop. The index variable K also points to members
of array A, and during one cycle through the innermost loop it also points
to the current maximum value in A.

We can preserve the identity of K by equating it to a storage variable
such as T. The proper place for this would be following line 150, the place
where the current maximum value itself is saved:

```
150 LET B(J)=A(K)
155 LET T=K
```

Running the program with these final modifications would yield:

```
RUN
YOU MAY ENTER UP TO 100 NOS, −1 ENDS LIST
```

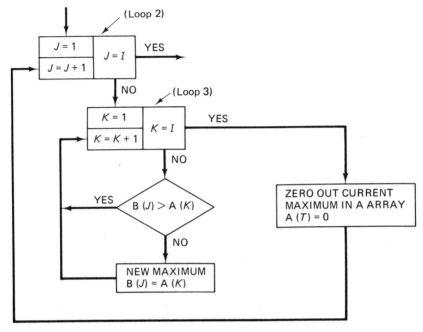

Fig. 4-5. Portion of number-sorting program flowchart, showing correct location of coding to zero out element of array A identified as current maximum value. Loop 2—outermost loop; loop 3—innermost loop.

```
? 1
? 2
? 3
? −1
J,K,B(J),A(K) 1 1 0 1
J,K,B(J),A(K) 1 2 1 2
J,K,B(J),A(K) 1 3 2 3
J,K,B(J),A(K) 1 4 3 −1
J,K,B(J),A(K) 2 1 0 1
J,K,B(J),A(K) 2 2 1 2
J,K,B(J),A(K) 2 3 2 0
J,K,B(J),A(K) 2 4 2 −1
J,K,B(J),A(K) 3 1 0 1
J,K,B(J),A(K) 3 2 1 0
J,K,B(J),A(K) 3 3 1 0
```

```
J,K,B(J),A(K) 3 4 1 −1
J,K,B(J),A(K) 4 1 0 0
J,K,B(J),A(K) 4 2 0 0
J,K,B(J),A(K) 4 3 0 0
J,K,B(J),A(K) 4 4 0 −1
3
2
1
0
READY
```

It looks as though the sorting program finally works, but we still have a cosmetic bug hanging on. Because the program must read in a −1 value as a signal to begin processing, it thinks that it has four values to sort instead of the actual three. Why? Because the index value *I* must be updated *before* a read statement is executed; otherwise the new value would write on top of a previously read-in value. The cure for this bug is simple and requires only that we reduce the value of *I* by one after the terminating −1 is read in:

```
80 IF A(I)=−1 THEN GOTO 110
    —
    —
110 REM SORT LIST OF NUMBERS
115 LET I=I−1
```

Can we say that the program is now debugged? We can say that for the values 1, 2, and 3, in that order, the program appears to be debugged. A more general test would be useful, however:

```
RUN
YOU MAY ENTER UP TO 100 NOS, −1 ENDS LIST
? 45
? 2.7
? 142
? 6
? 17
? −1
```

```
J,K,B(J),A(K) 1 1 0     45
J,K,B(J),A(K) 1 2 45    2.7
J,K,B(J),A(K) 1 3 45    142
J,K,B(J),A(K) 1 4 142 6
J,K,B(J),A(K) 1 5 142 17
J,K,B(J),A(K) 2 1 0     45
J,K,B(J),A(K) 2 2 45    2.7
J,K,B(J),A(K) 2 3 45    0
J,K,B(J),A(K) 2 4 45    6
J,K,B(J),A(K) 2 5 45    17
J,K,B(J),A(K) 3 1 0     0
J,K,B(J),A(K) 3 2 0     2.7
J,K,B(J),A(K) 3 3 2.7 0
J,K,B(J),A(K) 3 4 2.7 6
J,K,B(J),A(K) 3 5 6     17
J,K,B(J),A(K) 4 1 0     0
J,K,B(J),A(K) 4 2 0     2.7
J,K,B(J),A(K) 4 3 2.7 0
J,K,B(J),A(K) 4 4 2.7 6
J,K,B(J),A(K) 4 5 6     0
J,K,B(J),A(K) 5 1 0     0
J,K,B(J),A(K) 5 2 0     2.7
J,K,B(J),A(K) 5 3 2.7 0
J,K,B(J),A(K) 5 4 2.7 0
J,K,B(J),A(K) 5 5 2.7 0
142
45
17
6
2.7
READY
```

The answer is correct, but the volume of diagnostic printout has increased significantly. If we were to attempt to debug the program using a sample of 10 numbers, we would have to wade through 100 lines of print: the innermost loop executes 10 times for every single traverse of the outer loop, and the outer loop itself cycles through 10 times (10 times 10 equals 100).

This points up something that was mentioned before: *placement is critical.* Many times a bug can be traced to the vicinity of a series of concentric loops, and in that case the programmer faces a real challenge in determining when and where to make use of the print statement.

For example, consider the following excerpt from a geographical mapping program:

```
1010 REM PROCESS 100 X 100 MATRIX
1020 REM OF ALTITUDE VALUES
1030 REM IF VALUE IS MISSING
1040 REM INTERPOLATE FROM NEIGHBORS
1050 FOR I=1 TO 100
1060 FOR J=1 TO 100
1070 ON L5 GOTO 2030, 1090, 1235
1080 IF Z*R(J)>SQR(M/L9) THEN GOTO 1410
1090 REM INTERPOLATE VALUES
1100 FOR K=1 TO 8
1110 LET T1=M(I,J)*M(I−1,J)*M(I+1,J)/3
1120 LET T2=M(I−1,J+1)*M(I,J)*M(I+1,J−1)/3
1130 LET T3=M(I−1,J−1)*M(I,J)*M(I+1,J+1)/3
1140 LET T4=M(I,J+1)*M(I,J)*M(I,J−1)/3
1150 LET N=T1*T2*T3*T4/4
1160 NEXT K
```

There is enough going on in this one small section of code to generate literally thousands of lines of output from one print statement. In general it is not wise to place a print statement buried deep within a series of nested loops. If a print statement *must* be located inside a number of nested loops, it is advisable to put some kind of a clamp or switch on the statement so that it is only activated when there is a high probability that it will yield useful information. As an illustration, if we wanted to use a print statement to debug the following example, instead of writing

```
1155 PRINT"I,J,K,T1,T2,T3,T4,N"; I;J;K;T1;T2;T3;T4;N
```

we would be better off to write

```
1155 IF N<=0 THEN PRINT "I,J,K,T1,T2,T3,T4,N"; I;J;K;T1;T2;T3;T4;N
```

The second method would cause the diagnostic to be printed only in those cases where N was less than or equal to zero, a sure sign of trouble. Had we not clamped the print statement, the sheer volume of output produced would have been like a smokescreen, making the debugging task that much more difficult.

Correctly used, the print statement is perhaps the easiest debugging tool available. It is quick to apply and can yield much (sometimes too much) potentially useful information. The print statement is well suited to an interactive approach to debugging, which of course implies access to a functioning computer as a condition of its use.

5.

FORCING

It has been hinted at in previous chapters, and in some instances explicitly mentioned, that as an aid to easing the debugging task we should strive to eliminate as many unknowns as possible from the problem under investigation. This does not mean that we are to delete sections of the code because they are complicated; rather, when input variables are required by the program, we should supply as few values as possible and we should make them as simple as we can.

Simplification is the heart of *forcing*. For example, if the number 1 will work as an input variable, use it. If a program can be tested with three unknowns rather than ten, use the lower number.

Forcing means just what it says: by using as few input parameters as possible and by making the parameters as mathematically simple as possible, we are trying to play a game with loaded dice. In effect, we are trying to force a program to perform in a predetermined way; we want to be able to confidently predict the outcome of a certain program. If after doing all we can to force the program to yield the expected result, it still does not do so, then we know the program contains one or more bugs. It is the nature and magnitude of the discrepancy between expected result and actual result after forcing that gives us clues to the bug's identity, and that is what makes this technique so useful.

Consider for example a simple program to find the minimum, maximum, and average values of an arbitrarily long list of numbers. The listing for such a program is as follows (a flowchart corresponding to the code is in Fig. 5-1):

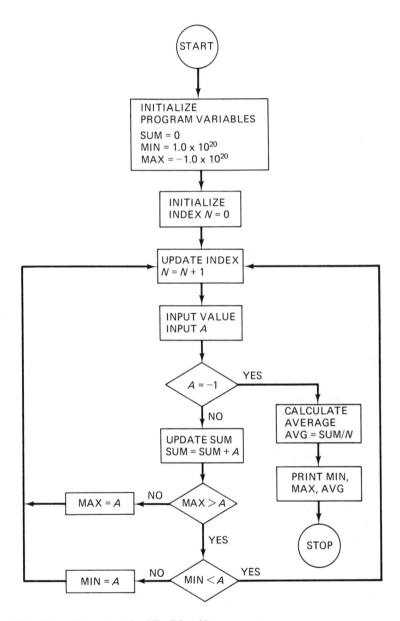

Fig. 5-1. Flowchart for Min/Max/Average program.

```
10   REM PROGRAM TO FIND MIN, MAX, AND AVERAGE
20   REM OF A LIST OF NUMBERS
30   PRINT "ENTER LIST OF NUMBERS, ENDING WITH −1"
40   REM INITIALIZE SUM, MIN, MAX, AND INDEX VARIABLES
50   LET S=0
60   LET M1=−1E20
70   LET M2=1E20
80   LET N=0
90   REM UPDATE INDEX VARIABLE AND INPUT VALUE
100   LET N=N+1
110   INPUT A
120   IF A=−1 THEN GOTO 220
130   REM UPDATE SUM
140   LET S=S+A
150   REM UPDATE MAX
160   IF M1>A THEN GOTO 90
170   LET M1=A
180   REM UPDATE MIN
190   IF M2<A THEN GOTO 90
200   LET M2=A
210   GOTO 90
220   REM CALCULATE AVERAGE
230   LET V=S/N
240   PRINT "MIN="; M2; "MAX="; M1; "AVERAGE="; V
250   END
```

A typical problem for this program to solve might be to find the minimum, maximum, and average values of the following list of numbers:

4302	6280	5619
1621	1904	9012
1411	3331	8631
2121	7014	8107

Using the list as input for the program we would find:

MIN=1411   MAX=9012   AVERAGE=4565.62

We can tell at a glance that the minimum and maximum values are correct, and we could add up all of the values and divide by their number to check the accuracy of the average-value computation. But what if the list were five times as long as it is? We might let ourselves be convinced that if the first two-thirds of the printout is correct, the rest of it is probably correct also.

We would be wrong in that assumption, however, because the average value is not correct in the example given. The average should be 4946.08, not 4565.62; there is a difference of 380.46.

What could cause such an error? The program is so simple, the bug responsible must be very elusive indeed. Had we remembered to follow the first rule of forcing—to simplify—we might have arrived at some significantly different conclusions.

Suppose we assume from the very beginning that the program has a bug in it (in general a wise philosophy for any programmer, no matter how experienced). Knowing that there is a bug hiding in the code, our job is to smoke it out and eliminate it. Through a judicious choice of input variables, designed to deliver only one easily predictable answer, our task will be made considerably less difficult.

As an example, we might test the program with only two values, 1 and 2, as follows:

```
RUN
ENTER LIST OF NUMBERS, ENDING WITH −1
? 1
? 2
? −1
MIN=1      MAX=2      AVERAGE=1
```

The average of 1 and 2 is 1.5, not 1. The equation for finding the average of a group of numbers is:

$$\text{AVERAGE} = \frac{\sum_{i=1}^{N} Xi}{N}$$

which translates as "the sum of the values divided by the number of values." The only way in which the average of 1 and 2 could equal 1 is if N, the number of values, was somehow set equal to S, the sum of the values. This is evident in line 230:

```
220   REM CALCULATE AVERAGE
230   LET V=S/N
```

Tracing through the flowchart in Fig. 5-1, and aided by the forced results, we easily spot the bug. The index variable N should be updated *after* an acceptable input value has been found, not before. In examples in previous chapters, index variables required updating before input of a new value, because the new values were being entered into arrays. However, in our current example there are no arrays; the index variable is used solely as a divisor quantity to keep track of the number of legitimate entries, and then to calculate the average. Relabeling statement 100 to become statement 125 will fix this bug, as shown in the revised flowchart, Fig. 5-2.

Not all programs make significant use of mathematical expressions; but those that do, such as the following example, are good candidates for the technique of forcing.

```
10    REM PROGRAM TO FIND THE ROOTS
20    REM OF A QUADRATIC EQUATION
30    PRINT "A QUADRATIC EQUATION HAS THE FORM"
40    PRINT "A*X*X*+B*X+C"
50    PRINT "PLEASE INPUT THE THREE COEFFICIENTS A,B,C"
60    INPUT A,B,C
70    REM CALCULATE DETERMINANT
80    LET D=(B*B−4*A*C)/(4*A*A)
90    LET D2=−B/2*A
100   IF D>=0 THEN GOTO 140
110   PRINT "X1="; D2; "+"; SQR(−D); "i"
120   PRINT "X2="; D3; "−"; SQR(−D); "i"
130   GOTO 210
140   IF D2>=0 THEN GOTO 170
150   LET X1=D2−SQR(D)
160   GOTO 180
170   LET X1=D2+SQR(D)
180   LET X2=C/X1*A
190   PRINT "X1="; X1
200   PRINT "X2="; X2
210   INPUT "ANOTHER CALCULATION, YES OR NO?", A$
220   IF A$="YES" THEN GOTO 50
230   END
```

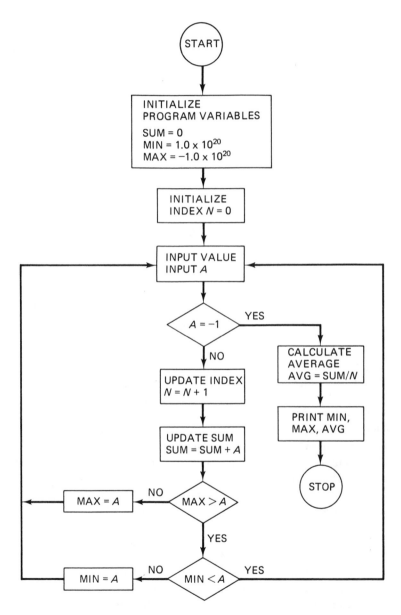

Fig. 5-2. Corrected flowchart for the Min/Max/Average program.

The program is fairly short, only 23 lines, but there is a lot going on within those lines. The equations being solved are given below.

$$D = \frac{B^2 - 4AC}{4A^2}$$

$$D_2 = \frac{-B}{2A}$$

For real roots:

$$X_1 = D_2 - \sqrt{D} \quad \text{if } D_2 < 0$$

$$X_1 = D_2 + \sqrt{D} \quad \text{if } D_2 \geqslant 0$$

$$X_2 = \frac{C}{AX_1}$$

And for imaginary roots:

$$X_1 = D_2 + \sqrt{-D}\, i$$

$$X_2 = D_2 - \sqrt{-D}\, i$$

$$where\ i = \sqrt{-1}$$

These equations are all linked together in the flowchart shown in Fig. 5-3. Compared to other flowcharts we have studied, Fig. 5-3 does not seem particularly complex. Note, however, that it is a purely mathematical flowchart, with none of the looping or array processing which has occurred so frequently in previous examples.

This all takes on greater meaning if we look at what it relates to in the physical world. Suppose we want to describe the motion of a comet entering our solar system from interstellar space. As it passes near the sun it is caught in the solar gravitational field, causing it to curve around the sun and be flung back out into space like a rock from a slingshot. The curve which corresponds to the meteor's trajectory is called a parabola, similar to the one drawn in Fig. 5-4.

The equation which describes a parabolic curve has the general form of $AX^2 + BX + C = Y$, and the program in this example finds the roots of that equation; the roots are the points where the curve crosses the X axis.

In Fig. 5-4 the equation of the curve is $X^2 + 3X - 4 = Y$, and the roots are X = −4 and X = 1. At the point where the curve crosses the X axis the value of Y is obviously zero. We can easily demonstrate that −4 and 1 are

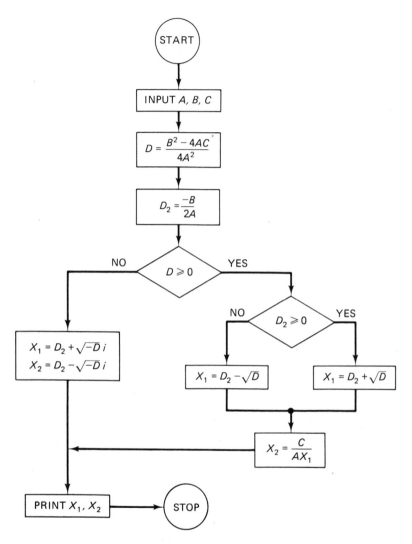

Fig. 5-3. Flowchart for the program to find the roots to a quadratic equation.

roots to $X^2 = 3X - 4 = Y$ by substituting those values into the equation for the curve and examining the result.

For $X = -4$

$$Y = X^2 + 3X - 4$$

$Y = (-4)^2 + 3(-4) - 4$

$Y = 16 - 12 - 4$

$Y = 0$

For $X = 1$

$Y = X^2 + 3X - 4$

$Y = (1)^2 + 3(1) - 4$

$Y = 1 + 3 - 4$

$Y = 0$

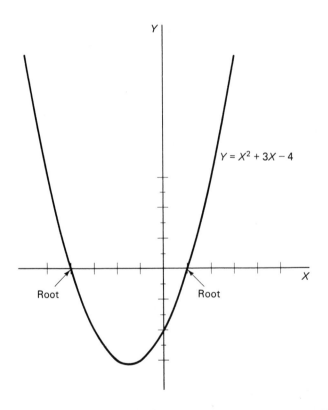

Fig. 5-4. Example of a parabolic curve, showing the two roots of the equation that describes it.

Since we know the roots to the quadratic equation $X^2 + 3X - 4$, suppose we use the values of its coefficients as input values to the root-finding program, thereby trying to force the program to yield our already known and predicted results.

```
RUN
A QUADRATIC EQUATION HAS THE FORM
A*X*X+B*X+C
PLEASE INPUT THE THREE COEFFICIENTS A,B,C
? 1
?? 3
?? -4
X1=1
X2=-4
ANOTHER CALCULATION? YES OR NO
```

It looks as though we have written a bug-free program; 1 and −4 are precisely the values we predicted. Remembering that the odds are strongly against a program being devoid of bugs on the first try, however, we decide to load the dice one more time and see if we can force the desired result.

The easiest way to construct a quadratic equation that will yield a nice, clean result is to work backwards from the answer. For instance, choosing as the two values 6 and −4, we would have:

$$Y = (X - 6)(X + 4)$$
$$= X^2 - 6X + 4X - 24$$
$$= X^2 - 2X - 24$$

Using these values to feed into our program, and typing in a yes response to the last query visible on the screen would result in:

```
ANOTHER CALCULATION?   YES OR NO   YES
? 1
?? -2
?? -24
X1=6
X2=-4
```

Once again the values are exactly as predicted. Against all odds we have apparently written a program without bugs. Flushed with success, we let our high-school age daughter use the program to do her geometry homework. She speeds through the assignment and is elated with the extra free time it gives her.

The next day, she curtly informs us that over half of her homework problems were incorrect. What could have gone wrong? A copy of the homework in hand, we return to the computer to track down this mysterious bug.

Among the problems that were solved correctly were:

$$X^2 - 5X + 6 \; ; \qquad X_1 = 3 \qquad X_2 = 2$$

$$X^2 - 16 \qquad ; \qquad X_1 = 4 \qquad X_2 = -4$$

$$X^2 - 2X - 15; \qquad X_1 = -3 \quad X_2 = 5$$

and among those problems solved incorrectly were:

$$2X^2 + 8X - 18$$

$$3X^2 - 14X + 8$$

Knowing which equations were not solved correctly, we could use them as test cases. For example, we could take the values 3, −14, and 8 to substitute into the equations and then arrive at a hand solution which could serve as the predicted results during a forced run.

Doing that, however, would be violating our own first rule in regard to forcing: make the test case as simple as possible. The simplest possible test case would be to set all coefficients equal to 1. Hand solving the series of equations using 1 is trivial, and yields the following results:

$$1. \quad D = \frac{B^2 - 4AC}{4A^2}$$

$$= \frac{1^2 - (4)\,(1)\,(1)}{4\,(1)^2}$$

$$= \frac{1 - 4}{4}$$

$$= \frac{-3}{4}$$

2. $D_2 = \dfrac{-B}{2A}$

$\quad\ \ = \dfrac{-1}{2\,(1)}$

$\quad\ \ = \dfrac{-1}{2}$

Since the determinant D is less than zero, we know that the two roots will be imaginary—that is, they will contain the variable i, which stands for the square root of -1. This is expressed mathematically as:

$X = D_2 \pm \sqrt{-D}\,i$

$\quad = \dfrac{-1}{2} \pm \sqrt{\dfrac{3}{4}}\,i$

$\quad = -.5 + .87\,i \qquad$ and $\qquad -.5 - .87\,i$

The program gives us:

```
ANOTHER CALCULATION?   YES OR NO   YES
? 1
?? 1
?? 1
X1=-.50+.87i
X2=-.50-.87i
```

Again, the program gives agreement with predicted results. Either (1) the program does work (although we can discount that theory based on the evidence from the homework assignment), (2) forcing as a debugging method is not applicable in this situation (remotely possible but not likely), or (3) we are somehow misapplying this particular technique, thus not seeing the types of results we should.

By forcing a program, by playing with a stacked deck, we want to not only cause the program to yield a specific answer, but we also want that answer to be arrived at in a particular way. Figure 5-5 is a reproduction of the flowchart for the quadratic solving program, only this time certain features have been emphasized. Note, for instance, that there are essentially three unique paths flowing from START to STOP. Each time we en-

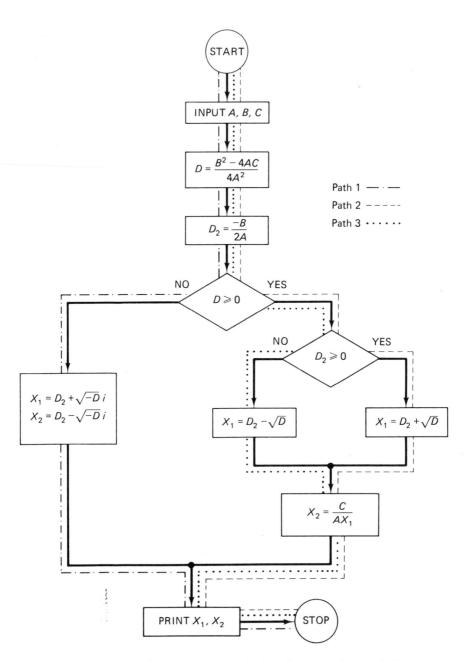

Fig. 5-5. Flowchart of program to calculate the roots of a quadratic equation, showing three possible paths from start to stop.

counter a decision block, such as "$D \unrhd 0$?," we are presented with another possible route through the program.

One objective of forcing is to exercise all possible paths through a program, one path at a time. This requires knowing how many paths exist (a flowchart is indispensable in this respect), and then it requires an understanding of what will cause a program to flow down one path as opposed to any other.

The factors which govern choice of paths in Fig. 5-5 are clear. The first division of paths depends upon whether D, the determinant, is positive or negative. Likewise, the second division of paths depends upon whether the quantity D_2 is positive or negative.

Looking again at the equation for the determinant, we can predict what sorts of values will cause it to be either positive or negative:

$$D = \frac{B^2 - 4AC}{4A^2}$$

In the dividend, B^2 will always be positive, no matter what the sign of B. Likewise, in the divisor, A^2 will always be positive independent of the sign of A. The controlling factor in deciding whether or not D will be positive or negative is therefore the expression:

$$- 4AC$$

The expression $-4AC$ must be both negative and larger in absolute value than B, if D is also to be negative—two requirements which can be met by an infinite number of combinations of values. However, our aim is to force D positive or negative in the simplest, most easily verifiable manner.

If we use $+1$ and -1, what combination would we require? By setting B equal to 1 or -1 (it makes no difference), B^2 will equal 1. For the determinant to point to real roots, then, $-4AC$ must be greater than or equal to -1; for imaginary roots, $-4AC$ will be less than -1.

According to the program, and as previously verified by hand calculations, the expression

$$X^2 + X + 1$$

has imaginary roots. Suppose we were to try all -1s, what sort of roots should we expect? For the expression

$$- X^2 - X - 1$$

the only coefficients which we will concern ourselves with at this point
are A and C, both equal to −1.

Substituting those values into −4AC, we have:

$$-4AC = -4(-1)(-1)$$

$$= -4$$

−4 is less than −1, so we predict that the answer would be imaginary
roots. If we now run the program we find:

```
ANOTHER CALCULATION?   YES OR NO   YES
? −1
?? −1
?? −1
X1=−.50+.87i
X2=−.50−.87i
```

Even with the change in sign of all three coefficients, it is the same
answer we got with A, B, and C equal to 1; and it is in fact correct, as we
can easily check by hand:

$$D = \frac{B^2 - 4AC}{4A^2}$$

$$= \frac{(-1)^2 - 4(-1)(-1)}{4(-1)^2}$$

$$= \frac{1-4}{4}$$

$$= \frac{-3}{4}$$

$$D^2 = \frac{-B}{2A}$$

$$= \frac{-(-1)}{2(-1)}$$

$$= \frac{1}{-2}$$

$$X = D^2 \pm \sqrt{-D}\,i$$

$$= \frac{-1}{2} \pm \sqrt{\frac{-(-3)}{4}}\,i$$

$$= -0.5 \pm \frac{3}{4}i$$

$$X_1 = -0.5 + .87i \qquad X_2 = -0.5 - 0.87i$$

Using coefficients of 1, since the absolute value of D will always be equal to ¾, and the absolute value of D_2 will always be equal to ½, we can see how working with all ones has simplified the computational task for us, making it easier to predict results than if we had to laboriously work through each equation by hand using large, unwieldy values.

Taking advantage of this, our next step is to construct a table of predicted versus actual results, the aim being to see if the bug can be forced out of hiding. The table of results for this particular program is reproduced in Fig. 5-6.

Once again, the actual results mirror the predicted results, indicating a perfect program—even though we know that a bug exists.

Although this is the sort of frustration that gives programmers ulcers, we should not be too quick to judge. The table of values is actually telling us quite a bit: whatever the bug is, it is not related to a problem having to do with improper calculation of sign. The problem instead has to do with the magnitude of the input variables.

The search for the bug is now complicated by the possibility that

TABLE OF PREDICTED VS ACTUAL RESULTS FOR $AX^2 + BX + C$						
Value of coefficients			Predicted		Actual	
A	B	C	X_1	X_2	X_1	X_2
1	1	1	$-0.5 + 87i$	$-0.5 - 0.87i$	$-0.5 + 0.87i$	$-0.5 - 0.87i$
1	1	1	-1.62	0.62	-1.62	0.62
1	-1	-1	$0.5 + 0.87i$	$0.5 - 0.87i$	$0.5 - 0.87i$	$0.5 - 0.87i$
-1	1	1	1.62	-0.62	1.62	-0.62
-1	-1	-1	$-0.5 + 0.87i$	$-0.5 - 0.87i$	$-0.5 + 0.87i$	$-0.5 - 0.87i$

Fig. 5-6. Forced values from the quadratic root program.

since the magnitude of the values is critical, there may be literally thousands of arbitrary combinations which will not exhibit the effects of the
bug. We recall, for instance, that the expression

$$X^2 - 2X - 15$$

yielded correct roots.

Since all ones (of whatever sign) used as coefficients did not reveal
the bug, then which other of the infinite combinations of variables should
we select for our next forcing run? As before, the guiding word should be
"simplify," and the most elementary combination of values besides all
ones is ones and twos.

Again, it is helpful to construct a table of predicted versus actual results. We will want to be as systematic as possible when gathering the
necessary data, and we will be especially on the alert for instances in
which the program supplies real roots rather than imaginary roots, and
instances in which the type of root is correct yet its value is not.

Figure 5-7 shows what such a table would look like. As we study the
information contained in this table of forced results, a definite pattern
begins to take shape. We note that a 2 in the B or C coefficient column
does not alter the actual result from that which we predicted it to be.

TABLE OF PREDICTED VS ACTUAL RESULTS $AX^2 + BX + C$						
Value of coefficients			Predicted		Actual	
A	B	C	X_1	X_2	X_1	X_2
1	1	−2	−2.0	1.0	−2.0	1.0
1	2	−1	−2.41	0.41	−2.41	0.41
2	1	−1	−1.0	0.5	−1.75	0.29
1	−1	2	$0.5 + 1.32i$	$0.5 - 1.32i$	$0.5 - 1.32i$	$0.5 - 1.32i$
1	−2	1	1.0	1.0	1.0	1.0
2	−1	1	$0.25 + 0.66i$	$0.25 - 0.66i$	$1.0 + 0.66i$	$1.0 - 0.66i$
−1	1	2	2.0	−1.0	2.0	−1.0
−1	2	1	2.41	−0.41	2.41	−0.41
−2	1	1	1.0	−0.5	1.75	−0.29

Fig. 5-7. Results of forcing as a debug method. Note the discrepancy
when A does not equal 1.

Also, it does not matter which coefficient is negative; the results still agree with the predictions.

However, whenever coefficient A is set equal to 2 the actual results are at variance with the predicted results. Indeed, this corresponds to the information we had about the program's performance from the homework problems. The problem

$$X^2 - 5X + 6$$

was correct, while

$$2X^2 + 8X - 18$$

was not.

We now have a good clue as to what the bug might be as we turn back to the program listing. We know now that whatever the bug is, the variable A is intimately connected with it. Fortunately, only three lines of code in the entire program contain that particular variable—lines 80, 90, and 180:

```
80   LET D=(B*B−4*A*C)/(4*A*A)
90   LET D2=−B/2*A
—
—
180   LET X2=C/X1*A
```

Before we get involved with playing computer, it is worth noting that Fig. 5-7 can tell us even more about the exact nature of the bug. Of course, after having seen the three offending lines of code, we might very well discover the bug just by inspection; but it is always a good idea to get in the habit of gleaning as much information as possible from the available diagnostic material.

Consider the following portion of Fig. 5-7:

	A	B	C	Predicted X_1	Predicted X_2	Actual X_1	Actual X_2
1.	2	1	1	−1.0	.5	−1.75	.29
2.	2	−1	1	.25+.66i	.25−.66i	1.0+.66i	1.0−.66i
3.	−2	1	1	1.0	−.5	1.75	−.29

Take, for example, lines 1 and 3: neither root of either case agrees with its predicted counterpart. But changing the sign of A from plus to minus flips the signs of X_1 and X_2 for the actual results just as it does for the predicted results. This implies that the quantity D_2, even though it may be of the wrong magnitude, is nonetheless of the correct sign. We know this because the sign of X_1 is determined by the sign of D_2, as we saw in Fig. 5-5.

Next, consider line 2: for both the roots of the actual and predicted results the imaginary component is the same $-.66i$. This implies that the quantity D is correct, removing line 80 from consideration, since for imaginary roots,

$$X = D_2 \pm \sqrt{-D}\, i$$

In this case, the evidence points directly to D_2 as being the home of at least one of the program's bugs.

In summary, then, all of the evidence from our forced data technique seems to indicate that the variable A is somehow being misused in the quadratic root-solving program, and furthermore that the most likely places the bug is hiding are at lines 90 and 180:

```
90   LET D2=-B/2*A
 —

 —
180  LET X2=C/X1*A
```

We note that the quantity X_1 is also computed incorrectly in those instances when the bug makes its presence felt, but since X_1 is a derived quantity based on D_2:

$$X_1 = D_2 \pm \sqrt{D}$$

it is unlikely that the bug would be found in any of the lines of code directly involved with computing X_1.

The cure for this particular bug is trivial; and surprisingly, that may have something to do with why it has escaped detection for so long. We recall first the hierarchy of mathematical operations in our SOL (and other computers):

Priority	Operation	Description
1	-	unitary negative
2	^	exponentiation
3	* , /	multiplication, division
4	+ , −	addition, subtraction

In the event that two operations of the same priority appear on the same line, they are evaluated as encountered, as the computer reads a line from left to right.

For line 90, then, the sequence of events would be:

```
FOR A=2
    B=1

90   LET D2=−B/2*A
 1)  −B/2=−½
         =−.5
 2)  −B/2*A=−.5*2
           =−1.0
```

This is not what would result had we evaluated the expression by hand:

$$FOR \quad A = 2$$
$$B = 1$$

$$D_2 = \frac{-B}{2A}$$

$$= \frac{-(1)}{2\,(2)}$$

$$= \frac{-1}{4}$$

$$= -.25$$

If we want the divisor to be evaluated in its entirety first—before it is divided into the dividend—then we must enclose all of its members in parentheses. The same reasoning holds true for line 180, and the corrected code would read as follows:

```
90   LET D2=−B/(2*A)
 —

 —

180   LET X2=C/(X1*A)
```

Running the program with these two alterations, and using as input variables sets of values from the table which we generated, we get the following results:

```
ANOTHER CALCULATION?   YES OR NO   YES
? −2
?? 1
?? 1
X1=1.0
X2=−.5
```

As we can see, this agrees with the predicted results in Fig. 5-7. Before we pronounce the program fixed, however, we should try a few more examples. Remember, we still want to force the program towards a specific result, rather than input random values and then have to perform potentially tedious hand calculations to verify the computer's results. As mentioned before, the easiest way to provide starting values that will yield easily verifiable results is to work backwards from the answer. In other words, we might do the following:

$$Y = (2X + 5)(3X − 2)$$
$$= 6X^2 + 15X − 4X − 10$$
$$= 6X^2 + 11X − 10$$

therefore,

$$A = 6$$
$$B = 11$$
$$C = −10$$

```
ANOTHER CALCULATION?   YES OR NO   YES
? 6
?? 11
?? −10
X1=−2.5
X2=.67
```

The roots of a quadratic equation are those points where the curve crosses the X axis, as we know. If −2.5 and 0.67 are correct roots to

$6X^2 + 11X - 10$, we should expect that the result of their substitution into the expression should equal zero:

FOR $X = -2.5$

$$Y = 6X^2 + 11X - 10$$
$$= 6(-2.5)^2 + 11(-2.5) - 10$$
$$= 6(6.25) - 27.5 - 10$$
$$= 37.5 - 27.5 - 10$$
$$Y = 0$$

FOR $X = 0.67$

$$Y = 6X^2 + 11X - 10$$
$$= 6(0.67)^2 + 11(0.67) - 10$$
$$= 6(.44) + 7.33 - 10$$
$$= 2.67 + 7.33 - 10$$
$$Y = 0$$

A few more such trials and we convince ourselves that the program has, in fact, been debugged.

We have seen how by structuring input data to cause a program to execute its code in a precisely predetermined way, hopefully arriving at a predetermined answer, we can make the step from bug to cure almost automatic. By (1) forcing a program through all of its possible execution paths one at a time, (2) systematically eliminating those branches of the program which are demonstrably bug-free, and then (3) narrowing down the remaining possibilities, we have established a powerful and effective debugging routine.

In most cases, forcing, like all the rest of the programmer's debugging techniques, is optional depending upon the specific circumstances and what the programmer feels like trying next. In some cases, however, forcing is mandatory; it is the only way a program can be debugged.

Consider, for example, the program outlined in flowchart form in Fig. 5-8. This is a flowchart for a version of the computer game, *Hunt the Wumpus*. Wumpus games have been around in many forms for a number of years. The object of the game is for us to get the wumpus before the wumpus gets (and presumably eats) us. Usually, we find ourselves in an intricately intertwined three-dimensional maze, full of trapdoors, bottomless pits, man-eating bats, winged snakes, and other assorted perils (not to mention the wumpus).

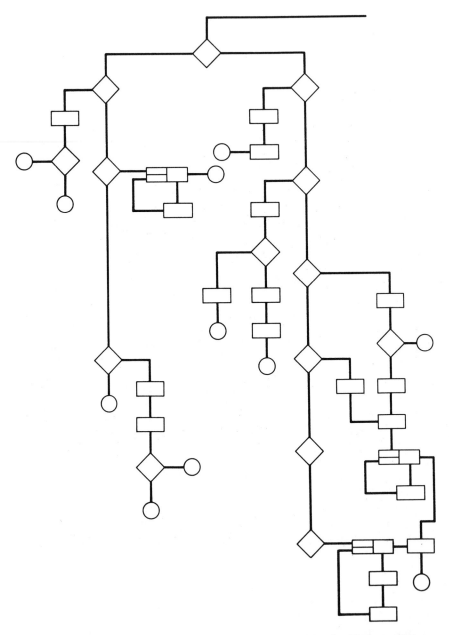

Fig. 5-8. Hypothetical flowchart for a game of "Hunt the Wumpus." Note the abundance of branches: A program such as this would be a perfect candidate for the debugging technique of forcing.

Fig. 5-8. *(Continued)*

A game this complex obviously requires a program with a large number of possible paths from start to finish. Since every move by either the computer or the player affects the flow of the game, there must be a considerable number of decision blocks, all interconnected in a manner nearly as complex as the maze in which the game is played.

Debugging a program of such complexity is itself a complex task, but it is at least brought within the range of manageability with the technique of forcing.

BLOCK DEBUGGING

Beginning with this chapter we will be concerning ourselves more with applied debugging methods rather than basic debugging tools. Techniques such as playing computer, inserting print statements, and forcing the flow of program execution all have their place in a normal debugging effort; to use one technique to the exclusion of all others is seldom the most efficient approach. Therefore, we will want to spend some time considering how the various techniques that we have so far been introduced to can be orchestrated into a single debugging plan.

PROGRAM TIERS OF COMPLEXITY

If we were to draw a hierarchy of program structure complexity, it might look something like Fig. 6-1. In this figure, we see that the simplest programs are linearly structured: they have one entrance, one exit, and one path of execution. The next level of complexity are linear programs with loops; there still is only one entrance, one exit, and one execution path, but now that path (or part of it) is executed more than one time within the body of the program.

The third level, the level at which most programs of general use begin, is that of branched program structure. Here, programs have been given some decision power; that is, they make choices and alter the path of execution based upon input or calculated values. Note that even though conditional branches are added, a definite increase in sophistication, the resulting program at the third level is still very much like that of the first level: once a path is chosen, execution continues linearly until it either encounters another conditional branch or reaches the end of the program.

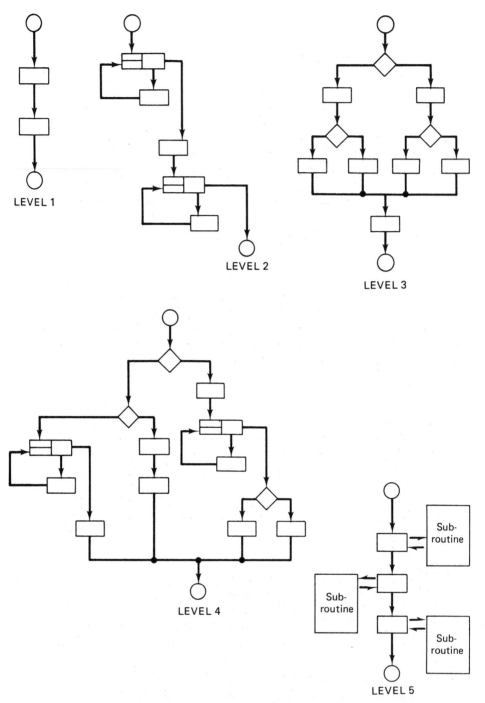

LEVEL 1

LEVEL 2

LEVEL 3

LEVEL 4

Sub-routine

Sub-routine

Sub-routine

LEVEL 5

Fig. 6-1. Comparative levels of program structure complexity.

The fourth level of complexity adds loops to conditional branches, making the program still more versatile. We are now able to selectively process arrays of numbers—as we might want to do in a game program, for example.

Level five returns to a somewhat modified linear program structure. At this level the main program proceeds from start to finish along a single path, but at certain points along the main program execution is transferred to separate blocks of code known as subroutines. Each subroutine executes just as if it were a separate program (which is what it is), and then passes the flow of execution back to the main program. The program we looked at in Chapter 1 to control the Smalltown model railroad has a level 5 structure, the only difference being that the main program has a long string of conditional branches which switch control of execution to one or another subroutine, depending upon the status of the train.

Beyond level 5, programs become more diverse and complex by adding more branches and loops to main programs, by making the subroutines equally involved, and by adding even more levels of subroutines: the main program transfers control to a subroutine which at some point in its path of execution transfers that control to yet another subroutine.

FUNCTIONAL CODE BLOCKS

The SOL version of extended BASIC includes entities known as user-definable functions, a feature also included in other BASIC packages. Functions can be thought of as modified subroutines; they are separate, specialized blocks of code which, when called into action by the main program, perform their required calculations and then return control of execution (along with whatever quantity they calculated) back to the main program. One difference between functions and subroutines, however, is that functions can be anywhere in a program, while subroutines are tied to particular statement numbers:

```
120   GOSUB 1040
130   L(I)=FNL(A,B,C)
```

In the first case at line 120, the code is saying "Go to the subroutine beginning at line 1040 and continue executing there." Line 130, however, says "Let L(*I*) be equal to the value of function L when function L uses for input parameters the quantities *A, B,* and *C.*" The function call makes no reference to a line number; the information for where the program must jump to if it is to evaluate function L is supplied as an intrinsic part of the FN statement.

Suppose we have a large body of information which we would like to categorize, collate, and keep open to easy access. The specific type of information might range anywhere from a file of research material for a scientist, to a case history file for a doctor, to a catalog of recordings for a musician. In each case, manual indexing and cross-referencing would work, but they are too time consuming to set up and maintain.

RECORD-KEEPING

What the various situations require is a computer-assisted filing system—one which can accept information according to a predetermined format, file the information away, and then selectively retrieve that information on the basis of certain supplied keywords.

The scientist, for example, might want to keep a reference collection of article reprints from the journals in his field. If he had available a full-time file clerk to take each reprint and generate for it a number of 3-by-5 index cards, each with the name of the author, title of the paper, name and issue of the journal, and a cross-idexed subject heading, there would be no problem.

But how much easier it would be if each reprint needed only to be assigned a unique locator number, and the file information—author's name, title of the paper, etc.—needed only to be entered once into a computerized file. Then, to access all of the papers relating to one specific topic, the scientists would need only to enter the subject heading into the computer, and the computer would search the file of reprint entries for those that matched.

Once written and debugged, this same basic program could be modified with little difficulty to handle the files of the doctor or the musician, or anyone else with a similar need.

A program versatile enough to do all that we have outlined would probably be at least moderately complex. The approach we take to debug such a program would therefore depend upon how we structure the program to accomplish its various tasks. In this case, a level 5 type of program would probably be the most efficient; by allocating well-defined tasks to specific subroutines we can maintain a clear focus on the various building blocks required to construct the program.

Block debugging is ideally suited to this sort of program. We first divide the overall program task into easily understood subtasks, and then we realize those subtasks in structures called subroutines or functions. Block debugging requires us to examine each subroutine separately, before it is inserted into the master program, to determine if the subroutine has any bugs. Block debugging can be used on a fully integrated master program simply by removing each subroutine one at a time from the main program and checking it for bugs; but block debugging is most profitably used when a program is first being written.

Suppose we return to the general record-keeping program mentioned earlier, and see how block debugging may be put to work. We remember from Chapter 1 that a programmer needs a set of specifications which the program is expected to meet before the first line of code can be written. Therefore:

> This program should be able to keep, update, and retrieve files of scientific article reprints. Each entry will contain the following information: title of article, name of author, publication name and date, and up to five cross-referenced headings. The bulk files will be kept on cassette tape, and the output will be arranged alphabetically. Programming language: Extended BASIC. Environment: SOL/20 microcomputer with 32K memory.

TASK IDENTIFICATION

Now that we know what the program must do, we can begin to work out the method of its actions and, *from* there, the structure which it will assume. We can draw a broad outline, as in Fig. 6-2, identifying the main subtasks of the program. We could stop there or continue to break down the program into even smaller, more manageable pieces; but to determine that possibility, we should first list in sufficient detail exactly what subtasks are required.

So far we have the two main headings:

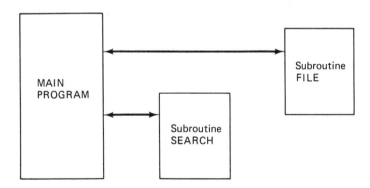

Fig. 6-2. Preliminary outline of the record-keeping program.

1. Make files

2. Search files

The first heading could be subdivided as follows:

1. Make files
   A. Make new files
   B. Add to old files

and each of those subdivisions could be amplified:

1. Make files
   A. Make new files
      1) Accept data from keyboard
      2) Format data into uniform record lengths
      3) Write formatted record onto tape
   B. Add to old files
      1) Transfer data from old file to new file
         a) read data from tape 1
         b) write data to tape 2
      2) Add new information to copy of file on tape 2
         a) perform sequence under A

We could subdivide the second heading:

2. Search files
   A. Search files for match with keyword
   B. Sort matching records alphabetically
   C. Print out result

and some of those subdivisions might also be expanded:

2. Search files
   A. Search files for match with keyword
      1) read in record from tape
      2) compare record headings with keyword
   B. Sort matching records alphabetically
   C. Print out result

First Level

We can now identify a larger number of subtasks, some of which might be better programmed as subroutines. One possible ordering scheme is shown in Fig. 6-3. We see that the program divides itself into three levels, the first level being the main program. The main program performs few, if any, computations or manipulations; it is instead like a master switch channeling the flow of execution down either one of two major paths. Once the subroutines have finished their efforts, the main program again plays the part of supervisor to determine whether there is more work yet to be done or all processing has been accomplished.

Second Level

The second level contains the two major subroutines which correspond to the two processing choices provided by the program: whether to write a new file, extend an old file, or search an old file for a specific keyword heading. Neither of these two subroutines does much in the way of nuts-and-bolts processing; rather, they are like second-echelon supervisors. They request information from the keyboard, and they work through a set of conditional branches to route the program flow.

Third Level

The third level of the program (in this example at least) is the most basic. Each subroutine performs a specific function without calling upon any subsidiary routines. If we were writing the program from scratch, or if we had been presented with the program fully written, we would take each subroutine block in turn, beginning with the blocks at the simplest level, and debug it.

THE DEBUGGING PROCESS

By convincing ourselves of the soundness of the individual building blocks, we hope to insure the soundness of the completed structure. Block debugging involves taking an existing subroutine, coding up a short supervisor routine called a driver, and then using the driver to put the subroutine through its paces. In this way, all of the subroutines common to a particular level may be tested independent of each other.

We will begin at the lowest program level and work upwards in complexity. In the record-keeping program, this would mean starting with the level 3 subroutines: READER, WRITER, FORMIN, and FORM-OUT. Once these are checked we can move up to the second level, and

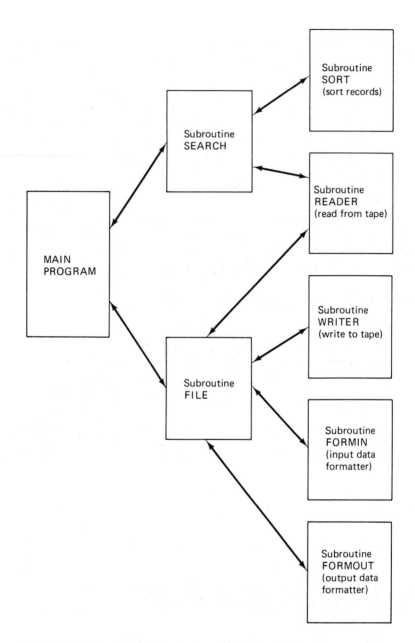

Fig. 6-3. Expanded block structure for the record-keeping program.

finally to the first level where we will integrate all of the subroutine building blocks under the master supervisory control of the main program.

Block debugging will be of greatest value at these lower levels; we may have to bring in other techniques as the subroutines become more complex.

Supervisor Routine

Driver programs are in general liberally sprinkled with print statements, and they also make considerable use of the technique of forcing. The purpose of a driver routine is to provide all of the values and variables which the subroutine under test will require to perform its task, call the subroutine into action, and finally display the results which the subroutine delivered. In much the same way that we constructed a table of actual and expected values in Chapter 5, driver routines often place the subroutine call inside one or more loops. Each time the subroutine is called, therefore, the input parameters change automatically, saving much hand effort and time.

For example, consider this subroutine:

```
500 REM SUBROUTINE TRIAREA
510 REM FINDS THE AREA OF TRIANGLE
520 LET C1=Y2-Y3
530 LET C2=Y3-Y1
540 LET C3=Y1-Y2
550 LET A=(X1*C1+X2*C2+X3*C3)*.5
560 RETURN
```

We note first that in BASIC the *return* statement signifies the lower bound of a subroutine, while there does not exist a unique statement which defines the beginning of a subroutine. A good general practice, then, is to identify the beginning of a subroutine with a line of comment, as was done in the example at line 500:

```
500 REM SUBROUTINE TRIAREA
```

The main program (or our driver program) would then access the subroutine with the command:

```
GOSUB 500
```

Distinguishing Subroutines

In BASIC, as mentioned before, the language makes no formal distinction between where a main program ends and where a subroutine begins. This is unlike other computer languages which consider main programs and subroutines to be semiautonomous units that only communicate through special reserved blocks of common memory storage. Statements in BASIC, then, whether they are part of driver programs, functions, or subroutines, must all have unique line numbers.

We could not, for example, use subroutine TRIAREA exactly as it appeared previously, using the following driver program:

```
500 REM THIS IS A DRIVER PROGRAM
510 REM TO TEST TRIAREA
520 FOR X1=1 TO 10
530 FOR X2=1 TO 10
540 FOR X3=1 TO 10
550 LET Y1=X1
560 LET Y2=X2
570 LET Y3=X3
580 GOSUB 500
590 PRINT A
600 NEXT X3
610 NEXT X2
620 NEXT X1
630 END
```

Since no two statements may have the same line number, we would get widely different results, depending upon which block of code we entered into the machine first. If we typed in the driver and then the subroutine, the lines of code in the subroutine would overwrite those of the driver, yielding:

```
500 REM SUBROUTINE TRIAREA
510 REM FINDS THE AREA OF A TRIANGLE
520 LET C1=Y2−Y3
530 LET C2=Y3−Y1
540 LET C3=Y1−Y2
550 LET A=(X1*C1+X2*C2+X3*C3)*.5
```

```
560 RETURN
570 LET Y3=X3
580 GOSUB 500
590 PRINT A
600 NEXT X3
610 NEXT X2
620 NEXT X1
630 END
```

This would result in a CS (control stack) error at line 560, which means that once the computer reached the statement

```
560 RETURN
```

it looked back for the address of the instruction to which it was supposed to jump in order to continue execution. Since the subroutine beginning at line 500 had not yet been called, the return address did not exist and the program bombed.

If we had typed in the subroutine first and then entered the driver, the like-numbered lines of the driver would have overwritten their counterparts in the subroutine, leaving in essence the driver routine. Executing this by itself would have thrown the computer into an endless loop since every time the flow of execution reached line 580 it would have been instructed to transfer control to the subroutine beginning at line 500.

A solution to the problem suggests itself: If we propose to write subroutines independent of the main program into which they will eventually be integrated (the basic premise of block debugging), then we should assign statement numbers which will guarantee that the subroutines are placed at the end of the (as yet unwritten) main program.

Subroutine TRIAREA may therefore be safely numbered beginning with line 500, as long as the main program begins somewhere after line 1 and does not extend beyond line 499.

There is only one more thing we must look out for before we move on to the actual block debugging of the record-keeping program. Suppose we renumber the statements of the previous driver routine as follows:

```
10 REM THIS IS A DRIVER PROGRAM
20 REM TO TEST TRIAREA
30 FOR X1=1 TO 10
40 FOR X2=1 TO 10
```

```
50 FOR X3=1 TO 10
60 LET Y1=X1
70 LET Y2=X2
80 LET Y3=X3
90 GOSUB 500
100 PRINT A
110 NEXT X3
120 NEXT X2
130 NEXT X1
140 END
```

We have eliminated any overlap between driver and subroutine, and both will execute perfectly. However, we must always keep in mind the lessons we learned in regard to forcing programs and the use of print statements. In the first case, we note that since the X and Y values are set equal to each other for the three end points that supposedly define the test triangle, the three points will all lie along the same line, X=Y, as in Fig. 6-4; and consequently the "triangles" thus constructed have no area.

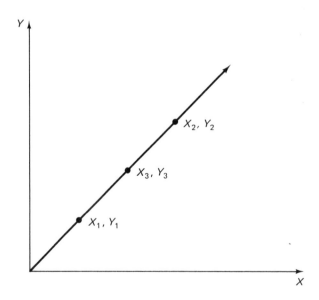

Fig. 6-4. The driver program to test the subroutine TRIAREA supplies points that all lie along the same line.

Also, since we planned our print statement deep within three nested FOR–NEXT loops, we will have 10 × 10 × 10, or 1000 lines of printout telling us that the area of a nonexistent triangle is 0.

Block Assignments

For the record-keeping program, in view of the program structure which we proposed in Fig. 6-3, we might decide to assign initial line numbers for the various subroutines as follows:

READER	1000
WRITER	2000
SEARCH	3000
SORT	4000
FILE	5000
FORMIN	6000
FORMOUT	7000

It is unlikely that any subroutine will be more than 1000 lines long, so we may feel safe that no two neighboring subroutines will find themselves competing for the same memory space.

We could conceivably begin block debugging with the lowest numbered subroutine, READER, and finish with the highest numbered subroutine, FORMOUT. Such an approach would not necessarily correspond to a progression from least to most complex, however, and would not therefore agree with our guidelines for block debugging.

The simplest subroutine is WRITER:

```
2000 REM SUBROUTINE WRITER
2010 REM WRITES A SINGLE LINE OF DATA
2020 REM TO TAPE (ALWAYS FILE #2)
2030 LET F$=H1$+H2$+H3$+H4$+H5$
2040 LET A$=F$+T$+N$+S$+D$
2050 PRINT #2;A$
2060 RETURN
```

The WRITER Subroutine

The question now: What sort of driver program do we write to correctly test this subroutine? Keeping in mind that the purpose of a driver is to

supply the input values required by the subroutine under test, we might
write the following:

```
10 REM DRIVER FOR WRITER
20 LET H1$="A"
30 LET H2$="B"
40 LET H3$="C"
50 LET H4$="D"
60 LET H5$="E"
70 LET T$="F"
80 LET N$="G"
90 LET S$="H"
100 LET D$="I"
110 GOSUB 2000
120 PRINT A$
130 END
```

The driver is simple and direct: it initializes the various unknowns
used by subroutine WRITER, it calls the subroutine, and it then displays
for us the resulting quantity from the subroutine. Running the driver
gives us:

```
FD ERROR IN LINE 2050
```

FD means format definition, a sort of catchall fatal-error flag which
in one possible interpretation means that the program tried to access a
file which was either unavailable for that particular operation, had not
been reopened after a *close* statement, or was unavailable owing to its
never having been requested in the first place.

Driver routines must provide for *all* of the needs of the subroutines
they control, not just initialization of variables. The FD error can be
erased with:

```
15 FILE #2; "OUT", 2
```

This tells the computer that a file called OUT, from now on to be referred
to simply as file #2, has been established and opened with *write* permission (2) granted. Running the program this time yields:

RUN
PREPARE TAPE UNIT 1 FOR WRITING TO: OUT

The computer wants us to load a blank tape into the cassette, press the record button, and then type any key on the console to tell the computer that all is ready. Since this is a test, we can simply type a key without loading a blank tape; the computer is easily fooled and will believe whatever we tell it. Execution continues:

ABCDEFGHI
READY

Apparently, subroutine WRITER works correctly. However, we have just engaged in an example of *blind debugging*. Blind debugging is not necessarily a practice to be avoided at all costs, but it is important that we be able to recognize when we are caught up in it. Specifically, in going through subroutine WRITER we noticed that it operated on nine unknown quantities: $H1\$$, $H2\$$, $H3\$$, $H4\$$, $H5\$$, $T\$$, $N\$$, $S\$$, and $D\$$. When we wrote the driver routine we provided values for those unknowns and, recalling the lessons of forcing, we made the values as simple as possible.

But could we have simplifed ourselves into a corner? In debugging we always face the conflict of simplicity versus reality. Perhaps if we had used a test case which more closely corresponded to reality we would not have gotten such reassuring results.

Identifying the Unknowns. If we go back to the paragraph of specifications for the record-keeping program, we can assign identities to the various unknown quantities of subroutine WRITER as follows:

$H1\$$=SUBJECT HEADING #1
$H2\$$=SUBJECT HEADING #2
$H3\$$=SUBJECT HEADING #3
$H4\$$=SUBJECT HEADING #4
$H5\$$=SUBJECT HEADING #5
$T\$$=TITLE
$S\$$=SOURCE
$D\$$=DATE

A more realistic set of initial values might therefore be:

```
20 LET H1$="CANCER"
30 LET H2$="CHEMOTHERAPY"
40 LET H3$="MITOCHONDRIA"
50 LET H4$="BRAUTMAN, J."
60 LET H5$="UCLA"
70 LET T$="NEW TREATMENT FOR CANCER"
80 LET N$="231"
90 LET S$="JOUR CHEM BIOL"
100 LET D$="FEB 78"
```

Execution.   Executing the driver and subroutine with these modifications would yield:

```
RUN
PREPARE TAPE UNIT 1 FOR WRITING TO: OUT
CANCERCHEM
READY
```

We should have gotten a lot more printout than merely CANCER-CHEM, but we notice that there are only ten digits in CANCERCHEM—a suspicious number which probably hints at the nature of the bug. Whatever it is, it would not have shown up had we continued to use one-letter values for each of the nine unknowns.

Checking the SOL Extended BASIC user's manual, we learn that:

The size of a string constant is limited only by its use in the program and the memory available.

This seems to be saying that if we set a string variable equal to a phrase containing 50 characters, and then print that variable out, we should be given the complete phrase.

Such does not seem to be the case with our test program, however. One sure way to force a string variable to be big enough to hold a particular phrase is to set its size with a dimension statement. We might therefore make the following modification to our driver routine:

```
5 DIM A$ (200)
```

A$ should now be large enough, so we run the program again:

RUN
PREPARE TAPE UNIT 1 FOR WRITING TO: OUT
CANCERCHEMNEW TREATM231JOUR CHEM FEB 78
READY

We found the rest of *A$*, but something is still not right. Our next step is to check into the subroutine itself for clues.

Using the Print Statement. Subroutine WRITER only has three lines of functional coding, which would not seemingly leave much room for a bug to hide:

```
2030 LET F$=H1$+H2$+H3$+H4$+H5$
2040 LET A$=F$+T$+N$+S$+D$
2050 PRINT #2;A$
```

Our most convenient tool here is the print statement. We know exactly what the various values are initialized to in the driver routine, so the logical first step is to simply print out all of those values at some point in the subroutine. One possible way of modifying subroutine WRITER with debug statements would be as follows:

```
2000 REM SUBROUTINE WRITER
2010 REM WRITES A SINGLE LINE OF DATA
2020 REM TO TAPE (ALWAYS FILE #2)
2030 LET F$=H1$+H2$+H3$+H4$+H5$
2031 PRINT "H1$";H1$
2032 PRINT "H2$";H2$
2033 PRINT "H3$";H3$
2034 PRINT "H4$";H4$
2035 PRINT "H5$";H5$
2040 LET A$=F$+T$+N$+S$+D$
2041 PRINT "F$";F$
2042 PRINT "T$";T$
2043 PRINT "N$";N$
2044 PRINT "S$";S$
2045 PRINT "D$";D$
2046 PRINT "A$";A$
```

```
2050 PRINT #2;A$
2060 RETURN
```

which would lead to:

```
RUN
PREPARE TAPE UNIT 1 FOR WRITING TO: OUT
H1$ CANCER
H2$ CHEMOTHERA
H3$ MITOCHONDR
H4$ BRAUTMAN, J
H5$ UCLA
F$ CANCERCHEM
T$ NEW TREATM
N$ 231
S$ JOUR CHEM
D$ FEB 78
A$ CANCERCHEMNEW TREATM231JOUR CHEM FEB 78
CANCERCHEMNEW TREATM231JOUR CHEM FEB 78
READY
```

We note that although *H2$* was initialized to CHEMOTHERAPY, it
appears in the debug printout as CHEMOTHERA, a 10-character word.
MITOCHONDRIA was also shortened to the 10-character MITO-
CHONDR. A clue such as this is too obvious to ignore; and indeed we
have discovered our bug. The fault lies not in the subroutine but in the
driver. String variables likely to contain more than 10 characters must be
specifically dimensioned to the required size, and the logical place to do
such dimensioning is in the main (or in thise case the driver) routine.

Line 5 of the driver routine therefore might be modifed and extended
as:

```
5 DIM H1$(20),H2$(20),H3$(20),H4$(20),H5$(20)
7 DIM F$(100),T$(40),N$(5),S$(20),D$(10),A$(175)
```

Running the two blocks of code now results in:

```
RUN
PREPARE TAPE UNIT 1 FOR WRITING TO: OUT
```

H1$ CANCER
H2$ CHEMOTHERAPY
H3$ MITOCHONDRIA
H4$ BRAUTMAN,J.
H5$ UCLA
F$ CANCERCHEMOTHERAPYMITOCHONDRIABRAUTMAN,J.UCLA
T$ NEW TREATMENT FOR CANCER
N$ 231
S$ JOUR CHEM BIOL
D$ FEB 78
A$ CANCERCHEMOTHERAPYMITOCHONDRIABRAUTMAN,J.UCLANEW
TREATMENT FOR CANCER231JOUR CHEM BIOLFEB 78
CANCERCHEMOTHERAPYMITOCHONDRIABRAUTMAN,J.UCLANEW
TREATMENT FOR CANCER231JOUR CHEM BIOLFEB 78
READY

At least the redimensioned variables are able to hold all the characters required of them. The process of adding string variables together, called *concatenation,* apparently ignores trailing blanks, leading (as we have just seen) to some considerable run-on sentences. Hopefully some other subroutine of the record-keeping program addresses the problem of trailing blanks, or else it is unclear how the computer would be able to perform a search for keywords among records of nonuniform size.

The READER Subroutine

We can, however, say that subroutine WRITER works. We then move on to the next test case, subroutine READER:

```
1000 REM SUBROUTINE READER
1010 REM READS DATA FROM TAPE (ALWAYS FILE #1)
1020 REM STORES A RECORD AT A TIME IN A$
1030 READ #1, A$
1040 IF EOF(1)=6 THEN GOTO 1150
1050 LET H1$=A$(1,10)
1060 LET H2$=A$(11,20)
1070 LET H3$=A$(21,30)
1080 LET H4$=A$(31,40)
1090 LET H5$=A$(41,50)
1100 LET T$=A$(51,80)
```

```
1110 LET N$=A$(81,85)
1120 LET S$=A$(86,100)
1130 LET D$=A$(101,110)
1140 GOTO 1160
1150 LET L$="EOF"
1160 RETURN
```

Just as it was WRITER's job to assemble a single record out of nine separate string variables and then write that composite out onto a mass storage device, so it is READER's job to read a single long record in from a storage medium such as cassette tape or floppy disk, and then dismember that one long record into nine simpler subunits.

In working at subroutine READER, we get our first detailed explanation of the layout of a record. Figure 6-5 graphically translates this information for us. Apparently we were correct in our hunch about there being another subroutine whose function is to massage the various entries into conforming to certain prescribed lengths, complete with trailing blanks if necessary, to fill up unused space.

When using the block method of debugging, it is important that we learn as much as we can about the inner workings of the subroutine under test before we try to debug it. This will become even clearer in later examples, as we move up the ladder of complexity through the record-keeping program.

Coding the Driver.   Using the information from Fig. 6-5, and combining it with the test case we constructed in the driver for subroutine WRITER, we code up the following driver for subroutine READER:

```
10 REM DRIVER ROUTINE TO TEST
20 REM SUBROUTINE READER
30 DIM A$(110),T$(30),S$(15)
40 FILE #1;"TEST",1
50 GOSUB 1000
60 PRINT "A$";A$
70 PRINT "H1$";H1$
80 PRINT "H2$";H2$
90 PRINT "H3$";H3$
100 PRINT "H4$";H4$
110 PRINT "H5$";H5$
120 PRINT "T$";T$
```

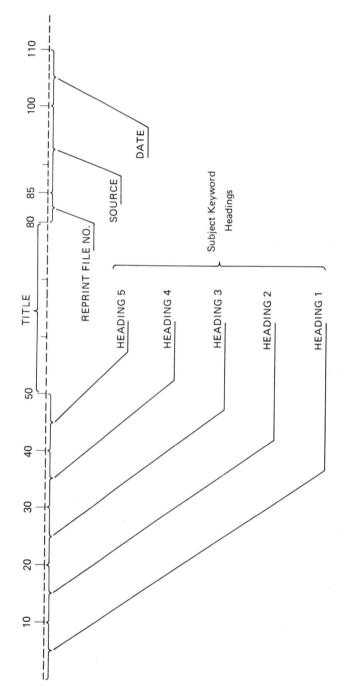

Fig. 6-5. Character space allocation scheme for a single 110-character record.

169

```
130 PRINT "N$";N$
140 PRINT "S$";S$
150 PRINT "D$";D$
160 DATA "CANCER        CHEMOTHERAMITOCHONDRBRAUTMAN,J
     UCLA          NEW TREATMENT FOR CANCER         231
     JOUR CHEM BIOL FEB 78    "
170 END
```

The driver routine is, as all good driver routines should be, fairly clear and to the point. The only potential area of confusion might be the data statement and the reasoning behind its peculiar construction. Figure 6-6 reproduces the data statement and illustrates why it looks as it does. When writing a driver, we must provide a subroutine with all the data it needs and in a form that it can use.

Driver Execution.   Suppose we try to execute the driver along with subroutine READER:

```
RUN
PREPARE TAPE UNIT 1 FOR READING FROM: TEST
OB ERROR AT LINE 1050
```

We should have suspected that something was wrong when the computer asked us to turn on tape unit 1 in preparation for the subroutine to read data from it. Since there is no data on the tape which we put in the tape recorder, the subroutine read in something less than a blank or a series of blanks: it read in what is called the *null string*, a string containing no characters whatsoever.

Line 1050 says to let $H1\$$ be equal to the first 10 characters of $A\$$. If $A\$$ were 110 characters long, as it should be, then this would pose no problem. But with $A\$$ equal to the null string, line 1050 is referencing characters in $A\$$ which do not exist. OB, therefore not surprisingly, means an out-of-bounds reference.

The Readable External File.   We could change subroutine READER so that it read from a data statement rather than an external memory device like a tape recorder, but that would be defeating the whole purpose of the subroutine and of block debugging as a technique. Instead, what we must do by way of the driver routine is create an external file that the subroutine *can* read.

One way to accomplish this would be as follows:

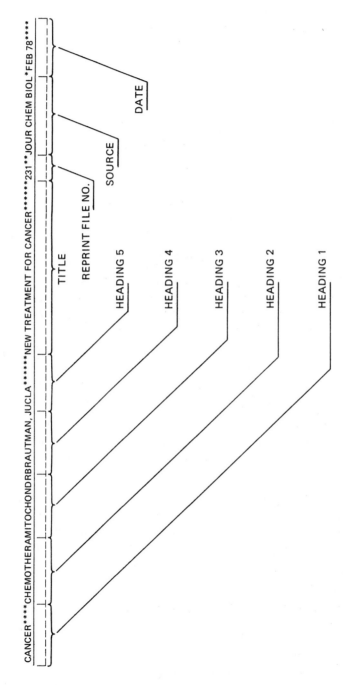

Fig. 6-6. Physical layout of sample record. Asterisks (*) indicate blanks.

```
10 REM DRIVER ROUTINE TO TEST
20 REM SUBROUTINE READER
30 DIM A$(110), T$(30), S$(15), Z$(110)
32 FILE #1;"TEST",2
34 READ Z$
36 PRINT #1;Z$
38 REWIND #1
40 CLOSE #1
42 FILE #1;"TEST",1
50 GOSUB 1000
```

and the rest of the driver would be as before.

The added lines of code may look cryptic and complicated, but they are essential to setting up a scratch file acceptable to subroutine READER, and they can be "decoded" as follows:

32 Declare file #1 (called TEST) to be open and to carry write (2) permission.

34 Read from the data statement at line 160, the string variable Z$.

36 Write (print) Z$ onto file #1

38 Rewind file #1 so that subroutine READER will be able to read from it at the beginning.

40 File #1 currently has write permission, but we will want to read from it. We must "erase" the write permission by closing the file.

42 We now reopen the file, this time with *read* (1) permission.

When debugging subroutine WRITER, we were able to fool the computer by typing a go-ahead to a tape handling request even though we had not performed the required task. When debugging subroutine READER, we will have to do what we are asked, however, or else the subroutine will not work.

We execute the two programs:

```
RUN
PREPARE TAPE UNIT 1 FOR WRITING TO: TEST
PREPARE TAPE UNIT 1 FOR REWINDING
PREPARE TAPE UNIT 1 FOR READING FROM: TEST
A$ CANCER      CHEMOTHERAMITOCHONDRBRAUTMAN,J.
```

```
UCLA        NEW TREATMENT FOR CANCER        231
JOUR CHEM BIOL FEB 78
H1$ CANCER
H2$ CHEMOTHERA
H3$ MITOCHONDR
H4$ BRAUTMAN,J
H5$ UCLA
T$ NEW TREATMENT FOR CANCER
N$ 231
S$ JOUR CHEM BIOL
D$ FEB 78
READY
```

And again, we may assume that the program has been debugged at this level.

The FORMIN Subroutine

The next two subroutines to consider are FORMIN and FORMOUT, the two level 3 subroutines directly under the control of FILE, the level 2 subroutine. FORMIN writes a fill-in-the-blank form on the CRT screen, and FORMOUT formats the entries thus obtained for transfer to subroutine WRITER.

FORMIN begins at line 6000, as follows:

```
6000 REM SUBROUTINE FORMIN
6010 REM FILL-IN FORM FOR INPUT DATA
6020 PRINT "&K"
6030 CURSOR 1,0
6040 PRINT "PLEASE ENTER THE INFORMATION AS REQUESTED"
6050 PRINT "A BLANK ON THE FIRST ENTRY ENDS THE LIST"
6060 PRINT "TITLE"
6070 CURSOR 5,0
6080 PRINT "FILE NUMBER"
6090 CURSOR 5,20
6100 PRINT "SOURCE"
6110 CURSOR 5,45
6120 PRINT "DATE"
```

```
6130 CURSOR 7,17
6140 PRINT "HEADINGS(TOTAL OF FIVE)"
6150 CURSOR 3,8
6160 INPUT T$
6170 IF T$="" THEN LET L2=1:GO TO 6340
6180 CURSOR 5,13
6190 INPUT N$
6200 CURSOR 5,28
6210 INPUT S$
6220 CURSOR 5,50
6230 INPUT D$
6240 CURSOR 8,0
6250 INPUT H1$
6260 CURSOR 8,20
6270 INPUT H2$
6280 CURSOR 8,40
6290 INPUT H3$
6300 CURSOR 10,10
6310 INPUT H4$
6320 CURSOR 10,30
6330 INPUT H5$
6340 RETURN
```

FORMIN Driver.   Subroutine FORMIN requires no files to read from or write to, but it does need some space reserved in memory for overlong string variables, like T$ and S$, similar to the two subroutines just previous. The driver routine for subroutine FORMIN can therefore be as simple as:

```
10 REM DRIVER TO TEST FORMIN
20 DIM T$(30), S$(15)
30 GOSUB 6000
40 PRINT "H1$";H1$
50 PRINT "H2$";H2$
60 PRINT "H3$";H3$
70 PRINT "H4$";H4$
80 PRINT "H5$";H5$
90 PRINT "T$";T$
```

```
100 PRINT "N$";N$
110 PRINT "S$";S$
120 PRINT "D$";D$
130 END
```

Execution.   If we now run the driver and its subroutine, we get the display reproduced in Fig. 6-7. The question mark just to the right of TITLE is the computer prompting us to input the requested information. We do so, and the display then looks like Fig. 6-8, showing that the prompt symbol has moved to the next field. We make the second entry and the display changes to that shown in Fig. 6-9.

Part of the display has been lost, and for no apparent reason: we did not type enough characters to overwrite either SOURCE or DATE, so why were those two items lost?

Unfortunately, the bug has its roots in the basic physical structure of the computer we are using, and is beyond our reach to correct or even modify. The electronic circuitry responsible for refreshing the CRT screen concerns itself only with those characters actually typed in to the computer (if the typed-in line begins midway across the screen, all characters already on the screen to the *left* of the typed-in line are considered part of this new line). The SOL shares this limitation with most other mi-

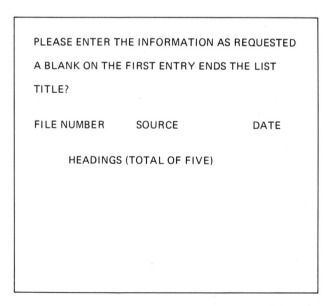

PLEASE ENTER THE INFORMATION AS REQUESTED

A BLANK ON THE FIRST ENTRY ENDS THE LIST

TITLE?

FILE NUMBER   SOURCE   DATE

         HEADINGS (TOTAL OF FIVE)

Fig. 6-7.   Input display generated by subroutine FORMIN under driver routine control.

PLEASE ENTER THE INFORMATION AS REQUESTED

A BLANK ON THE FIRST ENTRY ENDS THE LIST

TITLE NEW TREATMENT FOR CANCER

FILE NUMBER?   SOURCE   DATE

    HEADINGS (TOTAL OF FIVE)

Fig. 6-8. Input display generated by subroutine FORMIN under driver routine control, after first entry.

PLEASE ENTER THE INFORMATION AS REQUESTED

A BLANK ON THE FIRST ENTRY ENDS THE LIST

TITLE NEW TREATMENT FOR CANCER

FILE NUMBER 231   ?

    HEADINGS (TOTAL OF FIVE)

Fig. 6-9. Input display generated by subroutine FORMIN after second entry. Note the loss of SOURCE and DATE headings.

crocomputer systems; only when the price tag increases by an order of magnitude or so do we find features such as protected display areas and true tabular form data entry.

For our situation, however, we will have to think of alternate arrangements. One sure way to get around the line blanking is to put each input request on a separate display line. One such scheme is shown in Fig. 6-10, and the revised subroutine which would correspond to that is as follows:

```
6000 REM SUBROUTINE FORMIN
6010 REM FILL-IN FORM FOR INPUT DATA
6020 PRINT "&K"
6030 CURSOR 1,0
6040 PRINT "PLEASE ENTER THE INFORMATION AS REQUESTED"
6050 PRINT "A BLANK ON THE FIRST ENTRY ENDS LIST"
6060 PRINT "TITLE"
6070 CURSOR 5,0
6080 PRINT "FILE NUMBER"
6090 CURSOR 7,0
6100 PRINT "SOURCE"
```

PLEASE ENTER THE INFORMATION AS REQUESTED

A BLANK ON THE FIRST ENTRY ENDS THE LIST

TITLE

FILE NUMBER

SOURCE

DATE

HEADINGS (TOTAL OF FIVE)

Fig. 6-10. Revised input display generated by subroutine FORMIN.

```
6110 CURSOR 9,0
6120 PRINT "DATE"
6130 CURSOR 11,0
6140 PRINT "HEADINGS(TOTAL OF FIVE)"
6150 CURSOR 3,8
6160 INPUT T$
6170 IF T$=" " THEN LET L2=1:GOTO 6340
6180 CURSOR 5,13
6190 INPUT N$
6200 CURSOR 7,8
6210 INPUT S$
6220 CURSOR 9,6
6230 INPUT D$
6240 CURSOR 11,26
6250 INPUT H1$
6260 CURSOR 11,40
6270 INPUT H2$
6280 CURSOR 13,0
6290 INPUT H3$
6300 CURSOR 13,26
6310 INPUT H4$
6320 CURSOR 13,40
6330 INPUT H5$
6340 RETURN
```

The FORMOUT Subroutine

Subroutine FORMOUT is the complement to subroutine FORMIN. We know from before that each output record is composed of nine different elements; since a record is exactly 110 characters long, there must be some method for chopping off overly long elements or padding with blank spaces those elements which are too short, to bring the sum of all the elements up to 110 characters. Subroutine FORMOUT provides that method.

FORMOUT is basically a three-step linear program, with the three steps being repeated nine consecutive times. Figure 6-11 is a flowchart illustrating the subroutine, and its listing is as follows:

```
7000 REM SUBROUTINE FORMOUT
7010 REM THIS SUBROUTINE MOLDS DATA INTO
```

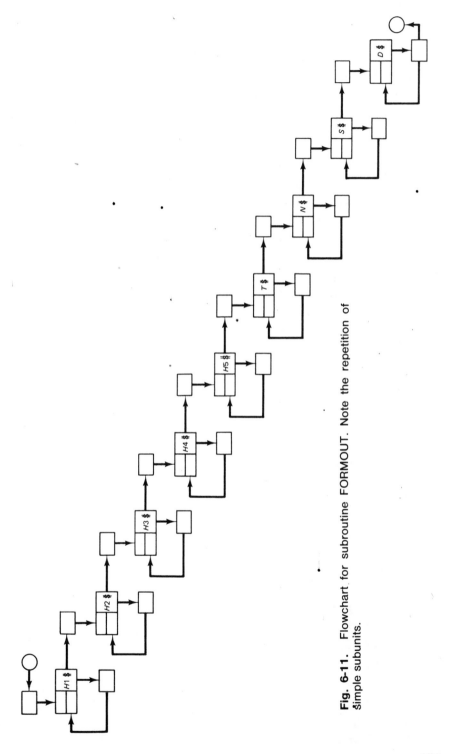

Fig. 6-11. Flowchart for subroutine FORMOUT. Note the repetition of simple subunits.

179

```
7020 REM PROPER FORMAT FOR OUTPUT INTO TAPE
7030 LET P$=" "
7040 LET L=LEN(H1$)
7050 LET J=10−L
7060 FOR I=1 TO 5
7070 LET H1$=H1$+P$
7080 NEXT I
7090 LET L=LEN(H2$)
7100 LET J=10−L
7110 FOR I=1 TO J
7120 LET H2$=H2$+P$
7130 NEXT I
7140 LET L=LEN(H3$)
7150 LET J=10−L
7160 FOR I=1 TO J
7170 LET H3$=H3$+P$
7180 NEXT I
7190 LET L=LEN(H4$)
7200 LET J=10−L
7210 FOR I=1 TO J
7220 LET H4$=H4$+P$
7230 NEXT I
7240 LET L=LEN(H5$)
7250 LET J=10−L
7260 FOR I=1 TO J
7270 LET H5$=H5$+P$
7280 NEXT I
7290 LET L=LEN(T$)
7300 LET J=30−L
7310 FOR I=1 TO J
7320 LET T$=T$+P$
7330 NEXT I
7340 LET L=LEN(N$)
7350 LET J=5−L
7360 FOR I=1 TO J
7370 LET N$=N$+P$
7380 NEXT I
7390 LET L=LEN(S$)
```

```
7400 LET J=15-L
7410 FOR I=1 TO J
7420 LET S$=S$+P$
7430 NEXT I
7440 LET L=LEN(D$)
7450 LET J=10-L
7460 FOR I=1 TO J
7470 LET D$=D$+P$
7480 NEXT I
7490 RETURN
```

FORMOUT Driver.   The driver for this subroutine will be very similar to those of previous examples. We still are required to supply nine string variables and to provide room in memory via a DIM statement for those string variables which exceed 10 characters in length. A good mixture of test values might be a few strings which are shorter than their required length and thus in need of padding, and others which are longer than necessary and therefore in need of clipping. The sample input which we used in the last few examples satisfies both of those needs.

We might therefore construct the following driver for subroutine FORMOUT:

```
10 REM DRIVER FOR SUBROUTINE FORMOUT
20 DIM T$(30),S$(15)
30 LET H1$="CANCER"
40 LET H2$="CHEMOTHERAPY"
50 LET H3$="MITOCHONDRIA"
60 LET H4$="BRAUTMAN,J."
70 LET H5$="UCLA"
80 LET T$="NEW TREATMENT FOR CANCER"
90 LET N$="231"
100 LET S$="JOUR CHEM BIOL"
110 LET D$="FEB 78"
120 GOSUB 7000
130 PRINT "FORMOUT SAYS"
140 PRINT "H1$"; H1$
150 PRINT "H2$"; H2$
160 PRINT "H3$"; H3$
170 PRINT "H4$"; H4$
```

```
180 PRINT "H5$"; H5$
190 PRINT "T$"; T$
200 PRINT "N$"; N$
210 PRINT "S$"; S$
220 PRINT "D$"; D$
230 END
```

By now the driver routines may be looking all very much alike; almost all the same statements have been used in each of those which we have considered so far. This should not be too surprising, since all of the subroutines which we have been debugging up to this point have been taken from the third level of subroutine complexity (Fig. 6-3), and all have also been in some way connected with input/output manipulations.

Execution. Executing this particular driver–subroutine combination would yield:

```
RUN
FORMOUT SAYS
H1$ CANCER
H2$ CHEMOTHERA
H3$ MITOCHONDR
H4$ BRAUTMAN,J
H5$ UCLA
T$ NEW TREATMENT FOR CANCER
N$ 231
S$ JOUR CHEM BIOL
D$ FEB 78
READY
```

Entries such as "CHEMOTHERAPY", "MITOCHONDRIA", and "BRAUTMAN, J." were clipped to only 10 characters each, the default length of a string variable. Since variables $H1\$$ through $H5\$$ are only supposed to be 10 characters long (Fig. 6-5), we had no need to specifically redimension the variables from their default dimensions.

We now know that words containing more than their allowed number of characters were clipped to conform to their allotted space, but we have no way of knowing if words containing fewer than their allowed number of characters (such as UCLA) were padded out to the right length. Why? Because the empty spaces will be padded with blanks, and blanks are just that: blank.

For debug purposes then, we should change line 7030 in subroutine FORMOUT to:

7030 LET P$="*"

Running the program a second time, we find:

```
RUN
FORMOUT SAYS
H1$ CANCER****
H2$ CHEMOTHERA
H3$ MITOCHONDR
H4$ BRAUTMAN,J
H5$ UCLA******
T$ NEW TREATMENT FOR CANCER******
N$ 231**
S$ JOUR CHEM BIOL*
D$ FEB 78****
READY
```

The results seem to indicate that subroutine FORMOUT is free of bugs, allowing us to move on to the next subroutine, SORT.

The SORT Subroutine

SORT is the last of the level 3 subroutines. Its input is the arbitrary number of records selected from the master tape file by subroutine SEARCH.

Note that in previous as well as upcoming discussions, we are not blindly asserting that "a record has 110 characters" for example, because we have the benefit of specification for each subroutine to tell us exactly what a particular subroutine needs for input and delivers as output, despite the fact that the subroutine in question might not yet even be written.

Bubble Sort.   Subroutine SORT uses an algorithm called a bubble sort. This differs from the sorting algorithm we encountered in Chapter 4, requiring much less memory space and running more efficiently. The two methods are contrasted in Fig. 6-12.

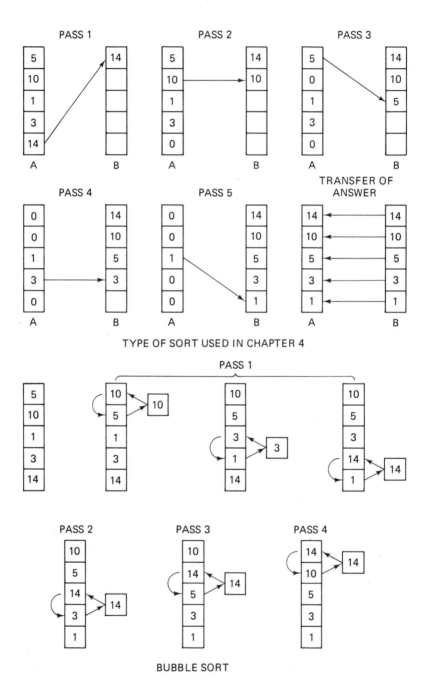

Fig. 6-12. Comparison of bubble sort and min/max sort.

The subroutine, which begins at line 4000, is as follows:

```
4000 REM SUBROUTINE SORT
4010 REM ALPHABETICALLY SORTS ENTRIES
4020 REM PRIOR TO PRINTOUT
4030 FOR J1=1 TO N
4040 LET N2=0
4050 FOR J2=1 TO N
4060 LET I2=(J2-1)*60+1
4070 LET V$=E$(I2,I2+59)
4080 LET V=ASC(V$)
4090 LET V2$=E$ (1+60,I2+119)
4100 LET V2=ASC(V2$)
4110 IF V>V2 THEN GO TO 4150
4120 LET N2=N2+1
4130 IF N2=N THEN GO TO 4220
4140 GOTO 4200
4150 LET L=I2+60
4160 LET H=I2+119
4170 LET T2$=E$(L,H)
4180 LET E$(L,H)=E$(I2,I2+59)
4190 LET E$(I2,I2+59)=T2$
4200 NEXT J2
4210 NEXT J1
4220 RETURN
```

The variable N, which serves as an upper bound to the loops beginning at 4030 and 4050, stands for the number of records which must be sorted. Lines 4060 through 4090 and line 4150 through 4190 display some fairly complicated indexing schemes. Suppose we consider only the following three lines:

```
4050 FOR J2=1 TO N
4060 LET I2=(J2-1)*60+1
4070 LET V$=E$(I2,I2+59)
```

We can construct a short table of representative values as follows:

J2	I2	V$
1	1	E$(1,60)
2	61	E$(61,120)
3	121	E$(121,180)
4	181	E$(181,240)

Each time the index variable J2 increments by 1, it specifies a new 60-character block of the string variable E$. These 60-character blocks are the items which will eventually be sorted, and they correspond to the 110-character blocks we encountered in READER and WRITER, minus the first 50 characters occupied by the five subject-heading keywords (each of which occupies 10 characters).

SORT Driver. When writing the driver routine to debug subroutine SORT, we will have to construct a string variable E$ with a series of 60-character records arranged as follows:

...(TITLE/NUMBER/SOURCE/DATE)(TITLE/NUMBER/SOURCE/DATE)...

We will also have to dimension the various string variables large enough and provide the subroutine with the value of N, the number of records to be sorted:

```
10 REM DRIVER FOR SUBROUTINE SORT
20 DIM E$(600),V$(60),V2$(60),T2$(60)
30 LET N=2
40 READ E$
50 PRINT "DRIVER SAYS E$=";E$
60 GOSUB 4000
70 PRINT "SORT SAYS E$=";E$
80 DATA "PHOSPHORYLATED ENZYME EFFECTS 192   JOUR
CHEM BIOL OCT 77      NEW TREATMENT FOR CANCER
    231 JOUR CHEM BIOL FEB 78        "
90 END
```

Execution. Running the program yields:

```
RUN
DRIVER SAYS E$=PHOSPHORYLATED ENZYME EFFECTS 192
```

JOUR CHEM BIOL OCT 77   NEW TREATMENT FOR CAN
CER   231   JOUR CHEM BIOL FEB 78
OB ERROR AT LINE 4090

The first thing for us to do is to get a listing of the two programs, since the bug could be something as trivial as a mistyped variable or number. The computer's response to our request:

```
LIST
10 REM DRIVER FOR SUBROUTINE SORT
20 DIM E$(600),V$(60),V2$(60),T2$(60)
30 LET N=2
40 READ E$
50 PRINT "DRIVER SAYS E$=";E$
60 GOSUB 4000
70 PRINT "SORT SAYS E$=";E$
LL ERROR
```

LL stands for line length. Although the data statement was accepted accurately (it was printed out correctly when we first tried to run the program), it is too long to be printed out in a *list* or in response to an *edit* command. There is a penalty, it seems, for being overly clever (or lazy). If we want to be able to list the program in its entirety we will have to break up the data statement at line 80 into a number of smaller statements. We will also have to add a few lines of code which will read the various small segments of test data and assemble them into the much longer string variable required by subroutine SORT.

One possible approach would be:

```
10 REM DRIVER FOR SUBROUTINE SORT
20 DIM E$(600),V$(60),V2$(60),T2$(60)
30 LET N=3
40 FOR I=1 TO N
50 READ V$
60 LET E$=E$+V$
70 NEXT I
80 LET V$=" "
90 PRINT "DRIVER SAYS E$=";E$
100 GOSUB 4000
```

```
110 PRINT "SORT SAYS E$=";E$
120 DATA "PHOSPHORYLATED ENZYME EFFECTS 192 JOUR CHEM
     BIOL OCT 77        "
130 DATA "NEW TREATMENT FOR CANCER        231    JOUR CHEM
     BIOL FEB 78    "
140 DATA "DNA DETERMINATION TECHNIQUES    402    JOUR
     MOLEC BIOLJAN 78        "
150 END
```

With the data statements shortened to manageable length, we can get a listing of the program with no trouble. Suppose we run the program again as a test; we have added a new piece of code, and for all we know the too-long data statements from before might have been partly responsible for the OB error.

```
RUN
DRIVER SAYS E$=PHOSPHORYLATED ENZYME EFFECTS 192
JOUR CHEM BIOL OCT 77      NEW TREATMENT FOR CANCER
          231    JOUR CHEM BIOL FEB 78      DNA DETERMINA
TION TECHNIQUES    402    JOUR MOLEC BIOLJAN 78
OB ERROR AT LINE 4090
```

The out-of-bounds (OB) error is still with us. Line 4090 is the second place in subroutine SORT that elements from string variable E$ are accessed:

```
4090 LET V2$=E$(I2+60,I2+119)
```

Not too far back we generated a table of values for $J2$, $I2$, and V$ as the index variable $J2$ incremented from 1 to N (actually we were playing computer—we just didn't call it that). Suppose we repeat that table, including V2$ this time, incrementing $J2$ from 1 to 3, the value of N specified in the driver routine:

J2	I2	V$	V2$
1	1	E$(1,60)	E$(61,120)
2	61	E$(61,120)	E$(121,180)
3	121	E$(121,180)	E$(181,240)

We know the exact content and length of E$, since we constructed it in the driver routine. It consists of the concatenation (addition) of three separate data statements, each of which is composed exactly 60 characters. There are as a result 60+60+60, or 180, characters in E$. In other words, E$ is exactly 180 characters long.

The bubble sort algorithm considers only neighboring elements of an array; it compares element N and element $N+1$. If (in this particular case) element $N+1$ is less than element N, the two switch places. If element $N+1$ is greater than element N, no action is taken and processing continues on to the next pair of elements, element $N+1$ and element $N+2$. In this manner, a list of numbers is sorted into smallest number at the first position and largest number at the last position.

In the case of the string variables which we are sorting, each element is actually 60 characters long, which explains the need for the count-by-60 indexing scheme of line 4060:

```
4060 LET I2=(J2−1)*60+1
```

As we saw in the table of values, each time the master index $J2$ increases by 1, the computed index $I2$ increases by 60. In this manner $I2$ is always pointing to the beginning of the next element in E$.

If we consider E$ to be made up of only three elements (regardless of how long each such element may be), then it is clear that the only side-by-side pairs of elements to be considered by the bubble sort algorithm are elements 1 and 2, and elements 2 and 3. The index variable $J2$, then, should only increment from 1 to 2, and not from 1 to 3. This is best pointed out by the table of values: if $J2$ is allowed to increment to 3, then the Nth element points to E$(121,180), while the Nth+1 element points to E$(181,240). In a string which contains only 180 characters, any reference to characters 181 through 240 is certainly out of bounds.

We can easily fix this bug by inserting one line of code into subroutine SORT as follows:

```
4025 LET N=N−1
```

Running the program with the change yields:

```
RUN
DRIVER SAYS E$=PHOSPHORYLATED ENZYME EFFECTS 192
JOUR CHEM BIOL OCT 77     NEW TREATMENT FOR CANCER
```

```
      231   JOUR CHEM BIOL FEB 78        DNA DETERMINA
TION TECHNIQUES   402   JOUR MOLEC BIOLJAN 78
SORT SAYS E$=DNA DETERMINATION TECHNIQUES   402
JOUR MOLEC BIOLJAN 78      NEW TREATMENT FOR CANCER
      231   JOUR CHEM BIOL FEB 78       PHOSPHORYLATE
D ENZYME EFFECTS 192   JOUR CHEM BIOL OCT 77
```

D before N before P; alphabetically correct—subroutine SORT also appears to be debugged and working.

Summary

We have now finished with all of the level 3 subroutines: those subroutines which are called by other, higher-up subroutines but which do not themselves invoke any subordinate programs. We have seen how block debugging allows us to isolate a subroutine from the program of which it is a part, and then test that subroutine under controlled conditions.

In that respect, driver routines are like artificial life support systems: they must provide all of the input parameters which the subroutines require (and which would normally be provided by the subroutine's calling program), and they must incorporate some sort of printout or display to inform the programmer if all the various functions of the subroutine under examination are being performed correctly.

Apart from that, driver routines are basically simple to construct and powerful in their application.

The record-keeping program which we have been working with still has three blocks of coding yet unchecked: the main program and the two level 2 subroutines, SEARCH and FILE. We could conceivably use block debugging and driver routines to check out SEARCH and FILE also, but as we will learn in Chapter 7, there are more efficient methods for programs of increased complexity.

7.

SNAPSHOTS

The print statement, in one form or another, is the most useful and therefore the most often used debugging tool available to the programmer. One particularly informative variation of the print statement is the *snapshot*.

A snapshot is similar in some respects to the breakpoint used to debug programs written in the much more primitive assembly-level language. Snapshots are uniquely useful to microcomputerists who program in BASIC or some other high-level language since they provide a dynamic overview of a program's function and status, and in some cases (depending upon the type of program and the nature of its bug) they can give the programmer considerable control over the flow of execution. This ability to observe what the program is doing and then influence its course of action as necessary is the power of using snapshots as a debugging technique.

We began in Chapter 6 to investigate a general-purpose record-keeping program. We saw how the program could be broken down into levels of varying complexity: the first level containing the main program, the second level containing the primary subroutines, and the third level containing those subroutines which share the characteristic of being called by other subroutines while they themselves called none.

We left Chapter 6 with three major blocks of code yet unchecked, the assertion having been made that more complex subroutines and programs were better debugged using methods other than block debugging. An examination of subroutine SEARCH clarifies this:

```
3000 REM SUBROUTINE SEARCH
3010 REM SEARCHES DATA ON FILE #1
3020 REM FOR A MATCH WITH KEYWORD
3030 FILE #1; "FLIES", 1
3040 PRINT "&K"
3050 PRINT "WHAT HEADING DO YOU WANT TO SEARCH FOR?"
3060 INPUT C$
3070 LET L$=" "
3075 LET E$=" "
3080 GOSUB 1000
3090 IF L$="EOF" THEN GOTO 3180
3100 IF C$=H1$ THEN GOTO 3160
3110 IF C$=H2$ THEN GOTO 3160
3120 IF C$=H3$ THEN GOTO 3160
3130 IF C$=H4$ THEN GOTO 3160
3140 IF C$=H5$ THEN GOTO 3160
3150 GOTO 3080
3160 LET E$=E$+T$+N$+S$+D$
3170 GOTO 3080
3180 LET L=LEN(E$)
3190 IF L=0 THEN GOTO 3270
3200 LET N=L/60
3210 GOSUB 4000
3220 FOR I=1 TO N
3230 LET J=(I-1)*60+1
3240 PRINT E$(J,J+59)
3250 NEXT I
3260 GOTO 3275
3270 PRINT "WE HAVE NO ENTRIES UNDER THAT HEADING"
3275 CLOSE #1
3280 PRINT "WOULD YOU LIKE TO SEARCH ANOTHER?"
3290 INPUT"TYPE YES OR NO",K$
3300 IF K$="YES" THEN GOTO 3030
3310 LET T=1
3320 RETURN
```

A driver routine for the subroutine would have to do more than just initialize a few variables and print out the results; it would also have to provide an acceptable response to lines 3080 and 3210:

```
3080 GOSUB 1000
3210 GOSUB 4000
```

Line 1000 is the beginning of subroutine READER, while line 4000 marks the beginning of subroutine SORT. We debugged both subroutines in Chapter 6, so we have a good idea of how they function and what kind of output we should expect from them. We could therefore use our knowledge to write a set of dummy subroutines: blocks of code which do not manipulate data like their real counterparts but merely initialize variables when called.

Such an approach is similar to forcing, since the results of a GOSUB statement are not being left to chance but are instead being explicitly established by the dummy routine.

Suppose we were to use a driver program and dummy subroutines to debug SEARCH. What difficulties, if any, would we encounter? Consider the following examples:

```
10 REM DRIVER TO TEST SEARCH
20 DIM E$(1200),T$(30),S$(15)
30 DIM A1$(40),A2$(40),B1$(40),B2$(40)
40 GOSUB 3000
50 END
—


—
1000 REM DUMMY READER
1010 LET T=T+1
1020 IF T=2 THEN LET L$="EOF":RESTORE:LET T=0:RETURN
1030 LET H1$="DNA            "
1040 LET H2$="CENTRIFUGA"
1050 LET H3$="SEDIMENTAT"
1060 LET H4$="NUCLEIC AC"
1070 LET H5$="TECHNIQUES"
1080 LET T$="DNA DETERMINATION TECHNIQUES    "
1090 LET N$="401    "
```

```
1100 LET S$="JOUR MOLEC BIOL"
1110 LET D$="JAN 78       "
1120 RETURN
```
—

—
```
4000 REM DUMMY SORT
4010 LET A1$="DNA DETERMINATION TECHNIQUES 401    "
4020 LET A2$="JOUR MOLEC BIOLJAN 78"
4030 LET E$=A1$+A2$
4040 RETURN
```

All three routines are uncomplicated and direct, with the driver routine being especially simple. All the prerequisites for the proper use of driver routines and forcing seem to be met. Executing these routines in conjunction with subroutine SEARCH yields:

RUN
PREPARE TAPE UNIT 1 FOR READING FROM: FILES

This is a request from subroutine SEARCH, not from our dummy read subroutine, and we know that the dummy READER is only reading from data statements, not from a tape unit. Consequently, we can get away with fooling the computer once again by typing a return.

WHAT HEADING DO YOU WANT TO SEARCH FOR?
?

We are still in subroutine SEARCH, at line 3060, and we are supposed to enter the keyword which will then be compared against the various subject headings as they are read from tape. Since in the dummy READER routine we have forced the program to input only the DNA DETERMINATION TECHNIQUES record, we should follow suit and enter a keyword which matched one of the forced record's headings. For example:

?CENTRIFUGATION

(The computer shortens the entry to the 10-character word CENTRI-FUGA, so we need not worry about making it comply exactly with what appears in the dummy READER routine.)

The computer continues with:

```
DNA DETERMINATION TECHNIQUES   401   JOUR MOLEC
BIOLJAN 78
WOULD YOU LIKE TO SEARCH ANOTHER?
TYPE YES OR NO NO
READY
```

Everything worked smoothly. If there is a drawback to using driver routines to debug more complicated subroutines, we do not seem to have yet discovered it.

Suppose we run the test again and choose a keyword for which we know there is no match:

```
RUN
PREPARE TAPE UNIT 1 FOR READING FROM: FILES
WHAT HEADING DO YOU WANT TO SEARCH FOR?
?CANCER
WE HAVE NO ENTRIES UNDER THAT·HEADING
WOULD YOU LIKE TO SEARCH ANOTHER?
TYPE YES OR NO
```

Once more, everything seems to check out. If we refer to the flow-chart of subroutine SEARCH in Figs. 7-1 and 7-2, we see that of the three possible paths of execution we have already tested two. A yes answer to the last query by the computer would test the one remaining path:

```
TYPE YES OR NO YES
PREPARE TAPE UNIT 1 FOR READING FROM: FILES
```

Again, since we are using an imaginary tape unit in our dummy routine, we can type in a return to clear this request (the RESTORE statement at line 1020 of the dummy READER routine performs essentially the same function as rewinding the tape; in both cases the READ statement turns back to the beginning of the data to look for the next block of input).

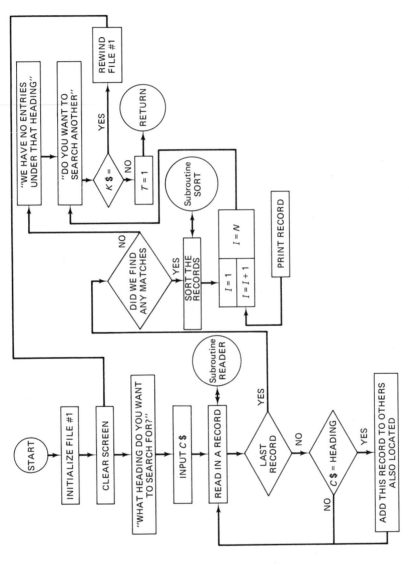

Fig. 7-1. Flowchart for subroutine SEARCH.

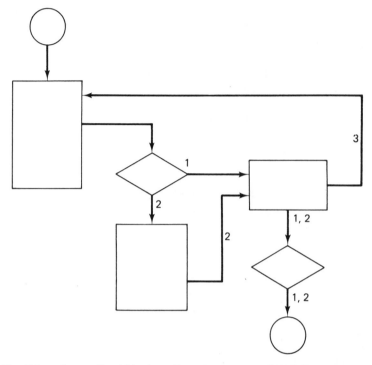

Fig. 7-2.   Generalized block outline of subroutine SEARCH, showing three possible paths of execution. Note how the paths join and separate. 1 = no matching record found. 2 = one or more records found that match the keyword locator. 3 = loop back to the beginning to search on another keyword.

Execution continues:

WHAT HEADING DO YOU WANT TO SEARCH FOR?
?SEDIMENTATION
DNA DETERMINATION TECHNIQUES   401   JOUR MOLEC
BIOLJAN 78
WOULD YOU LIKE TO SEARCH ANOTHER?
TYPE YES OR NO NO
READY

So far, all that we have seen argues against the statement that driver routines and dummy codes are not well suited to debugging complicated subroutines. Indeed, the opposite seems true: the driver and dummy routines were simple almost to the extreme. We traced through the structure of subroutine SEARCH in Fig. 7-1, and to all appearances every possible path of execution has been tried and found free of bugs.

On the basis of our tests, then, if we were to substitute the real subroutines READER and SORT for their dummy counterparts and run the program, we would predict that the result would execute free of errors; each individual block has been separately debugged, so the aggregate should also be bug-free. The driver routine will have to be modified, resulting in a block of code reminiscent of that used to debug subroutine READER in Chapter 6:

```
10 REM DRIVER FOR SUBROUTINE SEARCH
20 DIM E$(1200),V$(60),V2$(60),T$(30),S$(15),
A$(110),T2$(60)
30 FILE #1;"FILES",2
40 FOR I=1 TO 3
50 READ V$,V2$
60 LET E$=V$+V2$
70 PRINT #1,E$
80 NEXT I
90 CLOSE #1
100 LET V$=" "
110 LET V2$=" "
120 LET E$=" "
130 GOSUB 3000
140 DATA "ENZYMES    ATP        BIOCHEM    MITOCHON
DROXYDATION "
150 DATA "PHOSPHORYLATED ENZYME EFFECTS 192    JOU
R CHEM BIOL OCT 77        "
160 DATA "CANCER    CHEMOTHERAMITOCHONDRBRAUTMAN
,JUCLA          "
170 DATA "NEW TREATMENT FOR CANCER          231    JOUR
CHEM BIOL FEB 78        "
180 DATA "DNA          CENTRIFUGASEDIMENTATNUCLEIC
ACTECHNIQUES"
190 DATA "DNA DETERMINATION TECHNIQUES    401    JOU
R MOLEC BIOLJAN 78        "
200 END
```

Running the program yields:


```
RUN
PREPARE TAPE UNIT 1 FOR WRITING TO: FILES
```

Since subroutine READER must have a real tape file to read from, and since we are not using subroutine WRITER to create the file, we must create a file some other way. The current request is a result of line 30 of the driver routine:


```
30 FILE #1;"FILES",2
```

We are asking the computer to create a file called FILES, from here on out to be referred to simply as FILE #1, and to grant that file write-only permission. The computer complies with our request by setting up its own internal logical pathways to equate FILE #1 with FILES and with tape drive 1. We are then asked to perform the manual labor of inserting a cassette into the tape recorder and pressing the record button. We signal to the computer that we have completed our end of the bargain by striking any key on the keyboard.

Once the computer gets the go-ahead, it writes the test data from the driver routine onto tape. Completing this operation, control over the flow of execution is passed from the driver routine to subroutine SEARCH. Subroutine SEARCH assumes the existence of a valid tape file, so its first request is:


```
PREPARE TAPE UNIT 1 FOR READING FROM: FILES
```

Note that we have used the same name to identify the two files; the first file being the one we wrote in the driver routine and the second being the one we are reading from in subroutine SEARCH. What if we had given them different names, as:


```
30 FILE #1;"FILE1";2
3030 FILE #2;"FILE2";1
```

for the driver and subroutine SEARCH, respectively. We would also have to modify subroutine READER slightly:

1030 READ #2; A$

In this case, we would be directing the driver to write onto FILE #1 called FILE1, and we would be directing subroutine SEARCH to read from FILE #2, called FILE2. Perhaps we would see this as a logical way to avoid confusion between the two files and the operations which we perform on them.

Suppose we were to run the program with those changes:

```
RUN
PREPARE TAPE UNIT 1 FOR WRITING TO: FILE1
PREPARE TAPE UNIT 1 FOR READING FROM: FILE2
WHAT HEADING DO YOU WANT TO SEARCH FOR?
?CENTRIFUGATION
RD ERROR IN LINE 1030
```

RD stands for *read*, and an RD error is usually taken to mean that there was a piece of dust or some such thing which caused an irrecoverable error in the system routine which pulls data off of a tape and presents it to the user routine in a form that it can use. The recommended cure in the owner's manual is to rewind the tape and try again.

Unfortunately for us, no amount of rewinding and rereading would cure our particular manifestation of the RD error. A high-level language such as BASIC is essentially unintelligible nonsense to a computer. Before a computer can perform the mechanics of a READ statement, for example, the READ statement must be interpreted for the computer; decoded even further, in effect, down to the level of machine language instructions. A single word command in BASIC is thus broken down into a multiword list of instructions in machine code.

These intricacies are important to the programmer/debugger since they may significantly affect the results of statements as seemingly innocent as a PRINT or a READ.

The previous example of changing the file identification is a case in point. We might reason that "data is data" and if a certain block of data is written out onto tape, then it exists there in an unchanging form. If a subsequent program wants to read that block of data which now resides on tape, there should be no problem as long as the READ request matches in quantity and dimension the WRITE statement that created the block of data.

As we discovered in the example, however, there is a difference. A FILE statement does more than just match up a file number with a file name with a tape unit; it also sets a *flag*. When the computer comes to a PRINT statement, the block of machine-level code which results checks that flag to see if it is set. If the flag is set (meaning that this is the first PRINT statement encountered after the FILE statement), then before the object of the PRINT statement is written onto tape, the computer writes the name of the file.

A similar situation exists when the computer encounters a READ statement, such as:

```
1030 READ #2; A$
```

From the FILE statement which declared FILE #2 open and granted it read permission, the computer knows that "#2" refers to a file named FILE2. If this is the first READ statement encountered after the FILE statement, then before any variables are equated, the computer will first look for the file named FILE2. In the previous example, we wrote onto a file called FILE1; the program then tried to read from a file called FILE2, but there existed no file by that name. All the data contained in FILE1, even though it was the data we wanted the computer to use, was ignored. Eventually, the computer came to the end-of-file (EOF) put on the tape by the driver routine command:

```
90 CLOSE #1
```

The system read routine recognized the EOF mark, and since it had not come across any (what it considered to be) valid data up to that point, it signaled a fatal read error and halted execution.

Returning to the original example, then, the computer has just asked us to set the tape recorder up in the play mode with the tape positioned at the beginning of our data file. We comply, and:

```
PREPARE TAPE UNIT 1 FOR READING FROM: FILES
WHAT HEADING DO YOU WANT TO SEARCH FOR?
?CENTRIFUGATION
CS ERROR IN LINE 4210
```

We know that CENTRIFUGATION should be a valid entry, since it is an index heading for article number 401, DNA DETERMINATION TECH-NIQUES. Choice of keyword is probably not related to the bug in any case, since the error occurred at line 4210, the next-to-last line in subroutine SORT. For the error to be located in subroutine SORT is also something of a surprise, since we debugged that subroutine in Chapter 6.

CS stands for *control stack,* and an error there was indicated. CS refers to the instruction pointer of the central processing unit. The instruction pointer normally always contains the memory address of the next instruction, such as the destination of a jump statement or the home base of a return statement. One of the more nebulous of error codes, the SOL's Extended BASIC user's manual tells us that a CS error may be caused by any one of the following:

1. Return without a prior GOSUB statement
2. Incorrect FOR–NEXT nesting
3. Too many nested GOSUBs
4. Too many nested FOR–NEXT loops
5. Too many nested function calls

None of these possible causes seems applicable, as an examination of Fig. 7-3 confirms: subroutine SORT, being a level 3 subroutine (Chapter 6) does not invoke any lower-level subroutines; thus there are no GOSUB statements to worry about. Also, subroutine SORT contains only two FOR–NEXT loops, and both of those are properly nested.

Perhaps a second look at a listing of the subroutine will tell us something:

```
4000 REM SUBROUTINE SORT
4010 REM ALPHABETICALLY SORTS ENTRIES
4020 REM PRIOR TO PRINTOUT
4025 LET N=N−1
4030 FOR J1=1 TO N
4040 LET N2=0
4050 FOR J2=1 TO N
4060 LET I2=(J2−1)*60+1
4070 LET V$=E$(I2,I2+59)
4080 LET V=ASC(V$)
4090 LET V2$=E$(I2+60,I2+119)
4100 LET V2=ASC(V2$)
4110 IF V>V2 THEN GOTO 4150
4120 LET N2=N2+1
4130 IF N2=N THEN GOTO 4220
4140 GOTO 4200
```

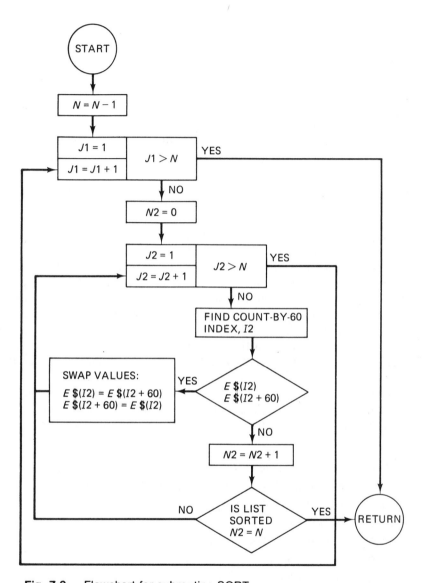

Fig. 7-3. Flowchart for subroutine SORT.

```
4150 LET L=I2+60
4160 LET H=I2+119
4170 LET T2$=E$(L,H)
4180 LET E$(L,H)=E$(I2,I2+59)
```

```
4190 LET E$(I2,I2+59)=T2$
4200 NEXT J2
4210 NEXT J1
4220 RETURN
```

Nothing presents itself as an obvious error, yet we know that the program bombed at line 4210. If this were a shorter and simpler program with a more definite lead as to the nature of the bug, we might want to consider dotting the program with print statements, similar to the approach of Chapter 4. We are restrained, though, by our uncertainty of where to place the print statements; also, there are so many variables whose values might give us a clue in our debugging that to insert print statements for each and every one could very well double the length of the program. The weakness of many individual print statements to debug this sort of program hints at the strength of snapshots.

Snapshots are basically a group of print statements gathered together in a single special-purpose subroutine. In BASIC, all variables are *global,* which is to say: a specific variable is not restricted to use in one particular subroutine; all subroutines which make up the program may refer to it, use it in calculations, or calculate new values to set it equal to. A snapshot routine, therefore, even though it might be called from subroutine SORT, would be able to correctly print out values of variables which only appeared in subroutine FILE, or the other way around.

In the current example we are only concerned with the driver routine and three subroutines: SEARCH, READER, and SORT. Before we begin, it might also be convenient to get a current listing of subroutine READER:

```
1000 REM SUBROUTINE READER
1010 REM READS DATA FROM TAPE (ALWAYS FILE #1)
1020 REM STORES A RECORD AT A TIME IN A$
1030 READ #1; A$
1040 IF EOF(1)=6 THEN GOTO 1150
1050 LET H1$=A$(1,10)
1060 LET H2$=A$(11,20)
1070 LET H3$=A$(21,30)
1080 LET H4$=A$(31,40)
1090 LET H5$=A$(41,50)
1100 LET T$=A$(51,80)
1110 LET N$=A$(81,85)
```

1120 LET S$=A$(86,100)
1130 LET D$=A$(101,110)
1140 GOTO 1160
1150 LET L$="EOF"
1160 RETURN

Based upon an examination of the three subroutines, the variables in Fig. 7-4 suggest themselves as candidates to be included in the snapshot. It is not unusual that most of the variables come from subroutine SORT. READER is perhaps the simplest routine in the entire program, and SEARCH is more supervisorial than computational in nature.

Like any other subroutine, the snapshot subroutine has to begin someplace. Earlier in Chapter 6 we decided that for the present situation, if we began our subroutines 1000 line numbers apart from each other, there would be no confusion or overlap of codes. Following that reasoning, we might decide to begin the snapshot routine at line 9000:

Variable	Original Location
A $	READER
L	SEARCH
E $	
C $	↓
*J*1	SORT
*J*2	
V $	
*V*2 $	
V	
*V*2	
*N*2	
L	
H	
N	↓

Fig. 7-4. Table of values to be displayed in debug snapshot. Note that most of the variables come from subroutine SORT.

```
9000 REM SNAPSHOT
9010 PRINT A$
9020 PRINT L;E$;C$
9030 PRINT V$;V2$;V;V2
9040 PRINT J1;J2;N2;L;H;N
9050 RETURN
```

We can almost guarantee that subroutine SNAPSHOT is free of bugs: it is only five lines long and performs no computations of any kind; it merely displays information to the outside world. What makes this or any other snapshot routine so useful is that it can be accessed from any point in any subroutine just by inserting the statement:

GOSUB 9000

Suppose we do that, indexing the statement line numbers as follows:

```
3145 GOSUB 9000
4024 GOSUB 9000
4055 GOSUB 9000
4105 GOSUB 9000
4195 GOSUB 9000
```

One of the subroutine calls has been placed in subroutine SEARCH, while the others have been located at what we hope to be advantageous spots in subroutine SORT. If we now rerun the program, we would have:

RUN
PREPARE TAPE UNIT 1 FOR WRITING TO: FILES

We already have a test record written to tape, and since we have no reason to believe that the record-creating portion of the driver routine is in any way related to the fatal CS error of subroutine SORT, we could safely "fool" the computer once again by hitting a key on the keyboard without first having set up the tape recorder as requested. In fact, if we find ourselves faced with having to run the program a number of times as we try to chase down the bug, we might want to consider bypassing the record-writing part of the driver routine altogether, as follows:

25 GOTO 130

But for the present we must be content with subterfuge.
    Execution continues:

PREPARE TAPE UNIT 1 FOR READING FROM: FILES

This request we must answer properly, by running the tape to the beginning of information and pressing the play button.

WHAT HEADING DO YOU WANT TO SEARCH FOR?
?CENTRIFUGATION

In under five seconds the following information would write itself onto the CRT screen:

ENZYMES   ATP   BIOCHEM   MITOCHONDROXYDA
TION PHOSPHORYLATED ENZYME EFFECTS 192   JOUR
CHEM BIOL OCT 77
0CENTRIFUGA
0 0
0 0 0 0 0 0
CANCER   CHEMOTHERAMITOCHONDRBRAUTMAN,J UCLA
        NEW TREATMENT FOR CANCER   231   JOUR
CHEM BIOL FEB 78
0CENTRIFUGA
0 0
0 0 0 0 0 0
DNA   CENTRIFUGASEDIMENTATNUCLEIC ACTECHN
IQUESDNA DETERMINATION TECHNIQUES   401   JOUR
MOLEC BIOLJAN 78 60DNA DETERMINATION TECHNIQU
ES   401   JOUR MOLEC BIOLJAN 78
CENTRIFUGA
0 0
0 0 0 60 0 0
CS ERROR IN LINE 4210

By the time the printing stopped, some of the information would have already been shoved off the top of the screen—a serious limit to the method's usefulness, since few microcomputerists can afford the considerable expense of a printer for permanent hard-copy output.

We have seen that snapshots are an efficient method of printing out large amounts of information, but it would seem that unless we can learn to read as fast as the computer can write, we will be hard pressed to absorb any of the torrent of information we can create with snapshots.

Then, too, there is a problem with the form of the output: unless we have a listing of the snapshot routine in front of us at all times, how will we remember which of the six displayed zeros is the value of J5? Or how can we tell if there is a variable J5 being displayed? In addition, although we can tell with little difficulty that the snapshot routine was called three different times, we have no idea of where it was called from.

Fortunately, none of these problems is difficult to solve. The form of the output can be corrected by printing out identifying information along with the variable, as follows:

```
9000   REM SNAPSHOT
9010   PRINT "A$=";A$
9020   PRINT "L,E$,C$=";L;E$;C$
9030   PRINT "V$,V2$,V,V2=";V$;V2$;V;V2
9040   PRINT "J1,J2,N2,L,H,N=";J1;J2;N2;L;H;N
9050   RETURN
```

A typical snapshot would now look like:

```
A$=ENZYMES   ATP      BIOCHEM   MITOCHONDRO
XYDATION PHOSPHORYLATED ENZYME EFFECTS 192
JOUR CHEM BIOL OCT 77
L,E$,C$=0CENTRIFUGA
V$,V2$,V,V2=0 0                              .
J1,J2,N2,L,H,N=0 0 0 0 0 0
```

The improvement is obvious, but not complete. Consider the line:

```
L,E$,C$=0CENTRIFUGA
```

L is apparently equal to zero, so it is printed out as 0. In addition, either *E$* or *C$* is blank, because the zero of *L* is followed by only one word. We may suspect that *E$* is the empty string variable (absolutely empty, containing not even a blank space) and that *C$* is the variable being displayed; but we cannot be sure based only upon the information given to us in the snapshot. This is another bug: a snapshot should ideally be self-contained: a bundle of useful information showing us the dynamic inner workings of the program it is called from.

All that is required to fix this particular bug is a simple rearrangement of the PRINT statements:

```
9000 REM SNAPSHOT
9010 PRINT "A$=";A$
9020 PRINT "L=";L;"E$=";E$;"C$=";C$
9030 PRINT "V$=";V$;"V2$=";V2$;"V=";V;"V2=";V2
9040 PRINT "J1=";J1;"J2=";J2;"N2=";N2;"L=";L;"
H=";H;"N=";N
9050 RETURN
```

Running the program with these changes would result in snapshots that looke like:

```
A$=ENZYMES   ATP       BIOCHEM   MITOCHONDROXY
DATION PHOSPHORYLATED ENZYME EFFECTS 192 JOUR
CHEM BIOL OCT 77
L=0E$= C$=CENTRIFUGA
V$= V2$= V=0V2=0
J1=0J2=0N2=0L=0H=0N=0
```

Now we know positively what each variable is equal to, although we still do not know where in the program the snapshot is being taken. However, we recall that in BASIC, variables are global and can be accessed by any subroutine at any point. Suppose, then, that as the first line of executable code (a nonremark statement) in each subroutine, we inserted the following line:

```
LET X$="(NAME OF SUBROUTINE)"
```

Specifically, for the subroutines which we are considering, we could add:

```
3021   LET X$="SEARCH"
4021   LET X$="SORT"
```

We would then follow that up with the addition of one more line of code to the snapshot routine:

```
9005   PRINT "SNAPSHOT CALLED FROM";X$
```

The difference is significant (note that we have bypassed the record-writing portion of the driver routine):

```
RUN
PREPARE TAPE UNIT 1 FOR READING FROM: FILES
WHAT HEADING DO YOU WANT TO SEARCH FOR?
?CENTRIFUGATION
SNAPSHOT CALLED FROM SEARCH
A$=ENZYMES   ATP        BIOCHEM   MITOCHONDROX
YDATION PHOSPHORYLATED ENZYME EFFECTS 192   JO
UR CHEM BIOL OCT 77
L=0E$= C$=CENTRIFUGA
V$= V2$= V=0V2=0
J1=0J2=0N2=0L=0H=0N=0
SNAPSHOT CALLED FROM SEARCH
A$=CANCER        CHEMOTHERAMITOCHONDRBRAUTMAN,JUC
LA         NEW TREATMENT FOR CANCER 231   JOUR CH
EM BIOL FEB 78
L=0E$= C$=CENTRIFUGA
V$= V2$= V=0V2=0
J1=0J2=0N2=0L=0H=0N=0
SNAPSHOT CALLED FROM SORT
A$=DNA          CENTRIFUGASEDIMENTATNUCLEIC ACTE
CHNIQUESDNA DETERMINATION TECHNIQUES 401 JOUR
MOLEC BIOLJAN 78      C$=CENTRIFUGA
V$= V2$= V=0V2=0
```

J1 = 0J2 = 0N2 = 0L = 60H = 0N = 0
CS ERROR IN LINE 4210

There is now far too much information to fit on the display screen at one time, which means that unless we have a printer hooked up to our computer, we will lose all but the last 16 lines of our debug output.

Suppose we had been able to capture the full round of output; we would soon notice that the snapshot has been taken twice in subroutine SEARCH and once in subroutine SORT. This is an important observation, since we would have expected a snapshot to be taken three times in subroutine SEARCH, once after each new record was read in. We note also that the record which is missing from the snapshots taken in subroutine SEARCH is the record containing the keyword CENTRIFUGA, which corresponds to the keyword we asked the computer to search for. Turning to the listing of subroutine SEARCH that contains the call to the snapshot routine, we try to use these facts to explain the whereabouts of the missing snapshot:


```
3060    INPUT C$
3070    LET L$=" "
3080    GOSUB 1000
3090    IF L$="EOF" THEN GOTO 3150
3100    IF C$=H1$ THEN GOTO 3160
3110    IF C$=H2$ THEN GOTO 3160
3120    IF C$=H3$ THEN GOTO 3160
3130    IF C$=H4$ THEN GOTO 3160
3140    IF C$=H5$ THEN GOTO 3160
3145    GOSUB 9000
3150    GOTO 3080
```


The bug is obvious: records 1 and 2 of the tape are printed out because neither of them contains headings which match the keyword *centrifugation* (or, as it appears in the program shortened to the 10-character default length, CENTRIFUGA). All of the conditional branches from line 3100 to line 3140 fail, execution continues to line 3145 where we take the snapshot, and then the program jumps back up to line 3080 to read in another record and begin again. When the third and final record is read in, the program continues to line 3110 where the test is met and execution skips over line 3145 to line 3160.

We seem to have forgotten one of the prime attributes of snapshots:

they are basically print statements. As such, they are as sensitive to the effects of placement as print statements—not in the sense of where the snapshot routine itself is placed, but rather where the call to the routine is located.

Instead of taking the snapshot at line 3145, then, we would be better advised to relocate it to line 3085, immediately after the program returns from reading in a new record.

The case of the one snapshot from subroutine SORT is different, however. We know that we placed four separate calls to the snapshot routine in subroutine SORT; the problem is to identify them, each one from the other. We might attempt a sophisticated solution to the problem—for example, entering the snapshot routine from different points, as follows:

```
9000 REM SNAPSHOT
9010 LET X=1
9020 GOTO 9080
9030 LET X=2
9040 GOTO 9080
9050 LET X=3
9060 GOTO 9080
9070 LET X=4
9080 PRINT "LOCATION";X
9090 PRINT "SNAPSHOT CALLED FROM";X$
```

The calls within the subroutines would have to be similarly modified to direct the flow of execution to the proper point, as:

```
3085 GOSUB 9090
4024 GOSUB 9010
4055 GOSUB 9030
4105 GOSUB 9050
4195 GOSUB 9070
```

It should be pointed out, however, that while such maneuvers may seem clever, they are self-defeating and should be viewed as very poor examples of programming technique. Entering a subroutine at a number of points weakens the concept of a subroutine as a one-entrance, one-exit block of code. It also weakens the subroutine itself by making it so specifically tied to its calling routine that it loses its general applicability.

Actually, the question of how to resolve which of the GOSUB calls in the subroutine invoked in the snapshot is answered as easily as the method we used to tag which subroutine was taking the snapshot. It requires an extra line of code before each GOSUB call, but it is accurate and easily implemented:

```
4000 REM SUBROUTINE SORT
4010 REM ALPHABETICALLY SORTS ENTRIES
4020 REM PRIOR TO PRINTOUT
4021 LET X$="SORT"
4022 LET X=4020
4024 GOSUB 9000
4025 LET N=N-1
4030 FOR J1=1 TO N
```

The addition of one more line to the snapshot routine completes the transformation:

```
9007 PRINT "AND FROM LINE";X
```

We have, without hamstringing the snapshot routine with specialized program-dependent coding, managed to uniquely identify each output generated by a snapshot. The one problem which we have not yet fixed is that of any output longer than 16 lines disappearing off the top of the CRT screen.

The language of BASIC has one command which would seem tailor-made for this application: the STOP command. This command stops program execution as soon as it is encountered, displays a short message telling us at what line execution was halted, and then waits for us to type in a *continue* command to resume execution. Suppose we add a STOP as the last line of the snapshot routine, and try running the program:

```
RUN
PREPARE TAPE UNIT 1 FOR READING FROM: FILES
WHAT HEADING DO YOU WANT TO SEARCH FOR?
?CENTRIFUGATION
SNAPSHOT CALLED FROM SEARCH
```

```
AND FROM LINE 3090
A$=ENZYMES   ATP        BIOCHEM   MITOCHONDROX
YDATION PHOSPHORYLATED ENZYME EFFECTS 192   JO
UR CHEM BIOL OCT 77
L=0E$=  C$=CENTRIFUGA
V$=  V2$=  V=0V2=0
J1=0J2=0N2=0L=0H=0N=0
STOP IN LINE 9045
CONTINUE
FD ERROR IN LINE 1030
```

We came across an FD error earlier, in Chapter 6. We recall that it stands for either *format definition* or *file declaration*. In effect this is an error in either an input or an output routine. The line that the program bombed at, 1030, is where subroutine READER reads in the next record from tape into the variable A$:

```
1030 READ #1;A$
```

Our getting caught by an FD error suggests that the program is trying to read from a file which has not been declared. We know that explanation to be false, though, since we declared FILE #1 open and with read permission granted in subroutine SEARCH:

```
3030 FILE #1:"FILES",1
```

One other possible explanation is that the STOP command not only halts execution of the program, but also closes all files which might have been previously declared open.

A way around this dilemma is right in front of us; we have been making extensive use of it without having realized its full potential. If we include in a program a statement such as:

```
INPUT A
```

the program will halt execution and wait patiently—forever if necessary—until we oblige it by entering a value from the keyboard. String variables are even more useful, since we need not hit any particular key at all to satisfy an input request. A numerical variable must be filled with a number or the computer will just respond with another prompt symbol until we get it right. A string variable, however, can be filled with anything, even nothing at all, just by hitting the RETURN key.

Instead of a STOP command at line 9045 then, we should use:

```
9045 INPUT Z$
```

Z$ is never used anywhere else in the entire record-keeping program; so now, when the program gets to line 9045 is will settle down into a comfortable idling routine without changing the status of any files. It will wait for us to give it the go-ahead to continue execution. To complete the effect, we might want to insert one more statement in the snapshot routine which would clear the screen each time a new snapshot is taken, as:

```
9005 PRINT "&K"
```

We are ready to try the snapshot one more time:

```
RUN
PREPARE TAPE UNIT 1 FOR READING FROM: FILES
WHAT HEADING DO YOU WANT TO SEARCH FOR?
?CENTRIFUGATION
SNAPSHOT CALLED FROM SEARCH
AND FROM LINE 3090
A$=ENZYMES   ATP        BIOCHEM   MITOCHONDROX
YDATION PHOSPHORYLATED ENZYME EFFECTS 192   JO
UR CHEM BIOL OCT 77
L=0E$=  C$=CENTRIFUGA
V$=  V2$=  V=0V2=0
J1=0J2=0N2=0L=0H=0N=0
```

The snapshot fits easily on the display screen of our computer, and we now may take as much time as we need to make notes and think about what the snapshot is telling us: execution is in a sort of suspended animation until we press the *return* key. We see that this snapshot was taken in subroutine SEARCH and line 3090, just after the point where subroutine READER was called and returned with a valid record, as shown to us

after the heading A$=. All of the other variables displayed in this snap-
shot are clearly labeled; and we note, for example, that C$, the keyword
from subroutine SEARCH is CENTRIFUGA, the 10-character truncation
of *centrifugation.* This is just as it should be. Also, all of the variables
from subroutine SORT, from V$ to N, are zero, just as they should be
since SORT has not yet been invoked.

We hit the *return* key, the screen is cleared, and almost immediately
the next snapshot appears:

```
SNAPSHOT CALLED FROM SEARCH
AND FROM LINE 3090
A$=CANCER        CHEMOTHERAMITOCHRONDRBRAUTMAN,J
UCLA        NEW TREATMENT FOR CANCER 231    JOU
R CHEM BIOL FEB 78
L=0E$= C$=CENTRIFUGA
V$= V2$= V=0V2=0
J1=0J2=0N2=0L=0H=0N=0
?
```

The only significant change between this snapshot and the last is that A$
now reflects the identity of the record just read in from tape by subroutine READER. We expect no changes in any of the other variables, and
indeed there are none. We type in a *return* to continue:

```
SNAPSHOT CALLED FROM SEARCH
AND FROM LINE 3090
A$=DNA          CENTRIFUGASEDIMENTATNUCLEIC AC
TECHNIQUESDNA DETERMINATION TECHNIQUES    401
JOUR MOLEC BIOLJAN 78
L=0E$= C$=CENTRIFUGA
V$= V2$= V=0V2=0
J1=0J2=0N2=0L=0H=0N=0
?
```

Since we know that there are three different records on the test file,
we should have expected to see three snapshots from subroutine
SEARCH, one for each record. Previously, however, we had seen only
two snapshots from SEARCH. Moving the snapshot to just below line

3090 of subroutine SEARCH corrected this problem, as evidenced by the third snapshot just displayed. As before, a *return* continues execution, and after a few seconds the previous snapshot clears and is replaced with:

```
SNAPSHOT CALLED FROM SORT
AND FROM LINE 4020
A$=DNA          CENTRIFUGASEDIMENTATNUCLEIC AC
TECHNIQUESDNA DETERMINATION TECHNIQUES    401
JOUR MOLEC BIOLJAN 78
L=60E$=DNA DETERMINATION TECHNIQUES    401    J
OUR MOLEC BIOLJAN78        C$=CENTRIFUGA
V$= V2$= V=0V2=0
J1=0J2=0N2=0L=60H=0N=1
?
```

At last we have identified the origin of the snapshot from SORT, knowledge which will take on greater meaning once we analyze the rest of the snapshot's output. We note for example that $A\$$, which was set by the last call to READER from SEARCH, remains unchanged from the last snapshot. This is as we would expect, since no line of subsequent coding changes its value. L, $E\$$, and $C\$$ are all variables which are set in subroutine SEARCH: $C\$$ is the keyword we are searching for, $E\$$ is the storage area for all those entries selected by SEARCH from the master tape file, and L is the length of $E\$$, a quantity later divided by 60 to determine the total number of entries culled from the master tape file. In the present case, we see that $E\$$ contains only one entry, number 401, entitled DNA DETERMINATION TECHNIQUES, and L is equal to 60, the exact length of one such entry.

As we move on to analyze the variables from subroutine SORT, we might want to turn to our most current listing of the subroutine:

```
4000 REM SUBROUTINE SORT
4010 REM ALPHABETICALLY SORTS ENTRIES
4020 REM PRIOR TO PRINTOUT
4021 LET X$="SORT"
4022 LET X=4020
4024 GOSUB 9000
4025 LET N=N-1
```

```
4030 FOR J1=1 TO N
4040 LET N2=0
4050 FOR J2=1 TO N
4052 LET X=4050
4055 GOSUB 9000
4060 LET I2=(J2-1)*60+1
4070 LET V$=E$(I2,I2+59)
4080 LET V=ASC(V$)
4090 LET V2$=E$(I2+60,I2+119)
4100 LET V2=ASC(V2$)
4102 LET X=4100
4105 GOSUB 9000
4110 IF V>V2 THEN GOTO 4150
4120 LET N2=N2+1
4130 IF N2=N THEN GOTO 4220
4140 GOTO 4200
4150 LET L=I2+60
4160 LET H=I2+119
4170 LET T2$=E$(L,H)
4180 LET E$(L,H)=E$(I2,I2+59)
4190 LET E$(I2,I2+59)=T2$
4192 LET X=4190
4195 GOSUB 9000
4200 NEXT J2
4210 NEXT J1
4220 RETURN
```

In the snapshot both V$ and V2$ are empty, and V and V2, the variables set equal to the lengths of V$ and V2$, are zero—which is not surprising since we have not yet entered the part of subroutine SORT that sets those values. For the same reasons, J1, J2, N2, and H are zero. We note that L equals 60; in subroutine SORT, L is not defined until line 4150, and we are a long way ahead of that, at line 4020. This may seem a puzzle until we recall that variables in BASIC are global, and wherever L appears in the program it will be equal to whatever value it was given whenever it was last accessed. The L of subroutine SORT is therefore the same L that appeared in subroutine SEARCH, so it naturally carries the same value: 60.

The last variable in the snapshot, N, is equal to 1. This is reasonable since it was set at line 3200 in subroutine SEARCH:

3200 LET N=L/60

Even a quick examination tells us that if *L* equals 60, then *N* must equal 1, just as it does.

So far, things appear to be normal. Another *return* and we have:

CS ERROR IN LINE 4210

The bug! There were three more snapshots in the subroutine, at lines 4055, 4105, and 4195, and we seem to have bypassed them all. Nothing immediately suggests itself as a cause, so the next logical step for us to take is to play computer for a bit and hope that by doing so an answer will appear.

We take the snapshot at line 4024 and then return to execute the next statement, 4025:

4025 LET N=N−1

We know that *N* was equal to 1 at the time of the snapshot; now one line later it is set equal to 1 − 1, or 0. The next line uses this new value of *N* as an upper limit to a FOR–NEXT loop:

4030 FOR J1=1 TO N

which in this particular case would be translated as:

4030 FOR J1=1 TO 0

We recall from Chapter 6 that *N* had to be reduced by 1 because of the mechanics of the bubble sort algorithm, but a terminating index which is less than the beginning index looks suspicious. Yet, the user's manual for the version of BASIC we are using clearly states:

If the starting value is greater than the ending value in the FOR statement, the statements in the loop are not executed.

If this were the whole story we would have nothing to complain about; but obviously some additional factor is affecting the outcome of this example. It is not insignificant that a second loop, interior to the loop beginning at line 4030, also uses *N* as an upper bound:

4050 FOR J2=1 TO N

The documentation seems to be saying that if the terminating value of the outermost loop is less than its beginning value, then statement 4050 would never even be executed and the program would skip immediately down to the end of the outermost FOR–NEXT loop—in this case, line 4210

4210 NEXT J1

This is exactly the behavior we would hope for if N had been set equal to 1 in subroutine SEARCH, since if we only located one entry out of the master tape file that matched our keyword, we would have no need to alphabetically sort it with respect to its neighbors.

Why then do we get the message CS ERROR IN LINE 4210? Suppose we write the following test program:

1 INPUT R
2 FOR I=1 TO R
3 PRINT I
4 NEXT R
5 PRINT "DONE"
6 END

If we number the statements exactly as shown, we can type them directly into the computer without having to worry about writing on top of some already existing lines of our main program. If we run the test program, we get:

RUN
?2
1
2
DONE
READY

Suppose we use a zero for input:

```
RUN
?0
DONE
READY
```

It performs exactly as the user's manual said it would: the FOR–NEXT loop was skipped entirely. What if we alter the test program to more closely approximate the situation facing us in subroutine SORT:

```
1 INPUT R
2 FOR I=1 TO R
3 FOR J=1 TO R
4 PRINT I;J
5 NEXT J
6 NEXT I
7 PRINT "DONE"
8 END
```

We then execute it with a value of 2:

```
RUN
?2
1 1
1 2
2 1
2 2
DONE
READY
```

Now with a value of zero:

```
RUN
?0
CS ERROR IN LINE 6
```

It seems we have found our bug. The most obvious remedy is to not execute subroutine SORT at all if subroutine SEARCH finds only one candidate which matches the requested keyword. We can circumvent SORT in either of two ways: (1) a conditional branch as the first executable statement of SORT, or (2) a conditional branch in subroutine SEARCH, immediately before the call to SORT.

For the sake of efficiency, the branch is best placed in the calling routine, SEARCH:

```
3200 LET N=L/60
3205 IF N=1 THEN GOTO 3220
3210 GOSUB 4000
3220 FOR J=1 TO N
```

Now if N equals 1, signifying only one entry, the program jumps directly to line 3220, where the loop that prints out the entries begins. Otherwise, subroutine SORT is called, the entries are arranged alphabetically, and then printed out.

Looking at this one section of code, however, we see something that hints at a potential bug: we know now that the program bombed in subroutine SORT because N, which was used as an upper bound for two loops, was decreased in value by 1, which in some cases caused it to go to zero. We fixed that by directing the program to skip over subroutine SORT if N was only equal to 1 to begin with. However, if N is equal to 2 (for example), SORT will be called, N will be reduced to 1, the two entries will be sorted alphabetically, and subroutine SORT will return control of execution to subroutine SEARCH at line 3220.

There, only one entry will be printed out instead of two, since N, the upper bound to the loop beginning at line 3220, will have been set to 1, thus causing the loop to execute only once. We can correct this by restoring N to its correct value after subroutine SORT has finished its work. We could restore N either as the last statement in SORT before it returns or as the first statement in SEARCH after SORT returns. To avoid confusion, the best choice of the two alternatives is in subroutine SORT; and the easiest way to accomplish that is to renumber the RETURN statement and give its old line number to the N-increase statement, as follows:

```
BEFORE: 4220 RETURN
AFTER:  4220 LET N=N+1
        4230 RETURN
```

Suppose we try to run the program again, incorporating all of the various changes we have made and using a different keyword, just for variety:

```
RUN
PREPARE TAPE UNIT 1 FOR READING FROM: FILES
WHAT HEADING DO YOU WANT TO SEARCH FOR?
?ATP
```

At this point the tape drive would begin to move on command from the computer; soon the screen would clear and the following would appear:

```
SNAPSHOT CALLED FROM SEARCH
AND FROM LINE 3090
A$=ENZYMES   ATP        BIOCHEM   MITOCHONDROX
YDATION PHOSPHORYLATED ENZYME EFFECTS 192   JOU
R CHEM BIOL OCT 77
L=0E$=C$=ATP
V$=V2$=V=0V2=0
J1=0J2=0N2=0L=0H=0N=0
?
```

We have come across a valid file, since we can see that the second heading in A$ matches our keyword, ATP. E$, which should eventually hold the title/number/source/date portion of the entry, is empty at this point since the program has not yet reached that section of code; we should, though, see it in the next snapshot. A *return* takes the program out of the idling mode:

```
SNAPSHOT CALLED FROM SEARCH
AND FROM LINE 3090
A$=CANCER       CHEMOTHERAMITOCHONDRBRAUTMAN,J
UCLA        NEW TREATMENT FOR CANCER 231   JOU
RNAL CHEM BIOL FEB 78
L=0 E$=C$=ATP
V$= V2$= V=0V2=0
J1=0J2=0N2=0L=0H=0N=0
?
```

Immediately we can see that something is not correct. The snapshot, by placing all of the pertinent information before us in a single easy-to-read form, has made the bug obvious, and even has suggested the cause. The entry displayed in the previous snapshot after A$= should have turned up in this snapshot after E$=, since our keyword matched a heading belonging to that entry.

We recall from Chapter 6, however, that the computer ignores trailing blanks after a string variable entry from the keyboard. When we wanted to make character strings of varying lengths conform to the uniform lengths required of records written out by subroutine WRITER, we had to process them through a special "massaging" subroutine, FORMOUT. In order to make the ATP of our keyword identically equal to the "ATP*******" (asterisks represent blank spaces) of the record heading, we will have to include in SEARCH a block of code nearly identical to the blocks of code found in FORMOUT, as follows:

```
3061 LET P$=" "
3062 LET L=LEN(C$)
3063 LET J=10-L
3064 FOR I=1 TO J
3065 LET C$=C$+P$
3066 NEXT I
```

Before we run the program again suppose we wanted to get rid of all the snapshots; would we have to hunt through the entire program and delete every call to the snapshot routine? Not at all: the most often used method is to insert a line of code just after the subroutine in question, as follows:

```
9000 REM SNAPSHOT
9001 GOTO 9050
```

This will be elaborated in Chapter 8. For now, however, whenever the snapshot routine is invoked, the computer will be directed to jump immediately down to line 9050, the RETURN statement for that subroutine. Execution will then immediately transfer back to the calling routine without any outward indication that it had ever left.

If we run the program, we get:

```
RUN
PREPARE TAPE UNIT 1 FOR READING FROM: FILES
```

```
WHAT HEADING DO YOU WANT TO SEARCH FOR?
?ATP
PHOSPHORYLATED ENZYME EFFECTS 192    JOUR CHEM
BIOL OCT 77
WOULD YOU LIKE TO SEARCH ANOTHER?
TYPE YES OR NO
```

It appears as though the subroutine works. In response to our keyword request of ATP we were presented with file number 192, PHOSPHORY-LATED ENZYME EFFECTS, the one correct choice out of the three available records on our test tape. Suppose we answer YES to the last question, and try to read two files. We will want to determine if: (1) the program will reinitialize itself correctly, (2) the proper files will be pulled from the master tape, and (3) if these files—there are two—are sorted in correct alphabetical order.

```
TYPE YES OR NO YES
PREPARE TAPE UNIT 1 FOR READING FROM: FILES
```

We must rewind the tape, position it at the beginning of information and press the play button:

```
WHAT HEADING DO YOU WANT TO SEARCH FOR?
?MITOCHONDRIA
NEW TREATMENT FOR CANCER 231    JOUR CHEM BIOL
FEB 78
PHOSPHORYLATED ENZYME EFFECTS 192    JOUR CHEM
BIOL OCT 77
WOULD YOU LIKE TO SEARCH ANOTHER?
TYPE YES OR NO NO
READY
```

Indeed, SEARCH has been successfully debugged using snapshots, as has the communications problem between SEARCH and its subroutine SORT. It is this facility for providing a dynamic overview of program–subroutine functioning that makes snapshots so useful. We could have achieved the same results with a number of print statements sprinkled throughout the two blocks of code, but not without paying a high price in maneuverability and efficiency; separate print statements would require as many switches as there were statements. Also, we need only formulate a snapshot once, and if, for example, we wished to display the same information from a number of different points in a program, we need only insert at each point a single GOSUB statement rather than an entire block of code.

Of the seven subroutines which make up the record-keeping program, we have to this point debugged six, leaving us with FILE, the one other level 2 subroutine, and finally the main program. Both of these two remaining blocks of code will be dealt with in the next chapter.

8.

DESIGNING-IN

Designing-in, the process of loading a program with "sleeping" debug statements, is an approach most often taken with programs that have a high probability of being changed or modified during their useful life. An example of such a program is the record-keeping program we have been working with in the last two chapters.

In its present form, the program is designed for a research scientist to keep a file of article reprints, but the same basic program structure could be adapted to keep track of recipes, court decisions, book titles, phonograph records, or any other collection of items which can be classified and sorted. Each new modification, however, opens doors to more bugs; it has been asserted and we have shown (especially in the chapter on *forcing*) that even though a program may appear to be debugged when run under a particular set of constraints—input value, index range, etc.— once those constraints are altered, new bugs are likely to appear.

Designing-in requires that we understand the code we write well enough to be able to recognize potential trouble spots, and then fill those spots with appropriate debuggers such as print statements or snapshots. In previous examples the method has been to write in a print statement when and where it was required, and then delete it from the program once its usefulness was over. When we apply the technique of designing-in, however, we will be permanently installing print statements in the code, but their activity will be regulated by logical "switches."

We have already seen an example of such a switch in Chapter 4:

```
1155  IF N<=0 THEN PRINT "I,J,K,T1,T2,T3,T4,N";I;J;K;T1;T2;T3;T4;N
```

When we encountered it previously we called it a *clamp* because we wanted to put a lid on what might potentially have been torrents of output: the print statement only becomes active if the value of N becomes less than or equal to zero. As it stands, this example is more like a warning bell that rings only when danger is upon us. At the same time, however, we do not want the printout to be always active. The compromise between constant debugger activity and debuggers which only appear at the last minute is reached by placing such debuggers under outside control.

In the current example, this would be the same as saying:

```
1155  IF D=1 THEN PRINT "I,J,K,T1,T2,T3,T4,N";I;J;K;T1;T2;T3;T4;N
```

The switch would be the variable *D*, and it would have to be set equal to 1 (for printout) or zero (for no debug printout) somewhere earlier in the program.

The only two routines left for us to debug from the record-keeping program are MAIN and FILE. FILE is the only remaining level 2 subroutine, so we will begin with it. (We recall from the master routine outline presented in Chapter 6 that subroutine FILE begins at line 5000.)

```
5000 REM SUBROUTINE FILE
5010 REM MAKES AND EXTENDS FILES
5020 REM READS FROM FILE #1, WRITES TO #2
5030 LET L2=0
5040 PRINT "PLEASE TYPE M TO MAKE A NEW FILE"
5050 PRINT "AND E TO EXTEND AN OLD FILE"
5060 INPUT B$
5070 IF B$="E" THEN GOTO 5170
5080 IF B$="M" THEN GOTO 5110
5090 PRINT "ONLY M OR E ALLOWED, PLEASE RETYPE"
5100 GOTO 5070
5110 FILE #2;"FILES",2
5120 GOSUB 6000
5130 IF L2=1 THEN GOTO 5260
5140 GOSUB 7000
5150 GOSUB 2000
5160 GOTO 5120
5170 FILE #1;"FILES",1
```

```
5180 GOSUB 1000
5190 IF EOF(1)=6 THEN GOTO 5220
5200 LET Z$=A$
5210 GOTO 5180
5220 REWIND #1
5230 GOSUB 1000
5240 IF A$=Z$ THEN CLOSE #1:GOTO 5110
5250 GOTO 5230
5260 CLOSE #2
5270 RETURN
```

Subroutine FILE supervises the transfer of program control to a number of different subroutines, an attribute we would expect from a level 2 routine such as this. Figure 8-1 illustrates the interplay between FILE and its subordinate routines with greater clarity. It might also help us at this point to recall from Chapter 6 the beginning line numbers of all the subroutines:

```
1000 READER: reads data from tape
2000 WRITER: writes a record of data
3000 SEARCH: searches tape file for record
4000 SORT: sorts records found in SEARCH
5000 FILE: makes or extends files
6000 FORMIN: input formatter for FILE
7000 FORMOUT: output formatter for FILE
```

Using this information, we can with little difficulty match the appropriate lines of code with their respective positions in the flowchart, Fig. 8-1. The first thing the subroutine must determine is whether a new file is to be created or an old file is to be extended; this is decided by the value of B$, which is input from the keyboard. If a new file is to be created, the program enters a process involving three steps that are repeated over and over again until the end of information is reached:

1. Input data from the keyboard (using FORMIN)
2. Format the data into uniform records of 110 characters each (using FORMOUT)
3. Write the formatted record to tape (using WRITER)

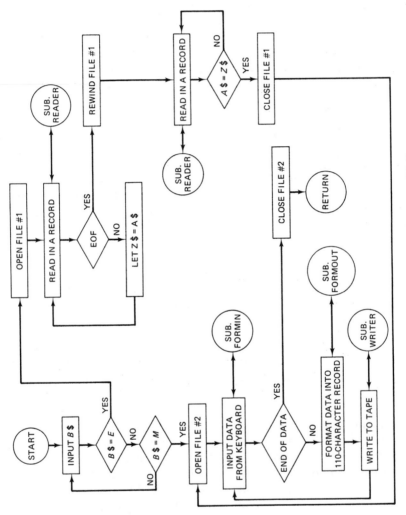

Fig. 8-1. Flowchart for subroutine FILE.

The process for extending an old file is much the same. The record-keeping program, as written, is intended for an application which uses cassette tape as the bulk data storage medium. Cassette tapes are a popular form of bulk memory, since their hardware is considerably less expensive than the next most popular alternative, the floppy disk. But cassettes also have a much slower access time than floppies, and they are much less sophisticated.

In order to extend an existing file, we must first determine where that file ends. Subroutine FILE's method of accomplishing this is roundabout but effective; it involves two consecutive reading passes over the tape before new information may be added. This is required because we cannot simply read in records until an end-of-file (EOF) mark is encountered, and then proceed to write more records onto the tape after it; the records which came after the EOF would be considered members of a new file and would therefore be ignored.

The first pass therefore sets up a temporary storage area into which a copy of the current record is placed after it is read into the program by subroutine READER. In this way, once the EOF is reached, the temporary array (Z$) contains a copy of the last record on the old file. Rewinding the tape to the beginning, we read it in a second time. This time, however, we know the identity of the record immediately preceding the EOF mark. We therefore compare each new record read in with the "marker" record in Z$; once we have reached that same record a second time, we turn off the tape deck and switch to the record mode, and in so doing we write over the old EOF mark and can extend the file.

By now, we recognize that in order to test a subroutine we need a driver routine which will set up all necessary array space, initialize required variables, and display appropriate diagnostic information at the conclusion of the program's execution. As it happens, we have only one other routine left besides subroutine FILE which has not yet been debugged: program MAIN. Program MAIN's purpose is to coordinate the flow of execution between the two major functions of creating files or searching files. In doing so, it so closely takes on the appearance of a driver routine that there is little reason to go to the trouble of constructing a special driver for FILE. Instead, we will find it easier to use MAIN:

```
10 REM GENERAL PURPOSE FILING PROGRAM
20 REM WITH SUBROUTINES AS FOLLOWS
30 REM —LINE/ NAME / DESCRIPTION—
40 REM 1000/READER/READ FROM TAPE
50 REM 2000/WRITER/WRITE TO TAPE
60 REM 3000/SEARCH/SEARCH TAPE
```

```
70 REM 4000/SORT/SORT RECORDS
80 REM 5000/FILE/MAKE OR EXTEND FILES
90 REM 6000/FORMIN/INPUT DATA FORMATTING
100 REM 7000/FORMOUT/OUTPUT DATA FORMATTING
110 DIM H1$(10),H2$(10),H3$(10),H4$(10),H5$(10)
120 DIM T$(30),N$(5),S$(15),D$(10),A$(110),Z$(110)
130 DIM E$(1200),F$(50),T2$(60)
140 PRINT "&K"
150 PRINT "TYPE R TO RETRIEVE AND F TO FILE"
160 INPUT B$
170 IF B$="R" THEN GOSUB 3000:GOTO 210
180 IF B$="F" THEN GOSUB 5000:GOTO 210
190 PRINT "SORRY, ONLY VALID CHOICES ARE R OR F.PLEASE
    RETYPE."
200 GOTO 160
210 PRINT "DO YOU WANT TO DO MORE? (YES OR NO)"
220 INPUT B$
230 IF B$="YES" THEN GOTO 140
240 END
```

The flowchart for program MAIN (Fig. 8-2) points up the simplicity of the routine. So far, we have not yet discussed the technique of designing in debuggers with respect to where it might be applied in the record-keeping program, and with good reason. We will first debug what remains of the program using techniques already familiar to us; once done, we will modify the program towards a new application and in so doing we will make considerable use of designing-in.

Loading the full program and running it yields:

```
RUN
TYPE R TO RETRIEVE AND F TO FILE
? F
PLEASE TYPE M TO MAKE A NEW FILE
AND E TO EXTEND AN OLD FILE
? M
PREPARE TAPE UNIT 1 FOR WRITING TO:FILES
```

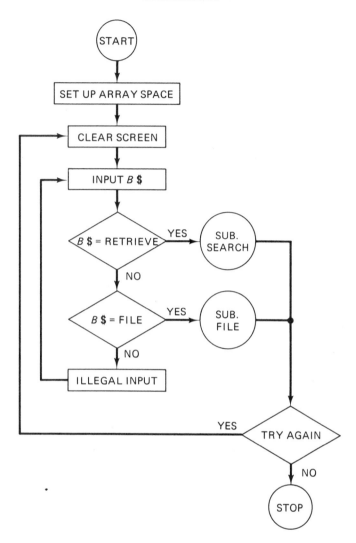

Fig. 8-2. Flowchart for program MAIN.

We press the record button on the tape recorder and hit a key to signal a go-ahead to the computer. The screen then clears and the tabular data form provided by subroutine FORMIN appears on the screen (Fig. 8-3). We provide the following input:

PLEASE ENTER THE INFORMATION AS REQUESTED

A BLANK ON THE FIRST ENTRY ENDS THE LIST

TITLE?

FILE NUMBER

SOURCE

DATE

HEADINGS (TOTAL OF 5)

Fig. 8-3.   Tabular data form as displayed on CRT screen.

TITLE? PHOSPHORYLATED ENZYME EFFECTS
FILE NUMBER? 192
SOURCE? JOUR CHEM BIOL
DATE? OCT 77
HEADINGS (TOTAL OF 5)?ENZYMES   ?ATP
?BIOCHEM   ?MITOCHONDRIA ?OXYDATION

Again the screen clears, and we continue:

TITLE? NEW TREATMENT FOR CANCER
FILE NUMBER? 231
SOURCE? JOUR CHEM BIOL
DATE? FEB 78
HEADINGS (TOTAL OF 5)?CANCER   ?CHEMOTHERAPY
?MITOCHONDRIA ?BRAUTMAN,J   ?UCLA

The screen clears again, the tape motor is activated to indicate that data is being written to tape, and the data form appears again. This time, however, we hit the return key without entering any data, signaling to the program that we wish to terminate the data entry phase. We recall from the listing of subroutine FORMIN given in Chapter 6 that making a blank entry for the title results in variable L2 being set equal to 1, and the transferring of execution control back from FORMIN to the routine which invoked it (in this case FILE):

```
6170 IF T$=" " THEN LET L2=1:GOTO 6340
—


—
6340 RETURN
```

Subroutine FILE also tests the value of L2 after each return from FORMIN, and if L2 should be equal to 1, indicating the end of input data, then FILE also terminates and returns control to its calling program (MAIN, in this case):

```
5120 GOSUB 6000
5130 IF L2=1 THEN GOTO 5280
—
—
5280 CLOSE #2
5290 RETURN
```

Upon reentering MAIN, the program responds with:

DO YOU WANT TO DO MORE? (YES OR NO)

In a general way we are again using the technique of forcing to test the various execution pathways of the record-keeping program. We are not rigorously following the guidelines of forcing, since we have not loaded variables with the simplest possible values to test the accuracy of certain computational procedures, as we did with the integer multiplication program. But we do have a good idea of what to expect from the program; we know what the final output should look like—assuming that all of the subroutines work correctly, communicate to each other without any garbling of data, and are invoked in the right sequence by the higher-level supervisory routines.

So far, then, we have tried to construct a file consisting of two records. We would next like to add to that file, extending its length by one record. We would therefore answer the program:

```
DO YOU WANT TO DO MORE? (YES OR NO)
? YES
TYPE R TO RETRIEVE AND F TO FILE
? F
```

which would bring us once again to subroutine FILE:

```
PLEASE TYPE M TO MAKE A NEW FILE
OR E TO EXTEND AN OLD FILE
? E
```

This will allow us to test the block of code from line 5170 to line 5250:

```
5170 FILE #1;"FILES",1
5180 GOSUB 1000
5190 IF EOF(1)=6 THEN GOTO 5220
5200 LET Z$=A$
5210 GOTO 5180
5220 REWIND #1
5230 GOSUB 1000
5240 IF A$=Z$ THEN CLOSE #1:GOTO 5110
5250 GOTO 5230
```

This section of code first declares file 1 to be open, to have the identifier name FILES, and to carry read-only permission. We have seen the file statement before, and so should be familiar with its operation. After returning from subroutine READER, the code performs a text to determine the status of file 1. EOF is a built-in function of SOL's Extended cassette Basic, and may return a number of different values:

Value of EOF	Meaning
0	File number was not declared
1	The last operation was FILE
2	The last operation was READ
3	The last operation was PRINT
4	The last operation was REWIND
5	not used
6	The last operation was READ EOF

Therefore, if the last operation did not result in reading an end-of-file mark, then the temporary record storage is updated and the next record is read in. If the last read operation yielded an end-of-file, then the program jumps to line 5220.

We recall that in order to extend a file we had to make two passes: one pass over the tape to identify the last record, then rewind to the beginning and make another pass over the tape to space up to that point but not beyond it. And in fact, in lines 5220 to 5250, that is exactly what the program does. Returning to the CRT display then, we would see:

```
PLEASE TYPE M TO MAKE A NEW FILE
OR E TO EXTEND AN OLD FILE
? E
PREPARE TAPE UNIT 1 FOR READING FROM: FILES
```

The tape would move forward, and after a short while:

```
PREPARE TAPE UNIT 1 FOR REWINDING
```

We have encountered this request before. We rewind the tape, and then signal the computer that we have finished by hitting any key on the keyboard.

We wait. Many long minutes go by and nothing seems to be happening. Usually this indicates an endless loop, but such would hardly seem to be the case in this instance. In any event, the only way to break out of whatever is locking up the machine is to hit the MODE SELECT key. Immediately the message is displayed:

```
RD ERROR IN LINE 1030
```

Apparently the program has been transferred to subroutine READER from subroutine FILE, and there it stayed. Fortunately, this bug can be solved with nothing more fancy than a bit of deduction, and all of the clues are before us.

When the program requested us to rewind tape 1, we did so and then signaled the computer of our accomplishment. Satisfied that all was as it should be, the program jumped to subroutine READER:

```
5230 GOSUB 1000
```

and then tried to read in the first record. This is where the hangup occurred. Since we had not pressed the play button on the tape recorder, the cassette did not move and no data flowed into the computer to satisfy the read statement in subroutine READER.

As mentioned before, cassette tapes are much less expensive than floppy disks, but they are also less efficient. Standard audio cassette tape recorders, when put to microcomputer applications, require a large amount of human intervention to push the proper buttons, and humans often require prompting. The bug therefore could be easily fixed with the addition of one statement which would execute immediately after the rewind operation:

```
5225  PRINT "PREPARE TAPE UNIT 1 FOR READING FROM: FILES"
5227  PAUSE 50
```

The pause statement causes the program to wait five seconds (fifty tenths) before continuing. Running the program with these modifications yields:

```
RUN
TYPE R TO RETRIEVE AND F TO FILE
? F
PLEASE TYPE M TO MAKE A NEW FILE
AND E TO EXTEND AN OLD FILE
? E
PREPARE TAPE UNIT 1 FOR READING FROM: FILES
```

The tape, which had been rewound, now moves forward, then stops:

```
PREPARE TAPE UNIT 1 FOR REWINDING
```

We rewind the tape and signal the computer. Then:

PREPARE TAPE UNIT 1 FOR READING FROM: FILES

This is our message, as opposed to the one just previous which was generated by the file statement. We have 5 seconds to comply, which should be ample time.

In a short time, another message appears:

PREPARE TAPE UNIT 1 FOR WRITING TO: FILES

If everything has worked correctly the program has now spaced up to the last record on the tape, and then halted. Once we switch the tape recorder over to the record mode, new information will be written over the old end-of-file mark, and a new EOF will be written at some point further along on the tape.

Once we have pressed the record button on the tape deck, we notify the computer. The screen then clears, and the data input form appears. So far everything seems to be functioning correctly. We fill in the form as follows:

TITLE? DNA DETERMINATION TECHNIQUES
FILE NUMBER? 401
SOURCE? JOUR MOLEC BIOL
DATE? JAN 78
HEADINGS (TOTAL OF 5)?DNA   ?CENTRIFUGATION
?SEDIMENTATION ?NUCLEIC ACID ?TECHNIQUES

The screen clears and the blank data input form reappears. As before, we end the data input phase by returning a null entry for the title, sending control of execution eventually back to MAIN:

DO YOU WANT TO DO MORE? (YES OR NO)
? YES
TYPE R TO RETRIEVE AND F TO FILE
?

By virtue of the debugging which we have already performed on all but two of the routines in the record-keeping program (those two routines being MAIN and FILE), we feel reasonably confident that events have progressed as they should and that consequently we have successfully created a file on the tape consisting of three separate records. However, since we have not used any print statements to check on the internal progress of the fully assembled program, we have no way of knowing for certain if we have succeeded. To check, then, we must exercise the retrieval pathway of the program to see what, if anything, is on the tape. We therefore answer the program's query:

TYPE R TO RETRIEVE AND F TO FILE
? R

and control of execution is transferred to subroutine SEARCH. The subroutine greets us with:

PREPARE TAPE UNIT 1 FOR READING FROM: FILES

We must of course rewind the tape before engaging the play button and signaling our *all clear* to the program. Here we come upon a bug of personal choice: it has to be assumed that if we ever plan to go to the search portion of the program directly from the file portion (and the means are provided to do just that), then we must be prepared to take it upon ourselves to remember the various tape handling chores which must be taken care of before execution may continue. While the program itself is without programming-related bugs, it could be argued that a prompt, similar to the one we placed in subroutine FILE (but this time telling us to rewind the tape), is necessary in order to address those occasions when execution would pass from FILE through MAIN to SEARCH.

For the present, however, we will assume that no such modification is required. Setting the tape up for a read, then, execution continues:

WHAT HEADING DO YOU WANT TO SEARCH FOR?

We choose a heading which corresponds to the last record, since that would tell us if we were able to overwrite the first EOF mark when we tried to extend the file:

WHAT HEADING DO YOU WANT TO SEARCH FOR?
? CENTRIFUGATION
DNA DETERMINATION TECHNIQUES   401   JOUR MOLEC

```
BIOLJAN 78
WOULD YOU LIKE TO SEARCH ANOTHER?
TYPE YES OR NO
```

The results look promising but we should also attempt to retrieve one or both of the first two records, just to convince ourselves that they, too, were not written over and obliterated when we extended the file.

```
TYPE YES OR NO YES
PREPARE TAPE UNIT 1 FOR READING FROM: FILES
```

Again, the program assumes that we realize that the tape must first be rewound to the beginning of information before another search can be initiated. Here, as before, we encounter a "personal choice bug" in which an explanatory print statement may be inserted to advise the operator of the additional tape handling which is required. Clearing the condition continues execution:

```
WHAT HEADING DO YOU WANT TO SEARCH FOR?
? MITOCHONDRIA
NEW TREATMENT FOR CANCER         231   JOUR CHEM
BIOL FEB 78
PHOSPHORYLATED ENZYME EFFECTS 192   JOUR CHEM
BIOL OCT 77
```

It would seem that the record-keeping program functions correctly; our confidence in the stability of the program will increase with the more trials the program is put to and passes.

Suppose we now want to modify the program to index and retrieve information about classical music recordings. We could begin by listing those categories we would like to use as retrieval headings:

Composer
Title of work
Performer
Form of composition

Also there might be some subsidiary headings which, while we might not want to use them as retrieval indexes, we would like to include as part of each entry to be printed out with the rest of the record:

Medium (whether record, cassette, or reel-to-reel tape)
Recording label
Label's stock number
Mode (quad/stereo/mono)

In addition, we would like the sorting process to extend to more than one level, so that if a number of entries are retrieved on the basis of composer, for example, they would be (1) sorted alphabetically by title and (2) further sorted alphabetically by performer (since often more than one artist will perform a particular work).

Already we can see that the modifications to our existing program will be extensive. Certainly it will be easier to turn the already written record-keeping routine to these new requirements than it would be to design a whole new program from scratch, but the magnitude of the proposed changes suggests that we will surely encounter a fair number of bugs.

Having listed the various items that we would like to appear in each entry, we can proceed to allocating space to each item. An important thing to keep in mind is the total memory space of the computer. Cassette tape is an essentially limitless depository of information, but the computer's internal memory is not without limits. We want to be able to store a very large quantity of data on some external device, and then extract some smaller subset of that information and store it inside the computer where we can sort it out and then display it. But along with the data, the computer's internal memory must also contain (1) the BASIC language program which manipulates the data and (2) the interpreter program which converts the BASIC statements to a form which the computer can understand.

This leads to some cryptic entries at times, made necessary by the tradeoff between not being able to fit all of the information into internal memory, or being able to squeeze in all of the essential information by shortening some of the items and leaving out others. In general, this requires the human operator to work a little harder to decipher the output; but that is not nearly as great a burden as it might sound, and it is almost always the most practical solution.

Consider the following typical block of information which must somehow be made to fit into a limited-length computer entry:

Saint-Saens' Piano Concerto No. 2, performed by Phillipe Entremont with the Philadelphia Orchestra conducted by Eugene Ormandy; Columbia stereo disk MS 6778.

One possible way to arrange the data would be:

COMPOSER: Saint-Saens
TITLE: Piano Concerto No. 2
PERFORMER: Phillipe Entremont
FORM: Concerto
MEDIUM: Record
LABEL: Columbia
STOCK NUMBER: MS6778
MODE: Stereo

We have filled all of the categories, but still something is lacking: we would also like to locate works performed by a particular conductor, such as Eugene Ormandy. In order to be able to sort out all recording made by a particular conductor we would have to have access to the conductor's name, and this is done by giving it the status of a retrieval heading. Suppose we expand the listing:

COMPOSER: Saint-Saens
TITLE: Piano Concerto No. 2
PERFORMER 1: Phillipe Entremont
PERFORMER 2: Eugene Ormandy/Philadelphia Orch.
FORM: Concerto
MEDIUM: Record
LABEL: Columbia
STOCK NUMBER: MS6778
MODE: Stereo

Only one other entry presents a problem:

FORM: Concerto

There are many different types of concertos; they have been written for almost every instrument found in the orchestra: piano, violin, oboe, flute, etc. We would therefore want the ability to retrieve either (1) all recordings of all concertos, no matter what the principal instrument, or (2) all piano concertos only. This requires that we either construct a program clever enough to take the entry:

FORM: Concerto, piano

and be able to read it either as "concerto, piano" or on other occasions simply "concerto," or that we add another *form* category just as we added another *performer* category. The second alternative is by far the easier to program, but we pay for the convenience with a bulkier total record. Even still, have we provided for all eventualities? Consider this entry:

> Die Zauberflote (The Magic Flute), an opera by Mozart. Conducted by Karl Bohm, with Evelyn Lear, Dietrich Fischer-Dieskau, and Fritz Wunderlich, on Deutsche Grammaphone disk 2709-017 in stereo.

To properly encompass all retrieval headings of interest for an entry such as this would require a form similar to the following:

	Characters
COMPOSER: Mozart	6
TITLE1: Die Zauberflote	15
TITLE2: The Magic Flute	15
PERFORMER1: Bohm, Karl	10
PERFORMER2: Lear, Evelyn	12
PERFORMER3: Fischer-Dieskau, Dietrich	25
PERFORMER4: Wunderlich, Fritz	17
FORM: Opera	5
MEDIUM: Record	6
LABEL: Deutsche Grammaphone Gesellschaft	33
STOCK NUMBER: 2907-017	8
MODE: Stereo	6
	158 total spaces

Suppose we construct the following general entry form:

Heading	Spaces allotted
COMPOSER:	15
TITLE1:	20
TITLE2:	20
PERFORMER1:	15
PERFORMER2:	15
PERFORMER3:	15
PERFORMER4:	15
FORM1:	15
FORM2:	15
MEDIUM:	10
LABEL:	15
STOCK NUMBER:	10
MODE:	10
	190 total spaces

When the record-keeping program was used to index scientific reprints, each record was only 110 characters long. But of those 110 characters, 50 did not have to be saved; they corresponded to the five keyword
headings (each 10 characters long) that were used during retrieval but
which were not displayed and hence could be disposed of before the
sorting process began.

For the music index, however, all of the headings contain information which will appear in the final listing. E$ is the array which accepts
the entries selected from the master file and holds them as they are rear-
ranged alphabetically by subroutine SORT. For the original article-indexing program, E$ was dimensioned to 1200 characters, large enough to
hold 120 entries of 10 characters each. If we carried over the same dimensioning to the music-indexing program, where each entry is potentially
now 190 characters long, we would only be able to contain roughly six
entries. Considering that Mozart wrote 40 symphonies, for example, we
would need 40 × 190, or 7600 words of memory. This is not unreasonable,
but it does point up the need to economize wherever possible.

Also, while we note that the grand total of available spaces for the
proposed format was greater than the number of spaces actually required
by the example (190 vs. 158), many of the individual entries were considerably longer than their allotted space would accommodate (Deutsche
Grammophone Gesellschaft, with 33 characters, was to fit in a slot only
15 characters wide).

One solution is to truncate many of the entry fields by abbreviating
the entires which fill them. For example, we drop first names of
performers:

Instead of	*We use*
Bohm, Karl	Bohm
Fischer-Dieskau, Dietrich	F-Dieskau

We can also gain room by using one-letter abbreviations for words
which, when taken in context, become self-explanatory:

Instead of	*We use*
Stereo	S
Cassette	C

Similar economies may be realized when it comes to identifying the different record labels. This may require an index sheet which the human
operator may refer to if necessary, but the saving in computer memory
space can be significant:

	Instead of	*We use*
	Deutsche Grammophone Gesellschaft	DGG
	Columbia	COL

Another way to conserve space is to allow only one entry for each main retrieval heading:

Heading	*Spaces allotted*
COMPOSER:	15
TITLE:	35
PERFORMER:	35
FORM:	10
MEDIUM:	1
LABEL:	3
STOCK NUMBER:	10
MODE:	1
	110 total spaces

How would the "Magic Flute" listing look with this format?

Heading: Entry	*Characters*
COMPOSER: Mozart	6
TITLE: Die Zauberflote/The Magic Flute	31
PERFORMER: Bohm/Lear/F-Dieskau/	
Wunderlich	30
FORM: Opera	5
MEDIUM: R	1
LABEL: DGG	3
STOCK NO: 2709-017	8
MODE: S	1
	85 total spaces

After padding the underlength entries to a uniform length, the completed record is only 110 characters long (80 less than originally proposed) and identical in length with the record length of the original article-indexing version of the program. Also the length of this unprocessed listing has been almost cut in half.

We now know enough about the requirements of our modified program definition to begin with the actual updating of the various subroutines. As we progress, we will be on the alert for potential trouble spots, and we will want to take care to guard these spots with some designed-in debuggers.

We will begin, as we did in Chapter 6, with subroutine WRITER:

```
2000 REM SUBROUTINE WRITER
2010 REM WRITES A SINGLE LINE OF DATA
2020 REM TO TAPE (ALWAYS FILE #2)
2030 LET F$=H1$+H2$+H3$+H4$+H5$
2040 LET A$=F$+T$+N$+S$+D$
2050 PRINT #2;A$
2060 RETURN
```

We recall that the variable names in this original version of the program were chosen to correspond to the values which they represent:

```
H1$ = 1st heading
H2$ = 2nd heading
H3$ = 3rd heading
H4$ = 4th heading
H5$ = 5th heading
T$  = Title
N$  = Number
S$  = Source
D$  = Date
```

Applying the same method, we might now want to use:

```
C$  = Composer
T$  = Title
P$  = Performer
F$  = Form
M1$ = Medium
L$  = Label
S$  = Stock No.
M2$ = Mode
```

Before we make such a change we must carefully weigh the consequences; we will be making the variables more easily identifiable, but we will also be disrupting much of the already existing code in other subroutines. Variables in BASIC are global, as we learned earlier, and the variables C$, P$, and L$ are already in use in other parts of the program. This will necessitate changing those variables whenever they appear elsewhere, which is not an impossible nor even particularly difficult task, but is an important one: one overlooked variable could spell disaster.

Suppose, however, that we decide to use the new naming scheme. Subroutine WRITER would have to be rewritten as follows:

```
2000 REM SUBROUTINE WRITER
2010 REM WRITES A SINGLE LINE OF DATA
2020 REM TO TAPE (ALWAYS FILE #2)
2030 LET A$=C$+T$+P$+F$+M1$+L$+S$+M2$
2040 PRINT #2;A$
2050 RETURN
```

In general form this differs very little from the original version. But because there may be some confusion caused by the redefinition of the variables, we should insert a debugger just in case.

We do not want a debugger which will always be on or which we will have to take down and individually activate or delete depending upon the status of the program. We came across this situation in Chapter 7 where we activated or deactivated a snapshot by either deleting or inserting a RETURN statement, respectively.

The solution once again is to take advantage of the fact that variables in BASIC are global. We can "switch" a debug statement on or off simply by tying its activity to the value of a particular variable. The control variable (which may be responsible for debug statements located in many subroutines) may in turn be read into the program just once, at the level of the main supervisory routine.

Suppose we call the control variable D, and insert the following lines of code:

```
2025 IF D=1 THEN GOSUB 2070
—

—
```

```
2070 REM WRITER DIAGNOSTICS
2080 PRINT "DEBUG FROM SUBROUTINE WRITER"
2090 PRINT "C$=";C$;"T$=";T$;"P$=";P$;"F$=";F$
2100 PRINT "M1$=";M1$;"L$=";L$;"S$=";S$;"M2$=";M2$
2110 RETURN
```

D will normally be initialized to zero, in which case the debug statement will be bypassed and execution will proceed normally. However, if *D* is set equal to 1 the debugger will be activated. In neither case will we be required to make any changes to the code or activate or deactivate the debuggers. This is a strong selling point, since each time we enter the code we run the risk of creating another bug.

The next subroutine to consider is subroutine READER:

```
1000 REM SUBROUTINE READER
1010 REM READS DATA FROM TAPE (ALWAYS FILE #1)
1020 REM STORES A RECORD AT A TIME IN A$
1030 READ #1;A$
1040 IF EOF(1)=6 THEN GOTO 1150
1050 LET H1$=A$(1,10)
1060 LET H2$=A$(11,20)
1070 LET H3$=A$(21,30)
1080 LET H4$=A$(31,40)
1090 LET H5$=A$(41,50)
1100 LET T$=A$(51,80)
1110 LET N$=A$(81,85)
1120 LET S$=A$(86,100)
1130 LET D$=A$(101,110)
1140 GOTO 1160
1150 LET L$="EOF"
1160 RETURN
```

The indexing scheme which separates the 110-character record into discrete subunits will have to be changed, since the original record is 120 characters long; also there are now 8 subunits as opposed to the original 9, and the new subunits are of widely varying lengths. We recall from Chapter 6 the physical layout of a single record; Fig. 8-4 compares the old and new formats. Taking all of the revised dimensions into consideration, we might rewrite subroutine READER as follows:

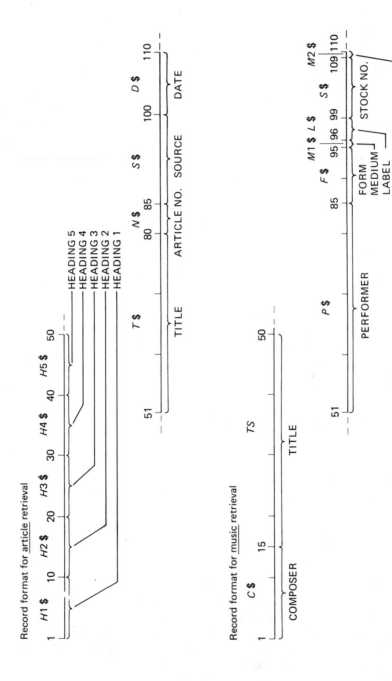

Fig. 8-4. Comparison of physical record layout for article-retrieval program vs. music-retrieval program.

```
1000 REM SUBROUTINE READER
1010 REM READS DATA FROM TAPE (ALWAYS FILE #1)
1020 REM STORES A RECORD AT A TIME IN A$
1030 READ #1;A$
1040 IF EOG(1)=6 THEN GOTO 1150
1050 LET C$=A$(1,15)
1060 LET T$=A$(16,50)
1070 LET P$=A$(51,85)
1080 LET F$=A$(86,95)
1090 LET M1$=A$(96)
1100 LET L$=A$(97,99)
1110 LET S$=A$(100,109)
1120 LET M2$=A$(110)
1130 GOTO 1160
1140 LET L2$="EOF"
1150 RETURN
```

In the old version, the variable L$ was an indicator to mark when the end of file had been reached, but in the modified application L$ relates to the record label identification. This means that a new variable had to be found for the EOF indicator. Thus:

```
1150 LET L$="EOF"
```

from the article-indexing application became

```
1140 LET L2$="EOF"
```

for the music-indexing application.

The debug statement for subroutine READER is simple:

```
1045 IF D=1 THEN PRINT "READER SAYS A$=";A$
```

As before, we use the variable D as the debug statement switch.

The next subroutine to consider is subroutine FORMIN. FORMIN is the subroutine which displays a data entry form on the CRT screen and then accepts input from the keyboard. The listing of subroutine FORMIN, taken from Chapter 6, is:

```
6000 REM SUBROUTINE FORMIN
6010 REM FILL IN FORM FOR INPUT DATA
6020 PRINT "&K"
6030 CURSOR 1,0
6040 PRINT "PLEASE ENTER THE INFORMATION AS REQUESTED"
6050 PRINT "A BLANK ON THE FIRST ENTRY ENDS THE LIST"
6060 PRINT "TITLE"
6070 CURSOR 5,0
6080 PRINT "FILE NUMBER"
6090 CURSOR 7,0
6100 PRINT "SOURCE"
6110 CURSOR 9,0
6120 PRINT "DATE"
6130 CURSOR 11,0
6140 PRINT "HEADINGS (TOTAL OF 5)"
6150 CURSOR 3,8
6160 INPUT T$
6170 IF T$="" THEN LET L2=1:GOTO 6340
6180 CURSOR 5,13
6190 INPUT N$
6200 CURSOR 7,8
6210 INPUT S$
6220 CURSOR 9,6
6230 INPUT D$
6240 CURSOR 11,26
6250 INPUT H1$
6260 CURSOR 11,40
6270 INPUT H2$
6280 CURSOR 13,0
6290 INPUT H3$
6300 CURSOR 13,26
6310 INPUT H4$
6320 CURSOR 13,40
6330 INPUT H5$
6340 RETURN
```

The revised program will be essentially the same as the original routine; the titling information will have to be changed to correspond to the

```
PLEASE ENTER THE INFORMATION AS REQUESTED

A BLANK ON THE FIRST ENTRY ENDS THE LIST

TITLE:


FILE NUMBER:

SOURCE:

DATE:

HEADINGS:  (TOTAL OF 5)
```

Fig. 8-5.   Data entry form as displayed on CRT screen for original article-indexing program.

music retrieval application, but the basic forms of the two subroutines will be identical. Figures 8-5 and 8-6 compare the old data entry format with the new and will help us as we rewrite subroutine FORMIN:

```
6000 REM SUBROUTINE FORMIN
6010 REM FILL IN FORM FOR INPUT DATA
6020 PRINT "&K"
6030 CURSOR 1,2
6040 PRINT "PLEASE ENTER THE INFORMATION AS REQUESTED"
6050 CURSOR 2,2
6060 PRINT "A BLANK ON THE FIRST ENTRY ENDS THE LIST"
6070 CURSOR 3,2
6080 PRINT "COMPOSER:"
6090 CURSOR 4,2
6100 PRINT "TITLE:"
6110 CURSOR 5,2
6120 PRINT "PERFORMER:"
6130 CURSOR 6,2
6140 PRINT "FORM:"
```

```
PLEASE ENTER THE INFORMATION AS REQUESTED

A BLANK ON THE FIRST ENTRY ENDS THE LIST

COMPOSER:


TITLE:

PERFORMER:

FORM:

LABEL:  (3 LETTER CODE)

STOCK NUMBER:

MEDIUM (R = RECORD, T = TAPE, C = CASSETTE)

MODE:  (Q = QUAD, S = STEREO, M = MONO)
```

Fig. 8-6. Data entry form as displayed on CRT screen for original music-indexing program.

```
6150 CURSOR 7,2
6160 PRINT "LABEL: (3 LETTER CODE)"
6170 CURSOR 8,2
6180 PRINT "STOCK NUMBER:"
6190 CURSOR 9,2
6200 PRINT "MEDIUM: (R=RECORD,T=TAPE,C=CASSETTE)"
6210 CURSOR 10,2
6220 PRINT "MODE: (Q=QUAD,S=STEREO,M=MONO)"
6230 CURSOR 3,12
6240 INPUT C$
6250 IF C$="" THEN LET L2=1:GOTO 6400
6260 CURSOR 4,9
6270 INPUT T$
6280 CURSOR 5,13
6290 INPUT P$
6300 CURSOR 6,8
6310 INPUT F$
6320 CURSOR 7,25
```

```
6330 INPUT L$
6340 CURSOR 8,24
6350 INPUT S$
6360 CURSOR 9,40
6370 INPUT M1$
6380 CURSOR 10,35
6390 INPUT M2$
6400 RETURN
```

A debug statement is not required but may as well be included for completeness. Any debugger which we would want to incorporate would only have to print out the variables C$, T$, P$, F$, L$, S$, M1$, and M2$—the identical variables which were displayed in subroutine WRITER. Instead of adding duplicate lines of code to an already lengthy program, suppose we use the same block of debugger code from subroutine WRITER after including one modification which will tell us from which subroutine the debugger is originating:

```
6395 IF D=1 THEN PRINT "DEBUG AT FORMIN":GOSUB 2090
```

The structure of the modified version of subroutine FORMOUT (much like the structure of the modified version of subroutine FORMIN) will be nearly unchanged from that of the original. The indexes will be changed, corresponding to the altered lengths of the variables, but in all other functional respects the two verions of subroutine FORMOUT will be the same. We will list here only the updated version:

```
7000 REM SUBROUTINE FORMOUT
7010 REM THIS SUBROUTINE MOLDS DATA INTO
7020 REM PROPER FORMAT FOR OUTPUT ONTO TAPE
7030 LET P2$=" "
7040 LET L=LEN(C$)
7050 LET J=15−L
7060 FOR I=1 TO J
7070 LET C$=C$+P2$
7080 NEXT I
7090 LET L=LEN(T$)
7100 LET J=35−L
```

```
7110 FOR I=1 TO J
7120 LET T$=T$+P2$
7130 NEXT I
7140 LET L=LEN(P$)
7150 LET J=35-L
7160 FOR I=1 TO J
7170 LET P$=P$+P2$
7180 NEXT I
7190 LET L=LEN(F$)
7200 LET J=10-L
7210 FOR I=1 TO J
7220 LET F$=F$+P2$
7230 NEXT I
7240 LET L=LEN(S$)
7250 LET J=10-L
7260 FOR I=1 TO J
7270 LET S$=S$+P2$
7280 NEXT I
7290 RETURN
```

The original subroutine ended at line 7490 in Chapter 6; the revised subroutine just listed ends at line 7290 and thus is shorter by 20 lines. This is an unusual discovery since the revised FORMIN subroutine was longer than its original version by 6 lines. The discrepancy is explained, however, once we realize that the variables L$, M1$, and M2$ were not included in our revision of FORMOUT. Since they are restricted to character lengths of 3, 1, and 1 spaces, they therefore have no place in a subroutine which is concerned with padding blank spaces around variable-length words to make them of a uniform length.

Again, the debugger which we used for FORMIN and WRITER may be profitably adapted to use in subroutine FORMOUT:

```
7285 IF D=1 THEN PRINT "DEBUG AT FORMOUT":GOSUB 2090
```

This will display for us the identities of the various input variables, but it will not tell us conclusively if FORMOUT has correctly performed its function. Taking a clue from Chapter 6, then, we can design in an additional feature to subroutine FORMOUT which will help us to ascertain absolutely if FORMOUT is doing its job:

```
7035 IF D=1 THEN LET P2$=''*''
```

Note also that the variable which contains the single blank space, P2$, has been changed from the P$ which appeared in the original version of FORMOUT; this is due to the conflict which came about after we changed the definition of P$ in subroutine READER.

Subroutine SORT is the only other level 3 subroutine left to modify for our music-indexing application of the record-keeping program. In its original version, it reads:

```
4000 REM SUBROUTINE SORT
4010 REM ALPHABETICALLY SORTS ENTRIES
4020 REM PRIOR TO PRINTOUT
4025 LET N=N−1
4030 FOR J1=1 TO N
4040 LET N2=0
4050 FOR J2=1 TO N
4060 LET I2=(J2−1)*60+1
4070 LET V$=E$(I2,I2+59)
4080 LET V=ASC(V$)
4090 LET V2$=E$(I2+60,I2+119)
4100 LET V2=ASC(V2$)
4110 IF V>V2 THEN GOTO 4150
4120 LET N2=N2+1
4130 IF N2=N THEN GOTO 4220
4140 GOTO 4200
4150 LET L=I2+60
4160 LET H=I2+119
4170 LET T2$=E$(L,H)
4180 LET E$(L,H)=E$(I2,I2+59)
4190 LET E$(I2,I2+59)=T2$
4200 NEXT J2
4210 NEXT J1
4220 LET N=N+1
4230 RETURN
```

We recall that the original subroutine SORT arranged the entries alphabetically by title of the article. In the ordering scheme proposed for the music-indexing application of the program, the new specifications call for a major sorting by composer, followed by a second-level sort on the basis of title, followed by yet another level of sort based on the name of the performer. A one-level sort would yield:

```
BEETHOVEN        SYMPHONY NO. 3
      KLEMPERER/PHILHARMONIA ORCH        SYMPHONY
      RANG35328     M
BEETHOVEN        PIANO CONCERTO NO. 5
      BRENDEL/WALBERG/VIENNA PRO MUSICA   CONCERTO/P
      RMURS3456     S
BEETHOVEN        SYMPHONY NO. 3
      FURTWANGLER/VIENNA PHIL             SYMPHONY
      RTURTV4343     M
IVES             VIOLIN SONATA NO. 1
      ZUKOFSKY/KALISH                     SONATA/VLN
      TNON73025-F-DPS
```

We note in this example that the sorting algorithm has placed Beethoven before Ives, as is alphabetically correct, but there is no definite order to the three Beethoven entries. The proposed three-level sort algorithm, however, attempts to solve this as follows:

```
BEETHOVEN        PIANO CONCERTO NO. 5
      BRENDEL/WALBERG/VIENNA PRO MUSICA   CONCERTO/P
      RMURS3456     S
BEETHOVEN        SYMPHONY NO. 3
      FURTWANGLER/VIENNA PHIL             SYMPHONY
      RTURTV4343     M
BEETHOVEN        SYMPHONY NO. 3
      KLEMPERER/PHILHARMONIA ORCH         SYMPHONY
      RANG35328     M
IVES             VIOLIN SONATA NO. 1
      ZUKOFSKY/KALISH                     SONATA/VLN
      TNON73025-F-DPS
```

Since, in the modified program, the full record is retained for pro-

cessing (as opposed to the abbreviated record which was used in the original subroutine) the index values will no longer specify 60-character
blocks but rather 110-character blocks. Also, the trilevel sort approach
requires a significant restructuring of the subroutine. Figures 8-7 and 8-8
compare and contrast the flowcharts for the original and the modified
SORT. The following is the revised code:

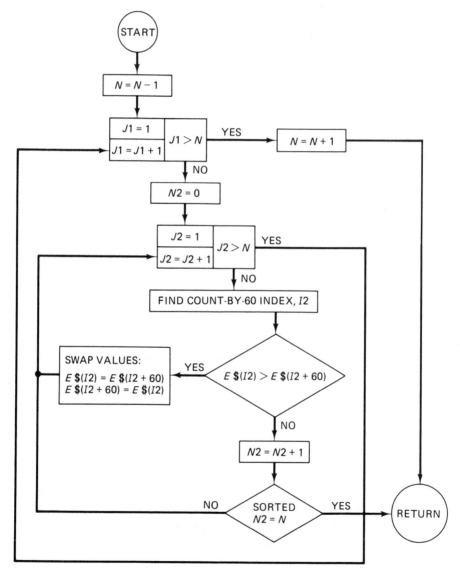

Fig. 8-7. Flowchart for original version of subroutine SORT.

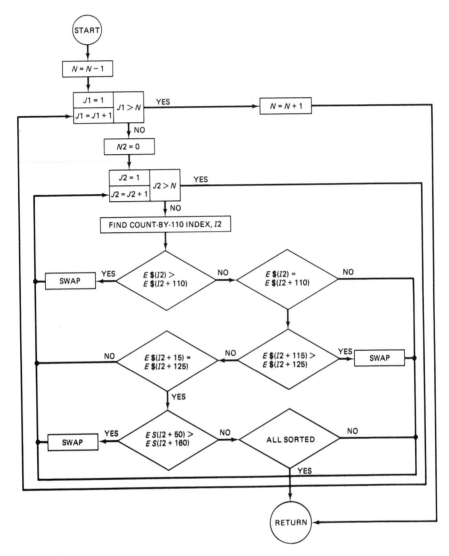

Fig. 8-8. Flowchart for subroutine SORT as it appears after modifications for music-indexing program. Note the trilevel sorting chain.

```
4000 REM SUBROUTINE SORT
4010 REM TRILEVEL SORT FOR ENTRIES
4020 REM PRIOR TO PRINTOUT
4030 LET N=N−1
```

```
4040 FOR J1=1 TO N
4050 LET N2=0
4060 FOR J2=1 TO N
4070 LET I2=(J2-1)*110+1
4080 LET L=I2+110
4090 LET H=I2+219
4100 LET X$=E$(I2)
4110 LET X=ASC(X$)
4120 LET X2$=E$(L)
4130 LET X2=ASC(X2$)
4140 LET Y$=E(I2+15)
4150 LET Y=ASC(Y$)
4160 LET Y2$=E$(L+15)
4170 LET Y2=ASC(Y2$)
4180 LET Z$=E$(I2+50)
4190 LET Z=ASC(Z$)
4200 LET Z2$=E$(L+50)
4210 LET Z2=ASC(Z2$)
4220 IF X>X2 THEN GOSUB 4500
4230 IF X=X2 THEN GOTO 4250
4240 GOTO 4290
4250 IF Y>Y2 THEN GOSUB 4500
4260 IF Y=Y2 THEN GOTO 4280
4270 GOTO 4290
4280 IF Z>Z2 THEN GOSUB 4500
4290 LET N2=N2+1
4300 IF N2=N THEN GOTO 4330
4310 NEXT J2
4320 NEXT J1
4330 LET N=N+1
4340 RETURN
4500 REM SUBROUTINE SWAP
4510 LET I3=I2+109
4520 LET T2$=E$(L,H)
4530 LET E$(L,H)=E$(I2,I3)
4540 LET E$(I2,I3)=T2$
4550 RETURN
```

Not only is the revised subroutine longer than the original version (due to the increased complexity of the task), but we have even added an entirely new subroutine.

Subroutine SWAP is no more than the block of code in the old version of subroutine SORT (lines 4150 through 4190). As we can see in Fig. 8-8, however, the revised subroutine accesses the block of code three times rather than just once. In general, if a segment of code is used more than once throughout a program, it is more efficient to raise the block of code to the status of subroutine rather than to write it out in full at each point in the program where it is referenced.

Because subroutine SORT has been changed so radically, we will want to include a number of designed-in debuggers, or at least one debugger which will display a large amount of information. We learned in Chapter 7, however, that simply displaying lots and lots of diagnostic printout is sometimes more a hindrance than a help, since it runs by so fast on the CRT screen that we are unable to assimilate it. The technique we developed in Chapter 7 to overcome these difficulties was the snapshot. A snapshot suitable for the revised subroutine might look like:

```
9000 REM SNAPSHOT
9010 PRINT "&K"
9020 PRINT "SNAPSHOT CALLED FROM SUBROUTINE";N$
9030 PRINT "AND FROM LINE";L2
9040 PRINT "A$";A$
9050 PRINT "E$";E$;"W$";W$
9060 PRINT "X$";X$;"X2$";X2$;"Y$";Y$;"Y2$";Y2$;"Z$";
     Z$;"Z2$";Z2$
9070 PRINT "X";X;"X2";X2;"Y";Y;"Y2";Y2;"Z";Z;"Z2";Z2
9080 PRINT "J1";J1;"J2";J2;"N";N;"N2";N2
9090 INPUT Q$
9100 RETURN
```

We recall that in Chapter 7, once the snapshot had outlived its usefulness, rather than delete it from the program entirely we inserted a jump statement as the first executable line of code in the subroutine, leaving the various "GOSUB 9000" statements which invoked the snapshot in place and unchanged. When designing-in, however, we approach the problem from a different viewpoint; we want the choice of whether or not to exercise the debug options to be under operator control. Therefore, instead of inserting the following statement-triplet into subroutine SORT as we did in the original version:

```
4027 LET X$="SORT"

—



—

4052 LET X=4050
4055 GOSUB 9000
```

we will now be inserting the statement:

```
4215 IF D=1 THEN LET N$="SORT":LET L2=4210:GOSUB 9000
```

Once again, the string of statements following the THEN will only be executed if D (the debug switch) is equal to 1. Otherwise, program execution will continue normally.

It is by now clearly evident that modifying the original article-indexing program to transform it into a music-indexing routine has been a nontrivial task. Certainly it has been easier than had we been forced to start from scratch, but every subroutine yet encountered has had to be modified in some way. There are now new variables to worry about, and many old variables have been redefined.

As we progress further up the hierarchy of subroutines, first to the level 2 subroutines FILE and SEARCH, and finally to the level 1 program, MAIN, we will note that fewer and less complicated alterations are required. Nonetheless, when we first type in a RUN command to check on the performance of our handiwork, we will likely be very grateful that we took the time to design in as many debug statements as we did. It is almost always easier to provide for debug statements while we are actively involved in writing or modifying a particular routine (and thus have a fresher knowledge of the intimate details of the code) than it is to return to it at some later date and try to retrace out steps to determine what exactly we were trying to do in a certain block of code.

The original SEARCH is as follows (the statements have been renumbered for clarity):

```
3000 REM SUBROUTINE SEARCH
3010 REM SEARCHES DATA ON FILE #1FOR
3020 REM A MATCH WITH KEYWORD
3030 FILE #1;"FILES",1
3040 PRINT "&K"
```

```
3050 PRINT "WHAT HEADING DO YOU WANT TO SEARCH FOR?"
3060 LET E$=""
3070 INPUT C$
3080 LET P$=""
3090 LET L=LEN(C$)
3100 LET J=10−L
3110 FOR I=1 TO J
3120 LET C$=C$+P$
3130 NEXT I
3140 LET L$=""
3150 GOSUB 1000
3160 IF L$="EOF" THEN GOTO 3250
3170 IF C$=H1$ THEN GOTO 3230
3180 IF C$=H2$ THEN GOTO 3230
3190 IF C$=H3$ THEN GOTO 3230
3200 IF C$=H4$ THEN GOTO 3230
3210 IF C$=H5$ THEN GOTO 3230
3220 GOTO 3140
3230 LET E$=E$+T$+N$+S$+D$
3240 GOTO 3140
3250 LET L=LEN(E$)
3260 IF L=0 THEN GOTO 3350
3270 LET N=L/60
3280 IF N=1 THEN GOTO 3300
3290 GOSUB 4000
3300 FOR I=1 TO N
3310 LET J=(I−1)*60+1
3320 PRINT E$(J,J+59)
3330 NEXT I
3340 GOTO 3360
3350 PRINT "WE HAVE NO ENTRIES UNDER THAT HEADING"
3360 CLOSE #1
3370 PRINT "WOULD YOU LIKE TO SEARCH ANOTHER?"
3380 INPUT "TYPE YES OR NO";K$
3390 IF K$="YES" THEN GOTO 3030
3400 RETURN
```

The revised subroutine SEARCH is:

```
3000 REM SUBROUTINE SEARCH
3020 REM SEARCHES DATA ON FILE #1 FOR
3020 REM A MATCH WITH KEYWORD
3030 FILE #1;"FILES",1
3040 PRINT "&K"
3050 PRINT "WHAT HEADING DO YOU WANT TO SEARCH FOR?"
3060 LET E$=""
3070 INPUT C$
3080 GOSUB 1000
3090 IF L2$="EOF" THEN GOTO 3150
3100 SEARCH C$,A$,R
3110 IF R>0 THEN GOTO 3130
3120 GOTO 3080
3130 LET E$=E$+A$
3140 GOTO 3080
3150 LET L=LEN(E$)
3160 IF L=0 THEN GOTO 3260
3170 LET N=L/110
3180 IF N=1 THEN GOTO 3200
3190 GOSUB 4000
3200 FOR I=1 TO N
3210 LET J=(I−1)*110+1
3220 PRINT E$(J,J+49)
3230 PRINT TAB(3);E$(J+50,J+109)
3240 NEXT I
3250 GOTO 3270
3260 PRINT "WE HAVE NO ENTRIES UNDER THAT HEADING"
3270 CLOSE #1
3280 PRINT "WOULD YOU LIKE TO SEARCH ANOTHER?"
3290 INPUT "TYPE YES OR NO";K$
3300 IF K$="YES" THEN GOTO 3030
3310 RETURN
```

Side-by-side comparison of the two versions suggests that there are only three areas of significant difference between them. First is the method of determining if the record just read in from tape has a component which matches the keyword entered from the console, and therefore qualifies as a record of interest. The article-indexing version compares keywords:

```
3170 IF C$=H1$ THEN GOTO 3230
3180 IF C$=H2$ THEN GOTO 3230
3190 IF C$=H3$ THEN GOTO 3230
3200 IF C$=H4$ THEN GOTO 3230
3210 IF C$=H5$ THEN GOTO 3230
```

The music-indexing version, however, treats the keyword as a substring, a lesser component of a greater whole, and then asks of each new record read in if it contains the keyword:

```
3100 SEARCH C$,A$,R
```

The SEARCH command searches string variable $A\$$ for an occurrence of $C\$$. If $C\$$ appears, then R is set to the character position where it begins. If $C\$$ is not in $A\$$, then R is set equal to zero. The SEARCH command seems a much more elegant approach than that which was used originally. However, the command was not used previously for a number of reasons. The article-indexing version retrieved records on the basis of precisely matching keywords which served as an adjective to describe the contents of the individual articles, but which were not included as part of the final display. The music-indexing version, though, searches and retrieves on the basis of nouns: title of work, name of composer, name of performer, even the name of the large form of the composition, such as opera or symphony. Also, unlike the first application, all of the information used as retrieval data forms an integral part of the final display; the record as it is read in from the master tape file, if it satisfies the search request, is transferred in its entirety to the temporary string storage variable, $E\$$, prior to sorting and display.

This leads to the next major difference between the two versions, and that is the manner in which the temporary storage variable is lengthened. Originally, only part of $A\$$ (the current record from the master file) was appended to $E\$$: the last 60 characters of the 110-character record. The first 50 characters represented the five 10-character adjective-type retrieval headings and were discarded since they had no place in the final display. The revised routine, as we know, saves the entire 110-character length of $A\$$:

```
Original:3230 LET E$=E$+T$+N$+S$+D$
Revised:3130 LET E$=E$+A$
```

Because the record lengths are different, the indexing scheme which divides E$ back into its constituent subunits and then displays the result had to be changed. Moreover, since the revised records are 110 characters long, and since the CRT screen display only accommodates 64 characters per line, it was decided to further subdivide the records into strings of 50 and 60 characters, and then offset the second half of the entry by three spaces. In this way, the entire record was split over two display lines without the confusion which might have occurred had both lines started at the same lefthand position.

For all that we made a number of changes to subroutine SEARCH, the debug statements which we design in may be fairly simple. In fact, we may do as we did when debugging the original version of SEARCH, and make use of the same snapshot which we used in SORT. The line of code required would be:

```
3095 IF D=1 THEN LET N$="SEARCH":LET L2=3090:GOSUB 9000
```

Subroutine FILE is listed in its entirety at the beginning of this chapter and so will not be relisted here. We recall from our earlier discussion regarding subroutine FILE that it is largely a supervisory program, more so than subroutine SEARCH. The prime function of subroutine FILE is to determine whether a new file is to be created or whether an old file is to be extended, and then to shunt the flow of program execution as required to accomplish the selected task. We may note that the length of physical layout of an individual record is immaterial to subroutine FILE as it performs its work. Therefore, it might not surprise us to learn that subroutine FILE requires no modifications whatsoever to effectively transfer its function from the article-indexing version to the music-indexing version of the program.

As for debug statements in subroutine FILE, perhaps the only variables of diagnostic interest in the program are the string variables A$ and Z$. Still using D as our debugger switch, we have:

```
5195  IF D=1 THEN PRINT "FILE, LINE 5190,A$=";A$
5235  IF D=1 THEN PRINT "FILE, LINE 5230,A$=";A$;
         "Z$=";Z$
```

Similarly, program MAIN is also discussed in the early pages of this chapter and it too requires little alteration. Indeed, the structure and logical flow of the program remain absolutely unchanged; the primary modification concerns the setting aside of memory space via the various dimension (DIM) statements:

Original:

```
110 DIM H1$(10),H2$(10),H3$(10),H4$(10),H5$(10)
120 DIM T$(30),N$(5),S$(15),D$(10),A$(110),Z$(110)
130 DIM E$(1200),F$(50),T2$(60)
```

Revised:

```
110 DIM C$(15),T$(35),P$(35),F$(10),M1$(1),L$(3)
120 DIM S$(10),M2$(1),A$(110),Z$(110)
130 DIM E$(4400),T2$(110)
```

The only other change to program MAIN involves D, the debug switch:

```
142 INPUT "IS THIS A DEBUG RUN? Y OR N",Q$
144 IF Q$="Y" THEN LET D=1 ELSE LET D=0
```

Having performed all of the necessary updates to the record-keeping program, suppose we try to execute it. The first thing we must do is create a file. Suppose further that we execute the program with no debuggers activated and see how far along we get:

```
RUN
IS THIS A DEBUG RUN? Y OR N ?N
TYPE R TO RETRIEVE AND F TO FILE
F
PLEASE TYPE M TO MAKE A NEW FILE
AND E TO EXTEND AN OLD FILE
M
```

At this point, the screen clears and the data entry form is displayed. We fill in its categories as follows:

COMPOSER: SAINT-SAENS
TITLE: PIANO CONCERTO NO 2
PERFORMER: ENTREMONT, ORMANDY/PHILADELPHIA ORCH
FORM: CNCRTO/PNO
LABEL: (3 LETTER CODE) COL
STOCK NUMBER: MS6778
MEDIUM: (R=RECORD,T=TAPE,C=CASSETTE) R
MODE: (Q=QUAD, S=STEREO, M=MONO) S

The screen clears:

COMPOSER: BEETHOVEN
TITLE: SYMPHONY NO 6 (PASTORAL)
PERFORMER: KLEMPERER/VIENNA SYM
FORM: SYMPHONY
LABEL: (3 LETTER CODE) YOR
STOCK NUMBER: PL6960
MEDIUM: (R=RECORD, T=TAPE, C=CASSETTE) R
MODE: (Q=QUAD, S=STEREO, M=MONO) M

(screen clears)

COMPOSER: BEETHOVEN
TITLE: SYMPHONY NO 3
PERFORMER: FURTWANGLER/VIENNA PHIL
FORM: SYMPHONY
LABEL: (3 LETTER CODE) TUR
STOCK NUMBER: TV4343
MEDIUM: (R=RECORD, T=TAPE, C=CASSETTE) R
MODE: (Q=QUAD, S=STEREO, M=MONO) M

(screen clears)

COMPOSER: TCHAIKOVSKY
TITLE: SYMPHONY NO 4

PERFORMER: ORMANDY/PHILADELPHIA ORCH
FORM: SYMPHONY
LABEL: (3 LETTER CODE) RCA
STOCK NUMBER: ARK1-0665
MEDIUM: (R=RECORD, T=TAPE, C=CASSETTE) C
MODE: (Q=QUAD, S=STEREO, M=MONO) S

(screen clears)

COMPOSER: BEETHOVEN
TITLE: PIANO CONCERTO NO 5
PERFORMER: BRENDEL, WALBERG/VIENNA PRO MUSICA
FORM: CNCRTO/PNO
LABEL: (3 LETTER CODE) MUR
STOCK NUMBER: S3456
MEDIUM: (R=RECORD, T=TAPE, C=CASSETTE) R
MODE: (Q=QUAD, S=STEREO, M=MONO) S

Again the screen clears, but when the data input form appears for the sixth time we type a carriage return for the first entry as a signal that we are out of data.

We stop for a moment to note the many cross-combinations provided by just these five entries: three symphonies, two piano concertos, two works performed by the same conductor, and three works written by the same composer. What makes the list especially valuable in our debugging effort is that the three symphonies are not all by the same composers; neither were the two piano concertos conducted by the same conductor nor played by the same pianists. The data provides enough permutations to successfully check out the operation of our program, while being simple enough for us to predict by inspection what the outcome of subroutines SEARCH and SORT should be. In other words, in addition to designing in a series of debug statements, we are also providing nonrandom input in a desire to force the flow of program execution along certain paths. As usual, the typical debugging effort involves more than one approach exclusively.

Execution continues:

DO YOU WANT TO DO MORE? (YES OR NO)

Having passed through the data collection phase with apparently no problems, we would like to switch over to the retrieval phase of the program and check that out. We answer, therefore:

DO YOU WANT TO DO MORE? (YES OR NO)
YES
TYPE R TO RETRIEVE AND F TO FILE
R
PREPARE TAPE UNIT 1 FOR READING FROM: FILES

We must rewind the tape, position it at the beginning of information, press the play button, and then hit any key to signal the go-ahead. We do so, and:

WHAT HEADING DO YOU WANT TO SEARCH FOR?
ORMANDY

We are asking the computer to search its files for all listings which include the conductor Eugene Ormandy. The tape begins to turn, and after a few moments we see:


```
BEETHOVEN        PIANO CONCERTO NO 5
     BRENDEL, WALBERG/VIENNA PRO MUSICA    CNCRTO/PNOR
MURS3456      S
BEETHOVEN        SYMPHONY NO 3
     FURTWANGLER/VIENNA PHIL        SYMPHONY    R
TURTV4343      M
BEETHOVEN        SYMPHONY NO 6 (PASTORAL)
     KLEMPERER/VIENNA SYM     SYMPHONY    RYORPL6960     M
SAINT-SAENS        PIANO CONCERTO NO 2
     ENTREMONT,ORMANDY/PHILADELPHIA    ORCHCNCRTO/PNOR
COLMS6778      S
TCHAIKOVSKY      SYMPHONY NO 4
     ORMANDY/PHILADELPHIA ORCH        SYMPHONY    C
RCAARK1-0665      S
```

While it is not diagnostic printout, we can still learn much about the functioning of our revised program by studying this sample of normal output. First, we can see that the three-level sorting modification seems to be working: the three Beethoven entries were sorted out before the Saint-Saens and the Tchaikovsky, and of the three Beethoven works, the two symphonies were sorted out after the piano concerto. In addition, of the two symphonies, the one directed by Furtwangler was sorted out before the one directed by Klemperer.

We can also see that subroutine SEARCH apparently did not function correctly: we asked for only those listings which contained the entry "Ormandy," but we were instead presented with every listing on the entire file.

Had we not taken the time to design in debuggers while we were modifying the code, we would now have to stop, retrace all of our steps, and insert a series of debuggers. Fortunately, all that we have to do now is "throw the debug switch" on our already existing debuggers and then rerun the program:

```
RUN
IS THIS A DEBUG RUN? Y OR N ?Y
TYPE R TO RETRIEVE AND F TO FILE
R
PREPARE TAPE UNIT 1 FOR READING FROM:FILES
WHAT HEADING DO YOU WANT TO SEARCH FOR?
```

Our new method of searching opens up avenues of selection which were unavailable to us in the original version. We can enter any substring we like, and if it is contained in the record on file, then that record will be retrieved. Suppose, then, that we search for all recordings of piano concertos. In the shorthand which we were forced to adopt because of memory space restrictions, piano concerto appears as CNCRTO/PNO, precisely 10 characters long. Thus we type in:

```
WHAT HEADING DO YOU WANT TO SEARCH FOR?
CNCRTO/PNO
```

The tape begins to move and soon the first debugger appears:

```
READER SAYS A$=SAINT-SAENS      PIANO CONCERTO NO 2
                ENTREMONT, ORMANDY/PHILADELPHIA ORCHCNC
RTO/PNORCOLMS6778      S
```

Almost as soon as it appears, though, it disappears, and is replaced by:

```
SNAPSHOT CALLED FROM SUBROUTINE SEARCH
AND FROM LINE 3090
A$ SAINT-SAENS      PIANO CONCERTO NO 2
    ENTREMONT,ORMANDY/PHILADELPHIA ORCHCNCRTO/PNORCO
LMS6778    S
E$ W$
X$ X2$ Y$ Y2$ Z$ Z2$
X 0 X2 0 Y 0 Y2 0 Z 0 Z2 0
J1 0 J2 0 N 0 N2 0
?
```

The snapshot waits patiently for us to read it, thanks to the trick we learned in Chapter 7. We can see that A$, the first record read in from the master tape file, is as it should be. The snapshot was taken at line 3090 in subroutine SEARCH, and it is not until line 3130 that E$ is filled with selected records:

```
3130 LET E$=E$+A$
```

Thus, even though the first record contains the keyword (CNCRTO/PNO) that we are searching for, we would not expect to find it in E$ yet. We type a *return* to continue execution. Almost instantly, the following appears:

```
READER SAYS A$=BEETHOVEN      SYMPHONY NO 6      (PASTO
RAL)              KLEMPERER/VIENNA SYM                  SY
MPHONYRYORPL6960      M
```

Once again, however, before we can get more than a fleeting glimpse of the printout, it vanishes and in its place we see:

```
SNAPSHOT CALLED FROM SUBROUTINE SEARCH
AND FROM LINE 3090
A$ BEETHOVEN      SYMPHONY NO 6 (PASTORAL)
KLEMPERER/VIENNA SYM              SYMPHONY   RYORP
L6960      M
E$ SAINT-SAENS      PIANO CONCERTO NO 2
```

```
      ENTREMONT,ORMANDY/PHILADELPHIA ORCHCNCRTO/PNORCO
LMS6778   S
W$
X$ X2$ Y$ Y2$ X$ Z2$
X 0 X2 0 Y 0 Y2 0 Z 0 Z2 0
J1 0 J2 0 N 0 N2 0
?
```

Before we address ourselves to this new snapshot, suppose we understand why the diagnostic printout from subroutine READER remains on the CRT screen for so short a time.

Subroutine READER is entered from subroutine SEARCH:

```
3000 REM SUBROUTINE SEARCH
      —



      —
3080 GOSUB 1000
```

Once in subroutine READER, the first task the program performs, after a valid read operation, is to print out a diagnostic (if the debug switch is on):

```
1000 REM SUBROUTINE READER
      —



      —
1030 READ #1;A$
      —



      —
1045 IF D=1 THEN PRINT "READER SAYS A$=";A$
```

Control then returns to subroutine SEARCH; and, a few lines after the call to subroutine READER:

3095 IF D=1 THEN LET N$="SEARCH":LET L2=3090:GOSUB 9000

The colon (:) allows more than one statement to be placed on a line. In the case of an IF–THEN statement, the use of a colon means that if the condition is true, all commands on the one line will be executed; if the condition is false, execution transfers to the next line.

The snapshot coming so close on the heels of the diagnostic from READER explains the latter's short lifespan; the first statement of the snapshot routine is a command to clear the screen:

9010 PRINT "&K"

If we want the READER diagnostic (and all of the other diagnostics, for that matter) to remain visible on the CRT screen for any length of time, then we should borrow a hint from the chapter on snapshots and append the following to each designed-in debugger:

:INPUT Q$

For READER we would thus have:

1045 IF D=1 THEN PRINT "READER SAYS A$=";A$:INPUT Q$

A couple of subroutines make use of the debug routine which we wrote into subroutine WRITER. For these subroutines (FORMIN, FORMOUT, and WRITER) we might add the following line to the diagnostic routine beginning at line 2070:

2070 REM WRITER DIAGNOSTICS

—

—

2105 INPUT Q$
2110 RETURN

Returning to the snapshot, then, we see that the record which once resided in A$ as a result of the previous READ statement has now been transferred to E$, since it contains the keyword CNCRTO/PNO. A$ con-

tains the result of the current READ statement, and we note that it agrees
with the diagnostic from subroutine READER.

We type in a carriage return to continue execution:

```
READER SAYS A$=TCHAIKOVSKY      SYMPHONY NO 4
                    ORMANDY/PHILADELPHIA ORCH          CRC
AARK1-0665 S
```

Again the diagnostic quickly disappears, but we know now how to correct it the next time. The snapshot follows:

```
SNAPSHOT CALLED FROM SUBROUTINE SEARCH
AND FROM LINE 3090
A$ TCHAIKOVSKY      SYMPHONY NO 4
   ORMANDY/PHILADELPHIA ORCH        CRCAARK1-0665 S
E$ SAINT-SAENS      PIANO CONCERTO NO 2
   ENTREMONT,ORMANDY/PHILADELPHIA ORCHCNCRTO/PNORCO
LMS6778      SBEETHOVEN      SYMPHONY NO 6 (PASTORAL)
                KLEMPERER/VIENNA SYM                    SYMPH
ONY   RYORPL6960      M
W$
X$ X2$ Y$ Y2$ Z$ Z2$
X 0 X2 0 Y 0 Y2 0 Z 0 Z2 0
J1 0 J2 0 N 0 N2 0
?
```

Our designed-in debuggers are doing their jobs well, for here we see
the evidence of our bug and perhaps even the clues which will lead to its
eradication. We observe that E$ now has two entries, although only the
first, the Saint-Saens piano concerto, is valid. Somehow, all records are
being appended to E$ whether they contain the keyword or not.

Closer inspection of the snapshot reveals another puzzling development: W$ is supposed to be the keyword as entered from the console, but
it is displayed as a blank. Perhaps in the snapshot routine we committed
a typographical error:

```
9000 REM SNAPSHOT
```
___

—

9050 PRINT "E$";E$;"W$";W$

Both the label and the variable are correct. Suppose we check sub-routine SEARCH, the subroutine responsible for accepting the keyword from the console:

3000 REM SUBROUTINE SEARCH

—

—

3050 PRINT "WHAT HEADING DO YOU WANT TO SEARCH FOR?"
3060 LET E$=""
3070 INPUT C$
3080 GOSUB 1000
3090 IF L2$="EOF" THEN GOTO 3150
3095 IF D=1 THEN LET N$="SEARCH":LET L2=3090:GOSUB 9000
3100 SEARCH C$,A$,R

We have found the bug. We are reading in C$ as the keyword instead of W$, and then testing (at line 3100) to determine if C$ is contained in A$. This in itself is not fatal, except for the fact that at line 3080, the next line after C$ is read in, control of program execution jumps to subroutine READER. We recall that under the revised scheme, C$ now stands for *composer*. Thus, even though we might have entered CNCRTO/PNO for C$ when we were asked for a keyword, the program promptly changed C$ to *Saint-Saens* after the first read. Every subsequent call to subroutine READER reinitialized C$ to the composer of the current work being read from the master file. Consequently, whenever a search of the current A$ was performed, C$ was always found to be a part of it. This in turn caused A$ to be appended to an ever-growing E$:

3100 SEARCH C$,A$,R
3110 IF R>0 THEN GOTO 3130

—

3130 LET E$=E$+A$

The cure is to replace the two occurrences of C\$ in subroutine SEARCH with the proper string variable, W\$.

We mentioned at the beginning of this chapter that one of the biggest challenges facing us when attempting to perform a significant program revision such as this one is being able to keep tabs on all of the many new and redefined variables. We have just seen an example of a situation where we were unable to keep track of all of the redefinitions, but thanks to our foresight when designing in a set of comprehensive diagnostic statements, the debugging task was relatively easy and straightforward.

PATCHES

There are situations when, despite our efforts to design and execute what we consider to be an intelligent and well-structured program, bugs appear that are either very elusive to understand or are very difficult to fix. On such occasions the programmer must often resort to a technique known as *patching*. Usually, when we speak of debugging we refer to the process of identifying a bug, tracing it to its source, and then correcting the problem. When we resort to patching a program, however, we are treating the symptoms rather than the cause; patches are not therefore a debugging technique in the strictest sense, yet they find common use in many debugging efforts.

Patches may at first seem like the easy way out; but in fact, they require a firm understanding of the code they are being applied to. Suppose we traced a bug to the following fragment of code:

```
1720 LET X2=SQR(32*Y)/M
1730 IF X2>10 THEN GOSUB 1500
```

Suppose further that we discovered that the bug that caused the program to fail is that the variable M occasionally takes on a negative or zero value. We might select any one of the following patches to use for the program:

1. `1715 IF M<=0 THEN LET M=1`
2. `1715 IF M<=0 THEN LET M=−M`
3. `1715 IF M<=0 THEN LET X2=1:GOTO 1730`

The list of possible patches is almost limitless. We might have the program do any number of tasks if M is less than or equal to 0; but any change we make with our patch, even if it seems as harmless as setting M equal to 1, will have repercussions later on in the program. The challenge when using patches is to make a change that will not only cure the symptoms being caused by the bug, but that will have the fewest and least damaging effects at subsequent points in the program.

EXAMPLE: MONITORING ROOM TEMPERATURE

Consider the following situation:

> We have been asked by a local company to computerize the environmental control in its new office building. The building is divided into four sections, each with its own heating and air-conditioning units. The optimum environmental temperature for office work is 74°F.

Suppose we accept the assignment and, upon further investigation, learn that each of the four work areas has its own temperature sensor, which reads in degrees Fahrenheit, to give us our monitor input. We also learn that interfacing has already been taken care of; we need only to place a value on one of the SOL's output ports (as we did in Chapter 1 when we controlled the model railroad) and the rest will be taken care of.

With the preliminaries decided, our next step is to draw up a flowchart, as in Fig. 9-1. We note that the flowchart is very straightforward; the entire program is essentially no more than one great loop, endlessly cycling through itself. Each sensor in turn is queried as to the temperature of its control space, and that reading is compared with the status of the corresponding air-conditioning and heating units. Based on the sensor inputs and the heater and air-conditioner status flags, either the heater is turned on and the air conditioner is turned off, or the air conditioner is turned on and the heater is turned off, or no action at all is taken.

The program is as follows:

```
10 REM TEMPERATURE CONTROL PROGRAM
20 REM FOR ACME WIDGETS INC.
30 REM I=SENSOR INDEX
40 REM J=HEATER INDEX
50 REM K=COOLER INDEX
60 REM PORTS 1-4: SENSORS
```

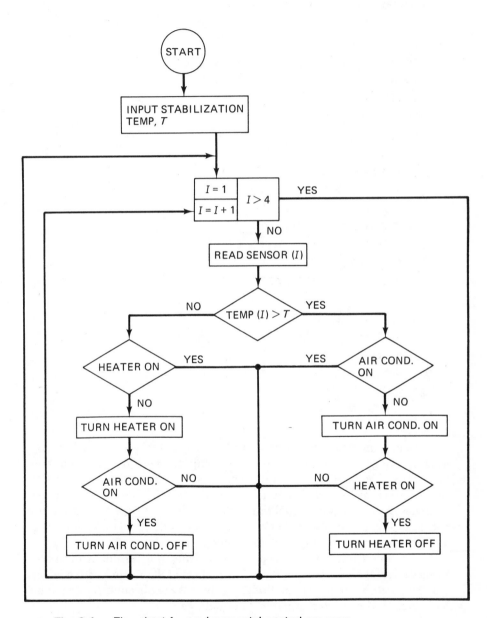

Fig. 9-1.   Flowchart for environmental control program.

```
70 REM PORTS 5-8:HEATERS
80 REM PORTS 9-12:COOLERS
90 PRINT "WHAT IS THE STABILIZATION TEMPERATURE?"
100 INPUT T
110 FOR I=1 TO 4
120 LET J=I+4
130 LET K=I+8
140 LET H=INP(J)
150 LET C=INP(K)
160 LET T2=INP(I)
170 IF T2>=T THEN GOTO 230
180 IF H=1 THEN GOTO 270
190 OUT J,1
200 IF C=0 THEN GOTO 270
210 OUT K,0
220 GOTO 270
230 IF C=1 THEN GOTO 270
240 OUT K,1
250 IF H=0 THEN GOTO 270
260 OUT J,0
270 NEXT I
280 GOTO 110
290 END
```

Tracing the program through, playing computer, we do not find any apparent bugs, and therefore load the computer with our program and type RUN. The interior temperature of the four offices starts out at 83°F, but as soon as our program takes over control, the air conditioner switches on and begins to cool things down. The president of Acme Widgets is happy, we receive a check for our labors, and everything looks like another success story for microcomputers.

Two hours later we get a phone call from the president of Acme Widgets saying that the offices have been alternately blasted with cold air and baked with hot air. To top things off, two of the air-conditioning units have broken down from apparent thermal overload.

Arriving at Acme Widgets, we hear the full story: For the first hour everything was fine as the air conditioners brought the temperature down to about 74°F. Suddenly one of the offices dropped below 74°, causing the heater to kick in to raise the temperature up to the stabilization point. The influx of warm air into the office displaced a large volume of cold air into one of the neighboring offices, causing it to become cooler than 74°F. This in turn caused the second office heater to engage.

Meanwhile, back in the first office the temperature sensor had been so placed that by the time the senor registered the stabilization temperature of 74°, the office itself was considerably warmer than that figure. The end result: a rolling hot and cold cycle moving from office to office. As each office approached stabilization, the effects of the neighboring office would be felt by the sensors and the system would attempt to compensate. But owing to the placement of the sensors, the compensation became overcompensation, which only fed and perpetuated the oscillations. Eventually, the temperature shifts became so sudden that the computer program was switching the air-conditioning units in and out of service so quickly that the compressors overloaded and caused the circuit breakers to open.

Sheepishly, we return to our program.

One thing to remember when using a computer to control real-world events is that the computer moves very fast in comparison to most natural events. This is especially the case with environmental control applications: the computer is querying the temperature sensors many hundreds of times each minute to see if the temperature has changed, yet it may take minutes for the air in a room to reach some sort of temperature equilibrium. During this time, drafts or eddies may cause the local air temperature around the sensor to fluctuate either over or under the stabilization point, causing the program to switch in hot or cool air, depending upon the conditions.

The bug in the program, then, is that we have a set of input parameters which cannot be controlled. When dealing with a human operator we can always have a bit of code which (1) tests to see if the input is acceptable, and (2) notifies the operator to try again if it is not. The difficulty with an environmental control program is that the inputs received from the sensors are all valid, but the rapidity of their fluctuations from one state to another causes the system as a whole to be unstable.

A patch is a convenient way to handle such a problem. We know why the program is failing, but there is no way for us to correct the basic cause of the bug: the physical realities of air mass mixing and convection. We therefore attack the problem from another angle; we patch the program in such a way as to minimize the random nature of the input data.

For example, one patch would have as its aim to slow down the program's cycling speed so as to smooth over and ignore short-lived temperature fluctuations. We cannot actually slow down the speed of execution, but we have previously come across a technique designed to throw stumbling blocks in the execution path and slow things down that way:

```
115 PAUSE 10
```

The statement is telling the program to pause during execution for 10 tenths of a second (or 1 second). One way we might make use of such a statement would be to use the statement as numbered, perhaps with a longer delay time:

```
115 PAUSE 50
```

Now, whenever the program reaches the top of the loop it will pause for 5 seconds before taking any readings and making any determinations based upon those readings.

We recall that one of the major items of caution involved with using patches is that we must always be on the alert for the consequences of our actions. Putting a pause statement in the program will certainly slow the rate of program execution, but will it solve the problem? Unfortunately, when programming for a real-time control application we cannot always make a change to the program and then run it to try it out. In the present situation, for example, it would look very bad for us if we were to reappear at Acme Widgets with a proposed solution for the bug if the air-conditioning units overloaded a second time. We might not get another chance.

To correctly and safely use a patch, therefore, we must have a solid enough understanding of the code and its function to be able to predict with reasonable certainty and effects of any patch we might make.

Suppose we try to predict the results of a pause statement. When we first begin the office temperature program, it will ask for the stabilization temperature and then wait 5 seconds before making the first set of measurements. Once the measurements are in (in less than 0.1 second), the program will decide whether the heater or the air conditioner should be turned on—or, if already on, whether they should remain on or be turned off. Immediately, the program branches back to the beginning of the loop to begin another traversal.

Before beginning the next pass through the loop, the program will again pause for 5 seconds. At the end of that time it will make the next pass through the loop; this process will be repeated indefinitely until the computer is turned off.

The problem of short-lived temperature fluctuations is still with us, however. We have slowed down the pace of the program only in the sense that we have separated periods of action by periods of inaction. We have no evidence to suggest that the temperature fluctuations will occur only during the pauses we've placed in the program. Fluctuations might just as well occur during the regular-speed passes through the measure-ment-and-control loop. That being the case, we are back to where we started from.

What we need to debug this program is a way to smooth out the minor temperature fluctuations to arrive at some average temperature reading for each sensor. One way to accomplish this might be:

```
153 LET T2=0
155 FOR L=1 TO 10
160 LET T2=INP(I)+T2
162 NEXT L
164 LET T2=T2/10
```

We now have the temperature reading set equal to the average of 10 consecutive readings. Still, however, the computer executes instructions so quickly that the 10 readings, which would require well under 1 second total to accomplish, might well be subject to the same short-lived temperature fluctuations. In order to spread our average out over a wider base, we could either take a much bigger sample—say 100 data points—or we could spread the 10 samples out over a longer time by using another pause, such as:

```
153 LET T2=0
155 FOR L=1 TO 10
157 PAUSE 10
160 LET T2=INP(I)+T2
162 NEXT L
164 LET T2=T2/10
```

By now we realize that physical phenomena, such as the air temperature in a group of offices, cannot be controlled as precisely as an event which takes place completely within the memory of the computer, such as the program in Chapter 3 which performed integer multiplication. We find, for example, that it is impractical to monitor room temperature on an instant-by-instant basis and to then apply corrections just as instantaneously, because the air mass in an office does not behave as a homogeneous whole.

Recognizing the limitation of our program, we also recognize that we would be unable to control the random natural events which in turn control the behavior of our program. The solution we adopt, then, is to use patches to treat the symptoms without correcting the causes of the bug.

ANOTHER EXAMPLE: DETERMINING STUDENTS' GRADES

Patches are so named because they are emergency stopgaps designed to bolster up "leaky" code. Frequently a program will be written that will function without problem for many applications—then suddenly a situation will arise which the designer had not anticipated, and the program will fail. Rather than rewrite the program (an alternative that would probably provide a stronger program but would also involve a fresh testing and debugging phase), the choice is made to code in a patch to take care of the special-case application and keep the program in service.

Consider the following example:

```
10 REM PROGRAM TO DETERMINE TEST GRADES
20 REM S=SCORE N=NUMBER AT THAT SCORE
30 DIM S(100), N(100)
40 LET I=1
50 INPUT "TEST SCORE?",S(I)
60 IF S(I)=900 THEN GOTO 100
70 INPUT "NUMBER RECEIVING THAT SCORE?",N(I)
80 LET I=I+1
90 GOTO 50
100 REM B1=SUM OF N*S
110 REM B2=SUM OF N
120 REM B3=SUM OF N*S*S
130 LET B1=0
140 LET B2=0
150 LET B3=0
160 FOR J=1 TO I
170 LET B1=B1+(S(J)*N(J))
180 LET B2=B2+N(J)
190 LET B3=B3+(S(J)*S(J)*N(J))
200 NEXT J
210 LET M=B1/B2
220 LET R=SQR((B3-B2*M*M)/(B2-1))
230 LET B=M+R
240 LET A=B+R
250 LET C=M-R
```

```
260 LET D=C−R
270 PRINT "A RANGES FROM";A;"TO 100"
280 PRINT "B RANGES FROM";B;"TO";A
290 PRINT "C RANGES FROM";C;"TO";B
300 PRINT "D RANGES FROM";D;"TO";C
310 PRINT "F RANGES FROM 0 TO";D
320 END
```

This program is supposed to determine the letter grade dividing lines for a sample of test scores (the flowchart for the program is in Fig. 9-2). The structure of the program is not complicated; pairs of grades and number of students receiving that grade are entered from the keyboard. The pairs of numbers continue to be accepted until a value of 900 is read in as a score. This terminates the data collection phase of the program and moves the processing to the data manipulation phase. In this phase a mean score M is calculated as well as the standard deviation from that score R. The letter grade dividing lines are calculated from the mean and the standard deviations.

Suppose we test the program on some typical test scores:

Data Set No. 1

Score	Number of Students Receiving Score
10	1
20	2
30	6
40	9
50	10
60	9
70	6
80	2
90	1

Running the program, we would find:

```
A RANGES FROM 84.5 TO 100
B RANGES FROM 67.3 TO 84.5
C RANGES FROM 32.7 TO 67.5
D RANGES FROM 15.5 TO 32.7
F RANGES FROM 0 TO 15.5
```

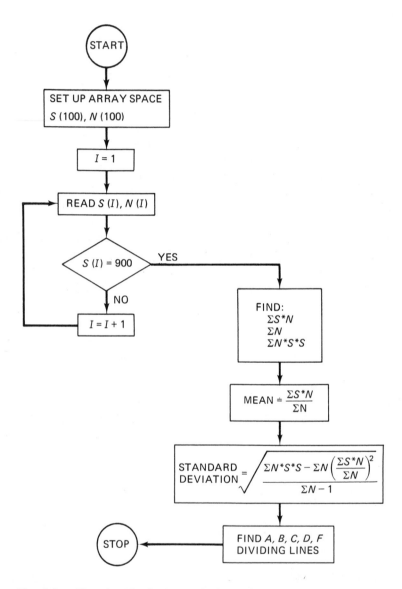

Fig. 9-2. Flowchart for letter grade determining program.

Number of students

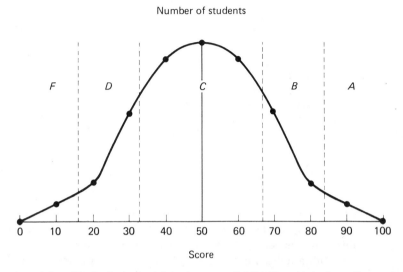

Score

Fig. 9-3. Typical students' test score distribution. Note how it approximates a bell-shaped curve. (Data Set No. 1 is displayed.)

The numbers look reasonable, and if we transfer them to a graph as in Fig. 9-3 we can confirm their correctness. Figure 9-3 illustrates a very important point about this particular program: the grade-finding program is based on the assumption that every group of students' test scores will, when graphed, closely approximate the statistically average bell-shaped curve. The program works well because the assumption is almost always valid, even for most normally encountered deviations.

Consider the following two sets of data:

Data Set No. 2

Score	Number of Students Receiving Score
25	2
40	4
50	7
60	10
70	9
80	6
90	2

Data Set No. 3

Score	Number of Students Receiving Score
10	1
20	4
30	7
40	9
50	5
60	3
70	1
80	1

Figure 9-4 illustrates what these two curves look like. We can see that while they both approximate the standard bell-shaped curve in general outline, neither one is centered around the score of 50, nor is either curve symmetrical. Nonetheless, we find upon running the program that it is sufficiently strong to deal with aberrations such as these and still yield usable results:

For Data Set No. 1

A RANGES FROM 92.9 TO 100

B RANGES FROM 77.1 TO 92.9

C RANGES FROM 45.4 TO 77.1

D RANGES FROM 29.6 TO 45.4

F RANGES FROM 0 TO 29.6

For Data Set No. 3

A RANGES FROM 71.4 TO 100

B RANGES FROM 55.7 TO 71.4

C RANGES FROM 24.3 TO 55.4

D RANGES FROM 8.6 TO 24.3

F RANGES FROM 0 TO 8.6

Comparison of the three examples of data sets points up some interesting differences and similarities. We know from the program listing that the various letter-grade divisions are all computed with reference to M, the mean value, and R, the standard deviation. It is therefore an easy-

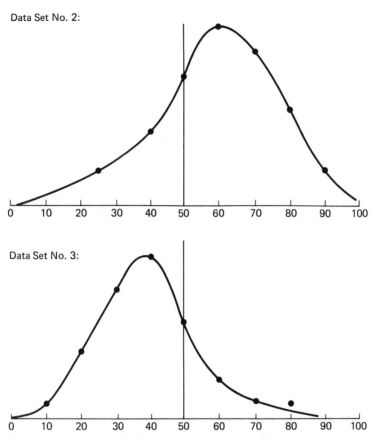

Data Set No. 2:

Data Set No. 3:

Fig. 9-4. Two examples of shifted data samples that are nonetheless handled successfully by the grading program.

enough exercise to work backwards from the printed output to determine what the values M and R were in each case.

Data Set No. 1

MEAN = (32.7+67.5)/2

= 100.2/2

= 50.1

STANDARD DEVIATION = 67.5−50.1

= 17.4

Data Set No. 2

MEAN = (45.4+77.1)/2

= 122.5/2

= 61.25

STANDARD DEVIATION = 77.1−61.25

= 15.75

Data Set No. 3

MEAN = (24.3+55.4)/2

= 79.7/2

= 39.85

STANDARD DEVIATION = 55.4−39.85

= 15.55

In all three cases the standard deviation is about 16 points in either direction from the mean value. The mean value, in contrast, is not at all the same value for each of the three examples, but its relevance to the data sets is clearly pointed out in Fig. 9-5, which superimposes the mean value as well as the letter grade dividing lines on top of the already presented curves of the three data sets.

We note that the mean value seems to fall on or near the maximum point of each curve, as would seem intuitively correct. In actuality, the line drawn at the mean value divides the curve into the halves of equal area. Of what special significance is this to us? After all, the program makes the assumption (which we have found to be reasonable) that for most cases the data will assume the general outline of a symmetrical bell-shaped curve. But consider the following example:

Data Set No. 4

Score	Number of Students Receiving Score
20	1
30	2
40	2
50	3
60	4
70	6
80	9
90	8
95	5
100	1

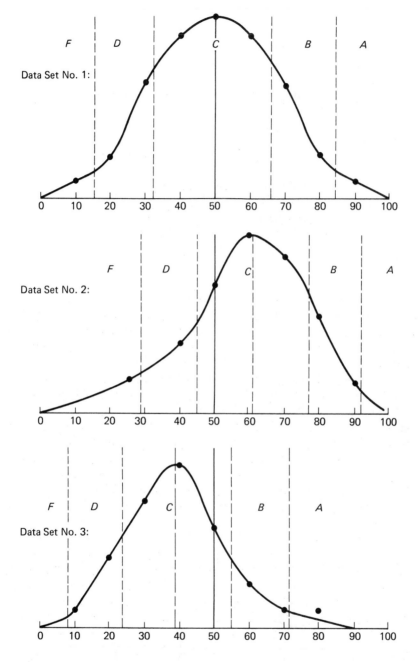

Fig. 9-5. Data Sets 1, 2 and 3 plotted with letter grade divisions superimposed. Note that in all cases the mean value closely approximates the maximum value.

The curve which represents this data is shown in Fig. 9-6. Note how the curve has been shoved over (skewed) onto the high end of the graph. In physical terms, the curve is telling us that for the examination in question, a disproportionate number of students scored very well. While the situation might be unusual it is by no means impossible and should therefore be provided for in the design of the grading program.

The output is as follows:

A RANGES FROM 113.9 TO 100
B RANGES FROM 93.4 TO 113.9
C RANGES FROM 52.2 TO 93.4
D RANGES FROM 31.7 TO 52.2
F RANGES FROM 0 TO 31.7

Obviously, this situation has not been provided for in the program. Mathematically, however, the program is correct; there is no bug of the sort we usually associate with malfunctioning programs. What we need is a patch to deal with the rare special occasion when data describing a highly skewed curve is fed into the program. The problem now is to determine what sort of patch should be instituted.

Suppose we begin by doing to this data set what we did to the three previous—working backwards from the printed result to discover the mean and standard deviation values:

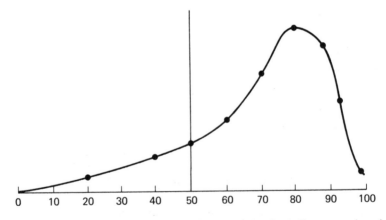

Fig. 9-6. The curve for Data Set No. 4. Note how the curve has been pushed over (skewed) to the high end of the graph.

Data Set No. 4

MEAN = (52.2+93.4)/2

$\quad\quad\quad$ = 145.6/2

$\quad\quad\quad$ = 72.8

STANDARD DEVIATION = 93.4−72.8

$\quad\quad\quad\quad\quad\quad\quad\quad\quad$ = 20.6

Immediately we can see that the standard deviation is not in line with the three previous examples, and a look at Fig. 9-7 tells even more. Before, the mean value calculated by the program had been very close to the maximum point on the curve. This was especially true for data set No. 1, which was a perfectly symmetrical group of data, and it continued to be true for data set Nos. 2 and 3 which, while not symmetrical, at least approximate a bell-shaped curve.

Data set No. 4, however, is very asymmetrical and the mean value reflects this deviation; it is significantly different from the maximum value of the curve. We now have a little more information than we did when we started, but the question still remains: What sort of patch should we use to correct the problem?

Actually, there is nothing we can do to modify the input to the program, since the input corresponds to a real event and cannot be modified. We might try some additional manipulation of the data once it is inside the program, but that would involve making additional assumptions (or modifying our original assumptions) regarding the statistical distribution

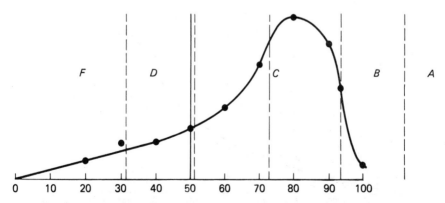

Fig. 9-7. Data Set No. 4 (skewed data) with grade divisions and mean value line superimposed. Note that the mean value is now significantly different from the maximum value (as compared to previous examples).

of test scores and the validity of methods based upon those distributions to determine letter grades. The mean-versus-standard-deviation method is one well-accepted approach; we must consider how a potential patch would affect that method.

Suppose we were to attempt the patch diagrammed in Fig. 9-8. It keeps all of the values on-scale but note how artificial the top-end divisions look; we would have to determine if this is an acceptable deviation from the mathematically determined values. The danger here is that our patch must include a warning which could be printed out each time the special coding is invoked. If it does not, the figures thus computed, since they are apparently computed by a program based on a supposed fair and equitable method of grade determination, might assume an undeserved air of respectability—to someone's possible harm.

Patches, because they are usually written to address the special-case occurrence, should always be clearly identified both inside the program and next to any output which they produce. Thus:

```
261 IF A<=100 THEN GOTO 270
262 LET S=100−M
263 LET R2=S/3
264 LET B=M+R2
265 LET A=B+R2
266 PRINT "**NOTE**"
267 PRINT "DATA ORIGINALLY OUT-OF-RANGE"
```

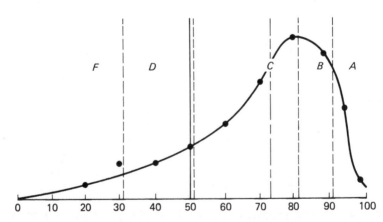

Fig. 9-8. Restructured grade divisions superimposed upon skewed data set. Note how the patch has artificially weighted the high end of the graph (above the mean score line).

```
268 PRINT "NEW BOUNDARIES COMPUTED"
269 PRINT "**NOTE**"
```

and the resulting printout for data set No. 4 would look like:

```
**NOTE**
DATA ORIGINALLY OUT-OF-RANGE
NEW BOUNDARIES COMPUTED
**NOTE**
A RANGES FROM 90.9 TO 100
B RANGES FROM 81.9 TO 90.9
C RANGES FROM 52.2 TO 81.9
D RANGES FROM 31.7 TO 52.2
F RANGES FROM 0 TO 31.7
```

Of course, not all patches must "fix" a particular program, especially when (as in this case) the patch makes such a severe modification of the program that the original rationale is sidetracked. In other words, it is sometimes most honorable if the patch does no more than admit defeat when defeat is obvious:

```
261 IF A<=100 THEN GOTO 270
262 IF D>=0 THEN GOTO 270
263 PRINT "SORRY, DATA IS TOO FAR OUT OF RANGE"
264 PRINT "AND CANNOT BE SUCCESSFULLY TREATED"
265 PRINT "SUGGEST YOU RESORT TO"
266 PRINT "HUMAN INTERPRETATION OF RESULTS"
267 GOTO 320
```

A FINAL EXAMPLE: TEACHING MUSICAL SCALES

Not all patches are written to help a program accommodate unexpected or uneven input from the real world, nor do all patches require potential compromise in the rationale of a particular program's construction. Consider the following program intended to teach musical scales. A look at the flowchart depicted in Fig. 9-9 helps to explain the program's operation.

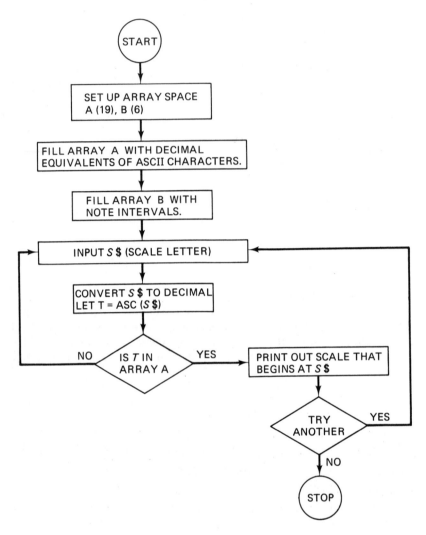

Fig. 9-9. Flowchart for music scale spelling program.

```
10 DIM A(19),B(6)
20 DATA 67.32,67.35,68.98,68.32,68.35,69.98
30 DATA 69.32,69.35,70.32,70.35,71.98,71.32
40 DATA 71.35,65.98,65.32,65.35,66.98,66.32,66.35
50 DATA 3,3,2,3,3,3
60 FOR I=1 TO 19
70 READ A(I)
```

```
80 NEXT I
90 FOR J=1 TO 6
100 READ B(J)
110 NEXT J
120 PRINT "WELCOME TO LEARN-A-SCALE"
130 PRINT "REPRESENT SHARPS WITH A SHIFTED 3 (#)"
140 PRINT "AND FLATS WITH A LOWER CASE B (b)"
150 PRINT "WHAT SCALE WOULD YOU LIKE TO SEE?"
160 INPUT S$
170 LET S=LEN(S$)
180 IF S=2 THEN GOTO 210
190 LET T=ASC(S$)+.32
200 GOTO 260
210 LET T1$=S$(1)
220 LET T2$=S$(2)
230 LET T1=ASC(T1$)
240 LET T2=ASC(T2$)
250 LET T=T1+T2/100
260 FOR I=1 TO 19
270 IF A(I)=T THEN GOTO 310
280 NEXT I
290 PRINT "SORRY, NO SUCH SCALE. TRY AGAIN":PAUSE 10
300 PRINT "&K"; GOTO 160
310 CURSOR 5,0
320 PRINT S$
330 CURSOR 5,3
340 FOR J=1 TO 6
350 LET K=3*J+3
360 LET N=B(J)
370 LET I=I+N
380 IF I>19 THEN LET I=I-19
390 LET T=A(I)
400 LET T1=INT(I)
410 LET T2=(T-T1)*100
420 SET DB=T1
430 SET DB=T2
440 CURSOR 5,K
450 NEXT J
```

```
460 PRINT S$
470 PRINT "ANOTHER SCALE? Y OR N"
480 INPUT B$
490 IF B$="Y" THEN PRINT "&K": GOTO 160
500 END
```

We associate the C-major scale with *do-re-mi-fa-sol-la-ti-do,* and it is "spelled" C-D-E-F-G-A-B-C. It is composed of seven notes, with one C on the bottom and another an octave higher on the top. Similarly, the G-major scale, for example, is spelled G-A-B-C-D-E-F#-G. The symbol F# stands for F sharp, and it represents a note which is one half-tone higher than the F appearing in the C-major scale. By the same token, there are notes which sound one half-tone lower than their root notes and they are called *flats,* marked by a *b.*

One curious quality about the spelling of musical scales is that some notes have dual identities. Thus we see, for example, in Fig. 9-10 that C# may also be considered Db. From a music theory viewpoint, the distinction is an important one, even though the scales C#-D#-E#-F#-G#-A#-B#-C# and Db-Eb-F-Gb-Ab-Bb-C-Db are the *same notes* when played on the piano. The two scales function differently, depending upon the key in a composition and may lead to entirely different tonal conclusions. A computer program which proposes to teach the spelling of musical scales must therefore take such nuances into account.

Another property of the musical scale is that the notes of a scale are not all equally spaced one from another. If we consider each key on the piano, whether black or white, to be half a step away from its neighbor, then we might consider a major scale to be laid out as follows:

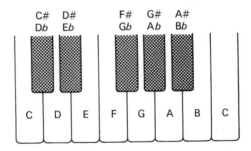

Fig. 9-10. The C-major scale as represented on the white keys of a piano. Some notes on the piano keyboard may take on variable identities, such as D#/Eb.

WHOLE STEP
WHOLE STEP
HALF STEP
WHOLE STEP
WHOLE STEP
WHOLE STEP
HALF STEP

This pattern is true for any major scale, no matter which key it begins on; and a successful music instruction program must also address this property.

Consider Fig. 9-11. It depicts all of the notes contained in one octave, including notes which have more than one identity, arrayed in a circle. We can see that by starting at any point on this circle and then following a clockwise path according to the whole-step–half-step pattern we can spell any of the major scales.

With the foregoing information as background we can now return to the program listing to determine more precisely how the program works. We begin with the data statements:

```
20 DATA 67.32,67.35,68.98,68.32,68.35,69.98
30 DATA 69.32,69.35,70.32,70.35,71.98,71.32
40 DATA 71.35,65.98,65.32,65.35,66.98,66.32,66.35
50 DATA 3,3,2,3,3,3
```

Lines 20, 30, and 40 are the decoded notes, while line 50 is the whole-step–half-step indexing pattern. The note values (which are later transferred into array A in lines 60 to 80) are the decimal equivalents of the ASCII alphabet, as follows:

A=65
B=66
C=67
D=68
E=69
F=70
G=71

In addition, to provide for all possibilities, all notes of the musical scale are considered in this program to consist of two characters and are

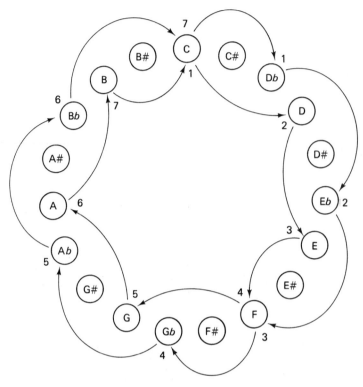

Inside: C D E F G A B C

Outside: D*b* E*b* F G*b* A*b* B*b* C D*b*

Fig. 9-11. One octave of notes on a piano keyboard arranged in a circle. By beginning at any note and travelling in a clockwise direction, any scale may be spelled out. In this diagram a whole step skips two notes, and a half step skips one note.

therefore represented as a two-digit whole number followed by a two-digit fraction:

$$A\# = 65.35$$
$$Db = 68.98$$
$$F = 70.32$$

according to the scheme

$$\# = .35$$
$$b = .98$$
$$\text{blank space} = .32$$

Whenever a letter is entered from the keyboard it is first converted to its decimal equivalent. It is then compared against all of the entries in array A to determine if it is a valid musical note:

```
160 INPUT=S$
170 LET S=LEN(S$)
180 IF S=2 THEN GOTO 210
190 LET T=ASC(S$)+.32
200 GOTO 260
210 LET T1$=S$(1)
220 LET T2$=S$(2)
230 LET T1=ASC(T1$)
240 LET T2=ASC(T2$)
250 LET T=T1+T2/100
260 FOR I=1 TO 19
270 IF A(I)=T THEN GOTO 310
280 NEXT I
290 PRINT "SORRY, NO SUCH SCALE. TRY AGAIN":PAUSE 10
```

We know from previous experience that when the computer accepts string-variable input from the keyboard it ignores trailing blanks. If we asked for the scale spelling of the key of D, for instance, S$ would be equal to D at line 160 which, if converted directly into decimal, would be 68. Certainly D is a valid note, but searching array A for its decimal equivalent of 68 would yield no match and would result in an error message (line 290). Therefore, line 190 takes all single-character entries and appends the decimal equivalent of a blank space onto them.

If an entry consists of two characters such as Bb, the block of code from lines 210 to 250 splits the two characters apart, separately converts each to its decimal value, and then recombines them into the four-digit number described earlier.

If this newly constructed number matches one of the numbers in array A, the computer proceeds to spell out the musical scale which begins with that note. Referring to Fig. 9-11, we realize that arranging the notes in a circle is a useful device for humans; but it is worthless to the computer, since data arrays in BASIC are linear, not circular. Suppose, for example, that we began at the top of the circle, at C, and counted clockwise around the circle. If we counted C as 1, then by the time we reached B# we would be at 19. Suppose we were to continue counting around the circle. 20 would bring us back to C, 21 would be C#, and 38 would be two revolutions around the circle, pointing again at B#. In

BASIC, however, if we reference A(19) we are pointing to B#, but if we reference A(21) we are pointing out-of-bounds—and execution halts on a fatal error.

The program gets around this difficulty by allowing us to conceptualize the notes in a circular array, while in actuality they are stored in an offset indexing and compensating scheme to stay within the confines of a 19-element array. For example, if we ask for the D-major scale, it converts the D of S$ into 68.32. Upon searching through array A the program finds that 68.32 occupies position 4 of the array; and using this value as its offset, it pulls consecutive increments from array B and adds them in sequence to the offset. In this way the program arrives at an index value which points to the next note in the scale of D-major.

We can play computer to see exactly how this works:

J (master loop index)	I (old pointer)	+	B(J) (increment)	=	I (new pointer)	A(I) (note)
1	4		3		7	E
2	7		3		10	F#
3	10		2		12	G
4	12		3		15	A
5	15		3		18	B
6	18		3		2	C#

We can see how linear array A is made to act as though it were circular. If I, the index variable that points to the notes in array A, becomes greater than 19 (the number of elements in array A) then I is reduced by 19. This has the effect of resetting the index pointer to the beginning of the array. The letter which names the scale, called the root (in this case D) is printed out separately before and after the loop indexed on J is executed, yielding:

D-E-F#-G-A-B-C#-D

Suppose we run the program:

```
RUN
WELCOME TO LEARN-A-SCALE
REPRESENT SHARPS WITH A SHIFTED 3 (#)
AND FLATS WITH A LOWER CASE B (b)
WHAT SCALE WOULD YOU LIKE TO SEE?
?C
```

```
C D E F G A B C
ANOTHER SCALE? Y or N Y
?G
G A B C D E F# G
ANOTHER SCALE? Y OR N Y
?Ab
Ab Bb C Db Eb F G Ab
ANOTHER SCALE? Y OR N Y
?Gb
Gb Ab Bb B# Db Eb F Gb
```

Even if we were not musicians we should be able to recognize that the Gb scale printed out by the computer is incorrect; intuition alone should tell us that no letter should appear twice in an alphabet. In the Gb scale just presented, however, B appears twice, first as Bb then as B#; they are not the same note but they are the same letter, and that is incorrect.

A music textbook would list for us all of the major scales:

```
C  D  EF  G   A   B   C
   D  EF#G  A   B   C# D
      E F# G# A  B   C# D# E
         G  A   B   C   D   E   F# G
            A   B   C# D   E   F# G# A
               B   C# D# E   F# G# A# B
                  C# D# E# F# G# A# B# C#
                     F# G# A# B   C# D# E# F#
Db Eb F Gb Ab  Bb C   Db
   Eb F G  Ab Bb C   D   Eb
      F  G  A   Bb C   D   E   F
         Gb Ab Bb Cb Db Eb F   Gb
            Ab Bb C   Db Eb F   G   Ab
               Bb C   D   Eb F   G   A   Bb
                  Cb Db Eb Fb Gb Ab Bb Cb
```

Before we were to release this program as a valid music instruction aid we would first have to test its ability to correctly reproduce each one of the 15 major scales just listed. In doing so we would discover that the computer performs correctly on all but just two of the scales: Gb-major and Cb-major. We have just seen the results of a request to write out the Gb scale; asking for the Cb scale leads to something else entirely:

WHAT SCALE WOULD YOU LIKE TO SEE?
?Cb
SORRY, NO SUCH SCALE. TRY AGAIN

    If there is not a Cb in the program, there should be, since it is listed as one of the 15 major scales. Referring again to Fig. 9-11 we see that Cb is in fact not on the graph, and closer inspection tells us that another note in the Cb scale, Fb, is also not included.

    Suppose we try to correct this oversight by adding Cb and Fb to the circle of notes, as in Fig. 9-12. Now absolutely all of the notes in an octave are represented. The diagram on the inside of the circle of notes shows what happens when we trace out the scale of C on the circle: all of the letters of the scale are now equally spaced apart from each other around the circle.

    If we use the same spacing scheme and try to trace out the Cb scale we get:

Cb–Db–Eb–Fb–Gb–Ab–Bb–Cb,

which we can check against our reference book to establish its correctness. Suppose we use the same spacing scheme to trace out the scale of A, shown in Fig. 9-12 by the arrows. This yields:

A-B-C-D-E-F-G-A

which is incorrect.

    Indeed, if we use the listing of the 15 major scales as a guide, and trace out the various scales on the revised circle of notes we would discover the following:

Name of Scale	Note Pattern Around Circle of Notes
C	3-3-3-3-3-3-3
D	3-4-2-3-3-4-2
E	4-3-2-3-4-3-2
G	3-3-3-3-3-4-2
A	3-4-2-3-4-3-2
B	4-3-2-4-3-3-2

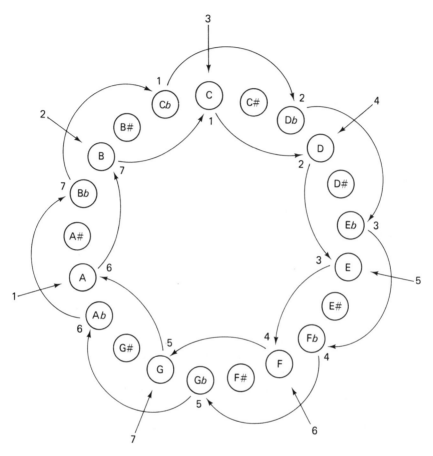

Inside: C D E F G A B C

Outside: C♭ D♭ E♭ F♭ G♭ A♭ B♭ C♭

Arrows: A B C D E F G A

Fig. 9-12.   Revised circle of notes, including all sharps and flats.

If we continued we would see that some of the patterns repeat; but clearly, if we were to use this method in our music instruction routine the program would require some extensive rewriting, and the result would not be nearly as clean as it is in its present state.

The best solution in this case, then, is to put in a patch and leave the rest of the program as it stands. The patch would only have to recognize the two special cases, G♭ and C♭; if either of those two notes were requested, the patch would skip all of the processing in the main body of the program and simply "brute force" an answer:

```
161 IF S$="Gb" THEN GOTO 462
162 IF S$="Cb" THEN GOTO 464
```

—

—

—

```
461 GOTO 470
462 PRINT "Gb Ab Bb Cb Db Eb F Gb"
463 GOTO 470
464 PRINT "Cb Db Eb Fb Gb Ab Bb Cb"
```

Before we leave the music instruction program we must attend to one other loose end. Our listing of major scales has only 15 entries, yet our circle of notes (the original version) numbers 19. If we further eliminate the two scales Cb and Gb, which we arrive at via brute force, it would seem to leave only 13 scales out of a potential 19. Where are the other six scales? If we ask for the scale of A#, for example, we would see:

```
WHAT SCALE WOULD YOU LIKE TO SEE?
?A#
A# B# Db D# E# Gb Ab A#
```

Actually, there is no such thing as an A#-major scale. If there were, it would have to be written thus:

$$A\# \ B\# \ C\#\# \ D\# \ E\# \ F\#\# \ G\#\# \ A\#$$

Because this scale must be written with double-sharped notes, it is not one of the 15 natural scales. Besides A#, rounding out the list of nonexistent major scales are B#, D#, E#, G#, and Fb. We might therefore want to include one additional patch which would recognize these impossible scales and take the appropriate action:

```
163 IF S$="B#" THEN GOTO 290
164 IF S$="D#" THEN GOTO 290
```

```
165 IF S$="E#" THEN GOTO 290
166 IF S$="G#" THEN GOTO 290
167 IF S$="Fb" THEN GOTO 290
—


—
290 PRINT "SORRY, NO SUCH SCALE. TRY AGAIN":PAUSE 10
```

With this final patch the music instruction program would be essentially debugged and ready to handle any situation.

We have seen in this chapter how patches are used to rescue a floundering program by forcing the code to handle specific situations which were not provided for by the original algorithm. Even with careful planning it often is very difficult for a programmer to see the problem from all possible sides and to provide for all possible applications to which the program must be put. Patches are therefore often used as a quick-and-dirty method of fixing up a program in the face of such unforeseen circumstances.

10.

PUTTING IT ALL TOGETHER

In the previous nine chapters we have examined a number of techniques for preventing, finding, and correcting errors (bugs) in a computer program; in this chapter we will integrate all that we have learned into a complete programming effort.

We begin with the specification:

> The program will simulate the ecological and environmental interactions between two competing groups. One group will be herbivorous (plant eating) while the other group will be carnivorous (meat eating). Group 1 will be prey to group 2. The program will provide tabular output describing group population sizes as a function of time.

We can now make up a list to amplify those aspects of the problem with which we feel the computer program might concern itself. We have been asked to construct an ecological/environmental model with the computer, and then to use that model to diagram and predict the results of a two-species interaction. The specification lists for us the three main elements of our model:

1. Quantity of plant life
2. Amount of species 1
3. Amount of species 2

We can expand each of these three main headings by listing below them the factors that affect and influence them:

1. Quantity of plant life
   1) Amount of land available to plants
   2) Quality of soil
   3) Amount and pattern of rainfall
   4) Amount and pattern of sunlight
   5) Number of destructive insects
2. Amount of species 1 (herbivores)
   1) Quantity of plant life
   2) Hunting pressure from animal group 2
   3) Birthrate
   4) Average natural lifespan
   5) Frequency and severity of disease
   6) Natural disaster (fire, flood, etc.)
3. Amount of species 2 (carnivores)
   1) Amount of animal group 1
   2) Birthrate
   3) Average natural lifespan
   4) Frequency and severity of disease
   5) Natural disaster (fire, flood, etc.)

Many of these subheadings are, in turn, influenced by additional factors, as well as by each other. For example:

> Amount of land available to plants
> is influenced by
>
> Amount of land occupied by animals,
> which in turn is influenced by
>
> Total number of animals,
> which is in part dependent upon
>
> Amount of species 1
> which, among other things, is influenced by
>
> Quantity of plant life
> which is a function of
>
> Amount of land available to plants.

Nothing in an ecological system functions with total independence: eliminating all of the pests in a section of cropland, for instance, might set off a disastrous chain reaction involving the birds which feed on those bugs, the mammals which feed on the birds, the parasites which depend upon the mammals, and so on.

For completeness, then, we would like our program to take into consideration all possible (or at least all relevant) interacting and competing influences. Unfortunately, such is not possible: not all relevant forces in any given ecological system are known, and for those which are known, scientists have an imperfect understanding of how they relate and even on how many levels they interact.

We will therefore have to make a number of simplifying assumptions when we construct our computer model of the two-species ecosystem. One way to do this is to separate the various parameters into two classes: those which are dependent upon each other, and those which are independent.

Thus we might say that the amount of species 2 would be dependent upon a number of factors, one of which is that species' birth rate. Yet for the purposes of our computer simulation, the birthrate will be established externally and will be independent of any influences from the program. This introduces inescapable artificiality into the simulation, which means that if the results are to be at all valid the simplifying assumptions which we make must at least be defensible.

In a way we are patching the program before it has even been written. We know from the outset that certain aspects of the program would be impossible to program correctly (with respect to the real world) because we do not know enough about the processes in nature to be able to accurately describe them for the computer. So we patch or brute-force that part of the problem based on our best guess as to what a reasonable value might be.

Suppose, therefore, that we classify the dependent and independent variables as follows:

Dependent Variables

Quantity of plant life
    Amount of land available to plants
    Grazing pressure from animal group 1
Amount of species 1
    Hunting pressure from animal group 2
Amount of species 2

Independent Variables

Plant life yield per unit area of land
Birth rate, group 1
Grazing pressure from group 1 (plants/animals)

Birth rate, group 2
Hunting pressure from group 2 (herbivores/carnivores)

In addition, we will want to classify some events as "chance" and will represent them in the program as being dependent upon some random-occurrence generator. Such "chance" items would include:

Frequency and severity of disease
Natural disaster (fire, flood, etc.)

By comparing this revised list with the original list, we can see that a number of factors which we at first determined to be significant have been left out:

Quality of soil
Amount and pattern of rainfall and sunlight
Number of destructive insects
Average natural lifespan for groups 1 and 2

These items have been cut from the program in the interest of simplification. Ideally, the assumptions we make when setting the values of the independent variables and when coding the mathematical relationships of the dependent variables will take into account these factors on the general level, at least, compensating for their not having been explicitly included.

Having discussed the preliminaries of the task we might return to the original specification and modify it to reflect our assessment of what can and cannot be reasonably done in a modest computer simulation. Thus we add to the original specification:

For the purpose of the simulation, environmental factors will be divided into interdependent, independent, and chance.

We would then list the factors which we had classified earlier.

Normally our next step would be to lay out a flowchart. For a simulation program, however, before we can arrive at any decisions about the order of statement we must plot out the interactions of the various subsections of code, as in Fig. 10-1. This figure clearly illustrates the distinction between dependent and independent elements: dependent elements have arrows flowing both towards and away from themselves, while independent elements have arrows which only flow away.

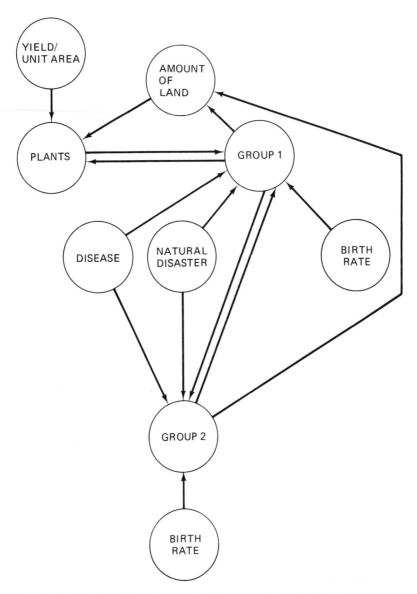

Fig. 10-1. Interaction diagram for the ecosystem simulation program.

Suppose from the block diagram in Fig. 10-1 we generate the flow-chart shown in Fig. 10-2. Note that we have identified the two groups in our simulation as moon rats and space bats. We could have used two more realistic groups such as rabbits and foxes, but such a choice would invalidate the design intention of the simulation program: to write a *general* program which simulates the gross interaction of a two-group system.

The resulting code might be as follows:

```
10 REM SIMULATION PROGRAM
20 REM SPACE BATS VS MOON RATS
30 LET L=10000,I=1,J=1,K=1
40 PRINT "TWO GROUP ECOSYSTEM SIMULATION"
50 PRINT "SPACE BATS VS MOON RATS"
60 PRINT "BATS EAT RATS AND RATS EAT PLANTS"
70 INPUT "INITIAL POPULATION OF RATS",R
80 INPUT "INITIAL POPULATION OF BATS",B
90 INPUT "RAT REPRODUCTION RATE(DAYS)",R1
100 INPUT "BAT REPRODUCTION RATE(DAYS)",B1
110 INPUT "NO. OF RATS/LITTER",R2
120 INPUT "NO. OF BATS/LITTER",B2
130 INPUT "RATS EATEN/BAT",R3
140 INPUT "PLANTS EATEN/RAT",P2
150 LET X=INT(10*RND(0) )
160 ON X GOTO 280,170,280,190,280,210,280,230,280
170 LET D=.1
180 GOTO 240
190 LET D=.2
200 GOTO 240
210 LET D=.3
220 GOTO 240
230 LET D=.4
240 LET X1=INT(10*RND(0) )/2
250 IF(10*X1)-(INT(X1) )*10=0 THEN LET D1=1 ELSE
LET D1=2
260 GOTO 290
270 REM NO DISASTER
280 LET D=0
```

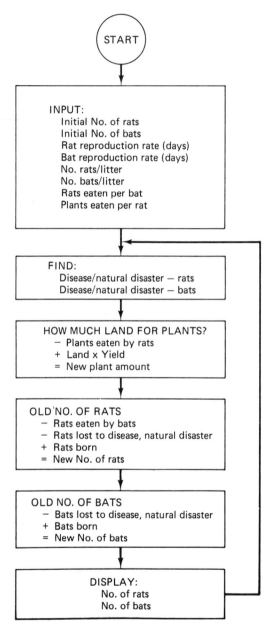

Fig. 10-2. Flowchart for two-species ecosystem model (Moon Rats vs. Space Bats).

```
290 LET L=L−(R*3.58E−8)−(B*1.07E−7)
300 LET P=P+(L*4E5)−(R*P2)
310 LET R=R−(B*R3)
320 IF I=R1 THEN LET I=0:LET R=R+(R*R2)
330 IF D1=1 THEN LET R=R−(R*D)
340 IF J=B1 THEN LET J=0:LET B=B+(B*B2)
350 IF D1=2 THEN LET B=B−(B*D)
360 PRINT "DAY, RATS VS BATS";K;R;B
370 LET I=I+1
380 LET J=J+1
390 LET K=K+1
400 GOTO 150
410 END
```

Before we can make any serious attempt to test this program we must first understand how it is written. We note, for example, that only eight of the 17 variables are described by internal documentation:

Variable	Description
R	Population of rats
B	Population of bats
R1	Rat reproduction rate (days)
B1	Bat reproduction rate (days)
R2	No. rats/litter
B2	No. bats/litter
R3	No. rats eaten/bat
P2	No. plants eaten/rat
X	?
D	?
X1	?
D1	?
L	?
P	?
I	?
J	?
K	?

If this simulation program belonged to someone else, and we came upon it "cold" and were asked to help debug it, we would likely find it very difficult to provide descriptions for the undocumented variables.

The variable X, for example, seems to have something to do with a random number:

150 LET X=INT(10*RND(0))

Once selected, X is used in a "computed GOTO" statement:

160 ON X GOTO 280,170,280,190,280,210,280,230,280

The flow of execution is switched down one of five different paths, depending upon the value of X. The difference in each path is the value to which the variable D is set, but since we also do not know the definition of variable D, the significance of the five paths is unclear.

Suppose we insert the following lines of documentation:

32 REM L=TOTAL LAND AREA AVAILABLE (SQ MILES)
34 REM I=RAT REPRODUCTION CYCLE COUNTER
36 REM J=BAT REPRODUCTION CYCLE COUNTER
38 REM K=INCREMENTING DAY COUNTER
155 REM X=RANDOM DETERMINATE FOR NATURAL DISASTERS
165 REM D=NATURAL DISASTER SEVERITY
245 REM X1=RANDOM SELECTION OF RATS OR BATS
255 REM D1=IF X1 IS EVEN, D1=1,RATS FEEL DISASTER
257 REM   IF X1 IS ODD, D1=2,BATS FEEL DISASTER
305 REM P=NO. OF PLANTS

Suppose further that we "verbalize" some of the equations. This technique is not often used, but in simulation or modeling programs, especially, it helps us as we try to place a real-world handle on the structured language of the mathematical statements. Thus

290 LET L=L−(R*3.58E−8)−(B*1.07E−7)

translates as: let the new quantity of land area available to the plants be equal to the old land area, minus the total area of land occupied by the rats and the bats put together. We also see in this equation two of the simplifying assumptions which we are forced to make: when computing the land area lost to rats and bats respectively, we assume 3.58×10^{-8} square

the statement would be executed it would produce a decimal fraction which could be used directly as the chance event severity coefficient.

Indeed, we may find that at some future time we may want to replace the original version with this one-line modification, but for the present we want to retain as much control over the program as possible. With the original version we can force the chance events variable into only one of five discrete values, rather than allow it to assume one of the many thousands of values generated by the RND function. Also, we have insured that the maximum amount of rats or bats lost to chance catastrophe will be limited to no more than 40%.

Before we move on to translating the mathematical sentences which describe the behavior of the bat population, we can see that, thanks to the documentation newly included in the program, we have discovered yet another error:

```
310 LET R=R−(B*R3)
320 IF I=R1 THEN LET I=0:LET R=R+(R*R2)
330 IF D1=1 THEN LET R=R−(R*D)
```

These three lines are the only lines which describe the changes that occur each cycle to the rat population, yet when we associate all of the variables with their definitions we find that nowhere does P, the number of plants, enter in. However, our group interaction diagram (Fig. 10-1) shows the number of plants as having a very definite effect upon the number of rats: if there are more rats than the plant population can support, the surplus rats can be expected to starve from lack of food.

Again we must make a simplifying assumption. In reality, if population outdistanced the food supply a general famine would result with only a small percentage of the population dying the first year (cycle), followed by a significantly increased percentage dying in the next year and years after if the famine persisted. However, we are already tied into the simplification that chance events which *do* occur last for only one cycle, and at no time do such events remove more than 40% of the population.

Suppose we adopt the following simplification in regard to the rat population/plant quantity balance:

```
IF R>P/P2 THEN LET R=.9*(P/P2)
```

We are saying that if the rat population is greater than the number of rats which the plant population can support (P/P2), then reduce the rat population to 9/10 of the maximum support number.

Having discovered a potential bug in the program, we have coded what we hope is a reasonable patch, but where in the program do we put it? Should it be inserted before line 310 where the rat population is adjusted to predation by bats, or after 310 and before 320 where the rat population is increased in response to the birthrate? Or perhaps after 320 and before 330, where the population decreases as a result of random natural disaster; or should it go at the end of all three lines?

Each suggested placement implies different interpretations of our understanding of the ecosystem we are trying to model; thus, each placement may lead to a significantly different outcome. Suppose we insert the patch between lines 310 and 320:

```
315 IF R>P/P2 THEN LET R=.9*(P/P2)
```

The computation of the bat population is handled similarly, except that bats are not subject to predation:

```
340 IF J=B1 THEN LET J=0:LET B=B+(B*B2)
350 IF D1=2 THEN LET B=B-(B*D)
```

In this case we are first increasing the bat population if the reproduction rate index matches the value supplied at the beginning of the simulation. We note that, as with the rats, we have made the simplifying assumption that every B1 number of cycles every member of the current bat population produces B2 number of offspring.

Line 350 refers to bat population losses resulting from chance natural disasters.

Comparing the code with the interaction diagram of Fig. 10-1, we notice that once again we have failed to include a necessary factor: the bat population is influenced by the size of the rat population in much the same way that the rats were influenced by the number of plants, yet the coded equations do not reflect this.

Realizing the implications of proper equation construction and placement, suppose we introduce the following statement:

```
335 IF B>R/R3 THEN LET B=.9*(R/R3)
```

All computer modeling schemes involve simplification, approximation, and in some cases, informed guesswork. This is especially true in our ecosystem simulation of moon rats vs. space bats; our goal is to illustrate general two-species interaction but in doing so we run the risk of simplifying ourselves to the level of nonsense. At the very least, we can expect a first trial execution of the program to exhibit a number of bugs.

Therefore, to save ourselves time and trouble later, we will now apply the techniques of earlier chapters and design in some debug snapshots which we can activate when the need arises.

Structurally, the program is short enough and simple enough that one snapshot routine will suffice; we have listed all of the pertinent variables but a short time ago. Quite the opposite of a tricky programming task, then, our snapshot routine will mainly be an exercise in clean, straightforward organization and display of diagnostic information.

One such design might be:

```
1000 REM SIMULATION SNAPSHOT
1010 REM ORGANIZE AND PRINTOUT
1020 REM ALL RELEVANT DATA
1030 PRINT "&K"
1040 PRINT "SNAPSHOT CALLED FROM LINE";Y
1050 PRINT "DAY=";K;"RAT INDEX=";I;"BAT INDEX=";J
1060 PRINT "RATS REPRODUCE EVERY";R1;"DAYS, YIELDING";
R2;"YOUNG"
1070 PRINT "BATS REPRODUCE EVERY";B1;"DAYS, YIELDING";
B2;"YOUNG"
1080 PRINT "BATS EAT";R3;"RATS, RATS EAT";P2;"PLANTS"
1090 PRINT "LAND FOR PLANTS=";L;"NO. PLANTS=";P
1100 PRINT "DISASTER SEVERITY=";D;"SELECTOR CODE=";D1
1110 PRINT "X=";X;"X1=";X1
1120 PRINT "NO. OF RATS=";R;"NO. OF BATS=";B
1130 INPUT Z$
1140 RETURN
```

Recalling the advice from earlier chapters regarding the placement of print statements and snapshots, and incorporating the changes already mentioned so far for this program, the revised listing looks as follows:

```
10 REM SIMULATION PROGRAM
20 REM SPACE BATS VS MOON RATS
```

```
30 LET L=10000,I=1,J=1,K=1
32 REM L=TOTAL LAND AREA AVAILABLE (SQ MILES)
34 REM I=RAT REPRODUCTION CYCLE COUNTER
36 REM J=BAT REPRODUCTION CYCLE COUNTER
38 REM K=INCREMENTING DAY COUNTER
40 PRINT "TWO GROUP ECOSYSTEM SIMULATION"
50 PRINT "SPACE BATS VS MOON RATS"
60 PRINT "BATS EAT RATS AND RATS EAT PLANTS"
70 INPUT "INITIAL POPULATION OF RATS",R
80 INPUT "INITIAL POPULATION OF BATS",B
90 INPUT "RAT REPRODUCTION RATE(DAYS)",R1
100 INPUT "BAT REPRODUCTION RATE(DAYS)",B1
110 INPUT "NO. OF RATS/LITTER",R2
120 INPUT "NO. OF BATS/LITTER",B2
130 INPUT "RATS EATEN/BAT",R3
140 INPUT "PLANTS EATEN/RAT",P2
145 INPUT "IS THIS A DEBUG RUN?(RETURN FOR NO)",Z$
147 IF Z$="" THEN LET Z=0:GOTO 150 ELSE LET Z=1
150 LET X=INT(10*RND(0) )
155 REM X=RANDOM DETERMINATE FOR NATURAL DISASTERS
157 IF Z=1 THEN LET Y=150:GOSUB 1000
160 ON X GOTO 280,170,280,190,280,210,280,230,280
165 REM D=NATURAL DISASTER SEVERITY
170 LET D=.1
180 GOTO 240
190 LET D=.2
200 GOTO 240
210 LET D=.3
220 GOTO 240
230 LET B=.4
240 LET X1=INT(10*RND(0) )/2
245 REM X1=RANDOM SELECTION OF RATS OR BATS
250 IF (10*X1)-(INT(X1) )*10=0 THEN LET D1=1 ELSE
LET D1=2
255 REM D1=IF X1 IS EVEN, D1=1, RATS FEEL DISASTER
257 REM IF X1 IS ODD, D1=2, BATS FEEL DISASTER
259 IF Z=1 THEN LET Y=250:GOSUB 1000
```

```
260 GOTO 290
270 REM NO DISASTER
280 LET D=0
290 LET L=L−(R*3.58E−8)−(B*1.07E−7)
300 LET P=P+(L*4E5)−(R*P2)
305 REM P=NO. OF PLANTS
310 LET R=R−(B*R3)
312 IF Z=1 THEN LET Y=310:GOSUB 1000
315 IF R>P/P2 THEN LET R=.9*(P/P2)
320 IF I=R1 THEN LET I=0:LET R=R+(R*R2)
325 IF Z=1 THEN LET Y=320:GOSUB 1000
330 IF D1=1 THEN LET R=R−(R*D)
332 IF Z=1 THEN LET Y=330:GOSUB 1000
335 IF B>R/R3 THEN LET B=.9*(R/R3)
340 IF J=B1 THEN LET J=0:LET B=B+(B*B2)
345 IF Z=1 THEN LET Y=340:GOSUB 1000
350 IF D1=2 THEN LET B=B−(B*D)
355 IF Z=1 THEN LET Y=350:GOSUB 1000:GOTO 370
360 PRINT "DAY, RATS VS BATS";K;R;B
370 LET I=I+1
380 LET J=J+1
390 LET K=K+1
400 GOTO 150
410 END
```

We are now ready to give our program a test run:

```
RUN
TWO GROUP ECOSYSTEM SIMULATION
SPACE BATS VS MOON RATS
BATS EAT RATS AND RATS EAT PLANTS
INITIAL POPULATION OF RATS?
```

As we know from previous chapters, choosing meaningful input values when initially testing a program is something of an art as well as a science. Common sense is always a good place to start, however, and in the present example it tells us that, to begin with, we probably do not want to have more bats than rats, nor even an equal number of each. Also, rats should reproduce faster and more heavily than the predator bats.

We might therefore continue as follows:

```
INITIAL POPULATION OF RATS 100
INITIAL POPULATION OF BATS 10
RAT REPRODUCTION RATE(DAYS) 2
BAT REPRODUCTION RATE(DAYS) 4
NO. RATS/LITTER 10
NO. BATS/LITTER 5
RATS EATEN/BAT 6
PLANTS EATEN/RAT 4
IS THIS A DEBUG RUN?(RETURN FOR NO) ?
```

If we answer yes to the last question, we will generate the snapshot debugger output which is referenced seven times in the simulation program. This could result in considerable quantities of output, so we decide for the present to avoid resorting to our designed-in debuggers unless absolutely necessary.

This is not a copout. In general, if a program can be debugged using only the programmer's tools of understanding, insight, and deduction, then it is only proper that it should be debugged that way. Among other things, such an approach weans the programmer away from an overdependence upon artifical aids and mechanical techniques. The more analytical brainwork a programmer invests in a particular routine, the less the likelihood of that routine exhibiting serious flaws.

We therefore hit a carriage return and the program continues:

```
DAY, RATS VS BATS 1     40      5.9999
BS ERROR IN LINE 240
```

Perhaps we made a typographical error when entering line 240, so we display the line and investigate:

```
240 LET X1 =INT(10*RND(0) )/2
```

Nothing appears to be wrong with line 240. RND(0) returns a randomly selected number, we multiply that number by 10, take the integer portion of that result, and divide it by 2 to determine if it is odd or even.

There is one possibility of error, however: the RND function returns numbers between 1 and 0. Suppose it returned 0.3478; the equation would be evaluated as:

$$RND(0) = 0.3478$$
$$10*RND(0) = 3.478$$
$$INT(10*RND(0)) = 3$$
$$INT(10*RND(0))/2 = 1.5$$

Suppose the value 0.0182 were returned:

$$RND(0) = 0.0182$$
$$10*RND(0) = 0.182$$
$$INT(10*RND(0)) = 0$$
$$INT(10*RND(0))/2 = 0/2 = ?$$

Division into zero should equal zero, but perhaps in this particular sort of mathematical construction the computer becomes confused and sends an error message. An easy way to check is to subdivide line 240 into a couple of shorter commands while at the same time putting in a patch which excludes all zero values:

```
240 LET T=INT(10*RND(0))
242 IF T=0 THEN GOTO 240
244 LET X1=T/2
```

We are ready to try again. The preliminary data input stage is the same as before, but the cycle-by-cycle listing has changed:

DAY, RATS VS BATS 1	40	4.799999
DAY, RATS VS BATS 2	123.20001	4.799999
DAY, RATS VS BATS 3	94.40001	3.8399999
DAY, RATS VS BATS 4	784.96012	23.04
DAY, RATS VS BATS 5	452.70408	23.04
DAY, RATS VS BATS 6	3459.1049	16.128
DAY, RATS VS BATS 7	2689.8695	16.128
DAY, RATS VS BATS 8	28525.117	96.768
DAY, RATS VS BATS 9	25149.158	96.768
DAY, RATS VS BATS 10	189177.83	96.768

Aside from the fact that this free-formatted output is messy and hard to read, and aside from the fact that there is no such thing as fractional rats or bats, it looks as though the program may be working. Both populations show a steady increase despite temporary setbacks due to natural disasters and predation.

The output form and the fractional rats and bats can be taken care of with a reworded print statement:

```
360 PRINT "DAY, RATS VS BATS"; %4I;K;%12I;R;B
```

The "%4I" and "%12I" establish formatted integer fields that are 4 and 12 characters wide, respectively. Running the program now yields:

```
DAY, RATS VS BATS 1               40
FO ERROR AT LINE 360
```

"FO" is a *field overflow* error, as explained in the SOL's Extended Cassette BASIC user's manual:

> An attempt has been made to print a number larger than extended BASIC's numerical field size.

Such an explanation hardly seems possible, since we know for a fact that the first time through the program the total bat population, which has not yet had a chance to be increased due to reproduction, cannot possibly be greater than 10. In an integer field of 12 characters we would not expect such a small number to cause an overflow.

If we refer to the user's manual for the precise description of the integer print specification, we find:

> Numbers will be printed in a field of width N. N must be between 1 and 26. If the value to be printed out is not an integer, an error message will be printed.

We seem to have found our bug. When we ran the program only two values were printed out:

```
DAY, RATS VS BATS 1               40
FO ERROR AT LINE 360
```

The integer 1 corresponds to day 1, and the integer 40 corresponds to 40 rats. The program bombed when it tried to print out the number of bats. Suppose, as in the first example, that B, the number of bats, was equal to 4.799999, a floating-point number rather than an integer. If such were the case, and in view of the user's manual discussion on integer formats, we would expect to see exactly what we did see.

If we wish to use an integer print format we must convert R and B to integers:

```
358 LET R=INT(R):LET B=INT(B)
```

Running the program with these changes, and using the same input data gives us:

DAY, RATS VS BATS 1	36	5
DAY, RATS VS BATS 2	66	4
DAY, RATS VS BATS 3	42	2
DAY, RATS VS BATS 4	330	12
DAY, RATS VS BATS 5	258	12
DAY, RATS VS BATS 6	2046	7
DAY, RATS VS BATS 7	1803	7
DAY, RATS VS BATS 8	19371	29
DAY, RATS VS BATS 9	19197	29
DAY, RATS VS BATS 10	209253	20

The output is considerably easier to read and we are at last dealing with whole rats and whole bats. Suppose we continue with the output:

DAY, RATS VS BATS 15	22754953	84
DAY, RATS VS BATS 16	250298940	302
DAY, RATS VS BATS 17	250297130	302
DAY, RATS VS BATS 18	2753248500	302
DAY, RATS VS BATS 19	1651948000	302
DAY, RATS VS BATS 20	18171408000	1812
DAY, RATS VS BATS 21	−2019155600	−302873340
DAY, RATS VS BATS 22	−2221071600	−199896440
DAY, RATS VS BATS 23	−613015800	−199896440
DAY, RATS VS BATS 24	6449990800	−1079440700
DAY, RATS VS BATS 25	−91953450	−1079440700

Previously we encountered fractional rats but now we have negative rats. Neither makes much sense. Referring to the program listing we can see that it is the negative rats which cause the bats to also be negative. This occurs at one of our original patches:

335 IF B>R/R3 THEN LET B=.9*(R/R3)

If the number of rats R becomes negative, then R/R3 will also be negative. The number of bats B will start out as a positive number, definitely greater than R's negative value. Thus the test at line 335 will be met and the number of bats will be reset to 0.9*(R/B), or:

B =0.9*(R/R3)
  =0.9*(−2019155600/6)
  =0.9*(−336525933.3)
  = −302873340

Checking with the output from the program, this is precisely the quantity of bats calculated for day 21. The patch for this can be fairly uncomplicated, the only difficulty being, once again, whether the simplifying assumption that we are being forced to make is going to be valid. Suppose we decide that if R ever becomes less than zero it should be reset to its initial value:

311 IF R<=0 THEN LET R=S

S is a storage variable which saves the value of R immediately after it is read in from the keyboard:

75 LET S=R

If we run the program now we get:

DAY, RATS VS BATS 1	28	4
DAY, RATS VS BATS 2	44	4
DAY, RATS VS BATS 3	20	2
DAY, RATS VS BATS 4	88	10

DAY, RATS VS BATS 5	25	3
DAY, RATS VS BATS 6	46	3
DAY, RATS VS BATS 7	28	3
DAY, RATS VS BATS 8	110	18
DAY, RATS VS BATS 9	2	0
DAY, RATS VS BATS 10	22	0
DAY, RATS VS BATS 11	22	0
DAY, RATS VS BATS 12	242	0

A relatively minor change to the program has resulted in a major change to its output. The rat population does not increase as dramatically as it did in the earlier example, but that could be due to chance events taking their toll. The bat population was reduced to zero by the ninth day and was unable to recover.

Normally this would be the time we would rerun the program with our debuggers turned on, but unfortunately that is the one thing we cannot do; every time we run the program we will get different results because of the two random number statements. We could try to force execution by writing in some statements that would bypass the random portions of the code, replacing them with exactly specified "chance" values. But there are 10 possible chance paths and 7 debug snapshots per cycle; since in the present example it took 8 cycles for the bug to show itself, the debug effort would be at the least tedious.

In this case our best bet is to play computer. We know that when the program reached line 360 of the eighth cycle the values of R and B were 110 and 18. The next cycle, cycle 9, would not be a reproduction cycle for either rats or bats (rats reproduce cycles 2,4,6,8,10, etc. and bats reproduce cycles 4,8,12,16, etc.), so the first thing the program would do in the new cycle is calculate a natural disaster severity quotient and determine which group, rats or bats, would be the group to suffer. Next, it would reduce the rat population by the amount lost through predation to the bats:

```
310 LET R=R−(B*R3)
```

We can substitute in our values for R and B from the previous cycle:

```
R = R−(B*R3)
  = 110−(18*6)
  = 110−108
R = 2
```

We calculate R to be equal to 2 at line 310. Since the print statement at line 360 shows the same value for R, we can deduce that whatever the severity coefficient (D), the rats/bats pointer (D1) was not equal to rats. We therefore bypass all the lines of code from 310 to 332, stopping at line 335:

335 IF B>R/R3 THEN LET B=.9*(R/R3)

The number of bats B equals 18, which is definitely greater than 2/6 or 0.33. The test condition is therefore met and we may calculate for ourselves:

$$B = 0.9*(R/R3)$$
$$= 0.9*(2/6)$$
$$= 0.9*.33$$
$$B = 0.3000$$

We recall that day 9 is not a reproduction day for bats, so B will not be increased by new additions. At best, if there are no chance natural disasters, we will be left with three-tenths of a bat—and even this meager sum would soon be erased because of the patch we put into the program earlier. We know from Chapter 9 that patches very often have serious consequences in places and in ways not originally anticipated, and this is one such case.

The culprit is line 358, the line we put in so that we could use the integer format when displaying our results:

358 LET R=INT(R):LET B=INT(B)

Clearly, if we take the integer portion of 0.30, we are left with zero. This explains our disappearing bats. What we need now is a patch similar to the one we used for negative rats:

352 IF B<=0 THEN LET B=S2

As before, S2 is a variable which stores the initial quantity of bats immediately after it is read in from the keyboard:

85 LET S2=B

We should now not expect to find any negative values for either rats or bats. Suppose we run the program once more:

```
RUN
TWO GROUP ECOSYSTEM SIMULATION
SPACE BATS VS MOON RATS
BATS EAT RATS AND RATS EAT PLANTS
INITIAL POPULATION OF RATS 100
INITIAL POPULATION OF BATS 10
RAT REPRODUCTION RATE(DAYS) 2
BAT REPRODUCTION RATE(DAYS) 4
NO. RATS/LITTER 10
NO. BATS/LITTER 5
RATS EATEN/BAT 6
PLANTS EATEN/RAT 4
IS THIS A DEBUG RUN? (RETURN FOR NO)
DAY, RATS VS BATS 1          40          5
DAY, RATS VS BATS 2          99          5
DAY, RATS VS BATS 3          69          5
DAY, RATS VS BATS 4         429         30
DAY, RATS VS BATS 5         249         27
DAY, RATS VS BATS 6         957         27
DAY, RATS VS BATS 7         795         18
DAY, RATS VS BATS 8        7557         64
DAY, RATS VS BATS 9        6455         64
DAY, RATS VS BATS 10      66781         64
```

So far things look good. Skipping ahead to day 20 we see:

```
DAY, RATS VS BATS 20        9565476300        6738
DAY, RATS VS BATS 21        5891331900        6738
DAY, RATS VS BATS 22       43534147000        6738
DAY, RATS VS BATS 23      −34519689000          10
DAY, RATS VS BATS 24      −29010886000          10
DAY, RATS VS BATS 25               90          10
DAY, RATS VS BATS 26              198          10
```

DAY, RATS VS BATS 27	138	9
DAY, RATS VS BATS 28	924	54
DAY, RATS VS BATS 29	420	54
DAY, RATS VS BATS 30	739	54

In spite of our last few patches the rat population has once again taken on a negative value. We note, however, that this time the negative rats did not drive the bat population figure negative also. It is a good bet that any bug this persistent would show up again if we were to rerun the problem, random execution paths or not. Therefore, suppose we turn on the snapshot debuggers, and try again:

RUN

—

—

IS THIS A DEBUG RUN?(RETURN FOR NO) YES

The screen clears and the first snapshot appears:

SNAPSHOT CALLED FROM LINE 150
DAY=1 RAT INDEX=1 BAT INDEX=1
RATS REPRODUCE EVERY 2 DAYS, YIELDING 10 YOUNG
BATS REPRODUCE EVERY 4 DAYS, YIELDING 5 YOUNG
BATS EAT 6 RATS, RATS EAT 4 PLANTS
LAND FOR PLANTS=10000 NO. PLANTS=0
DISASTER SEVERITY=0   SELECTOR CODE=0
X=8   X1=0
NO. OF RATS=100 NO. OF BATS=10
?

The snapshot displays all pertinent data and clearly labels all values to avoid ambiguities. There are no plants yet, since the snapshot was taken at line 150 and the number of plants is not computed until line 300. Similarly, the random disaster variables D, $D1$, and $X1$ are followed by zeros.

As the snapshots flash by, seven per cycle, it is a good idea for us to construct a table of values to follow the calculation's progress:

Day	Rats	Bats
1	40	10
2	24	3.6
3	26.4	3.6
4	10	3.888
5	100	3.1104
6	805.2422	3.1104
7	786.57984	2.79936
8	8467.6205	11.757312
9	8397.9766	11.757312
10	91591.86	11.757312
11	91521.316	7.054387
12	1006268.8	42.326322
13	1006014.8	42.326322
14	11063369	42.326322
15	7744180	42.326322
16	85183186	253.95793
17	51108997	253.95793
18	5.621822E8	253.95793
19	5.6218083E8	228.56214
20	6.1839741E9	959.961
21	5.5655715E9	959.961
22	6.1221223E10	959.961

Suddenly, after 157 snapshots, something quite unexpected shows up:

```
SNAPSHOT CALLED FROM LINE 320
DAY=23 RAT INDEX=1 BAT INDEX=3
RATS REPRODUCE EVERY 2 DAYS, YIELDING 10 YOUNG
BATS REPRODUCE EVERY 4 DAYS, YIELDING 5 YOUNG
BATS EAT 6 RATS, RATS EAT 4 PLANTS
LAND FOR PLANTS=7341.7608 NO. PLANTS=−2.0639957E11
DISASTER SEVERITY=0    SELECTOR CODE=1
X=3   X1=4
NO. OF RATS=−4.6439903E10 NO. BATS=959.961
```

Both the number of plants and the number of rats have gone negative. If we now expand our table of values and continue on, in a short while we learn something even more interesting:

Day	Line	Land	Plants	Rats	Bats
23	320	7341.7608	$-2.0639E11$	$-4.6439E10$	959.61
23	330	7341.7608	$-2.0639E11$	$-4.6439E10$	959.61
23	340	7341.7608	$-2.0639E11$	$-4.6439E10$	$-6.9659E9$
23	350	7341.7608	$-2.0639E11$	$-4.6439E10$	10
24	150	7341.7608	$-2.0639E11$	$-4.6439E10$	10
24	250	7341.7608	$-2.0639E11$	$-4.6439E10$	10
24	310	9004.3093	$-1.7030E10$	100	10
24	320	9004.3093	$-1.7030E10$	$-4.2169E10$	10
24	330	9004.3093	$-1.7030E10$	$-4.2169E10$	10
24	340	9004.3093	$-1.7030E10$	$-4.2169E10$	$-3.7952E10$
24	350	9004.3093	$-1.7030E10$	$-4.2169E10$	10
25	150	9004.3093	$-1.7030E10$	$-4.2169E10$	10
25	250	9004.3093	$-1.7030E10$	$-4.2169E10$	10
25	310	10513.982	$1.5584E11$	100	10

On day 22 there 6.12211×10^{10} rats. On day 23 there were supposedly minus 4.6439×10^{10} rats. We can trace the beginning of the trouble to line 300:

```
300 LET P=P+(L*4E5)-(R*P2)
```

The quantity of rats carried over from the previous day is 6.1×10^{10}, which combined with a land area of roughly 7342 (as we can see in our snapshot) caused the value of plants to go negative:

$$
\begin{aligned}
P &= P+(L*4E5)-(R*P2) \\
  &= P+(7342*4E5)-(6.1E10*6) \\
  &= P+2.94E9-3.66E11 \\
  &= P-3.63E11
\end{aligned}
$$

Working backwards from the printed value for P given in the snapshot ($-2.06E11$), we can deduce that at the time cycle 23 began there were only $1.57E11$ plants available, not enough to offset the imaginary negative plants calculated by the program.

We were tripped up by another one of our previous patches, at line 315. Negative plants caused negative rats:

```
315 IF R>P/P2 THEN LET R=.9*(P/P2)
```

Variable R came into line 315 as a positive value, which caused the condition to be met and R to become negative. We recall that we wrote line

315 into the program to guard against overgrazing by a too-high rat population, and we see again that a patch does not operate in a vacuum: a patch may later have consequences quite unforeseen at the time it is installed.

A few lines later, at line 335, the negative value of R causes the bats to become negative also, as we saw in our expanded table of snapshots printouts:

335 IF B>R/R3 THEN LET B=.9*(R/R3)

Fortunately the bats are saved by the zero-or-minus value clamp we installed at line 352:

352 IF B<=0 THEN LET B=S2

If we look more closely at our expanded table of values we note a few inconsistencies. For example, the table indicates a snapshot taken at line 350; this was true in the original version of the program before we installed the zero-or-negative value clamp at line 352. For clarity's sake we should really change line 355 to read:

355 IF Z=1 THEN LET Y=352:GOSUB 1000:GOTO 370

The proper line number would then be displayed in the snapshot. A similar situation exists for the snapshot called at line 335.

The rats were not caught because even though we installed a similar zero-or-minus value clamp for R we did so at line 311, just two lines *before* R became negative.

It takes two cycles for the program to correct itself, and it does so in an unusual way. First, the large negative value for R causes L, the land area, to increase from 7341 to 10514; 514 square miles more land than is even possible. In addition to negative animals, the program is creating land mass from thin air:

290 LET L=L−(R*3.58E−8)−(B*1.0E−7)

This sudden increase in land area, coupled with the massive infusion of plants caused by the noneating of -4.2×10^{10} rats, finally sends the plant population back into the realm of positive numbers at line 300:

300 LET P=P+(L*4E5)−(R*P2)

The very next line, 311, is our zero-or-minus value clamp on R. This time its effect holds since there are no more negative plants to unbalance the system. The rat population is reduced to its initial value of 100, and processing continues. Everything is as it should be save that the moon has permanently expanded by 514 square miles.

The way to prevent this scenario from repeating is to move line 315 to line 322, thus preventing the rat population from becoming so large that it drives the plant numbers negative. Line 315 was a patch which was intended to do just that but we neglected to place it *after* the rat population was increased by reproduction.

Suppose we now run the program again:

RUN

TWO GROUP ECOSYSTEM SIMULATION

SPACE BATS VS MOON RATS

BATS EAT RATS AND RATS EAT PLANTS

INITIAL POPULATION OF RATS 100

INITIAL POPULATION OF BATS 10

RAT REPRODUCTION RATE(DAYS) 2

BAT REPRODUCTION RATE(DAYS) 4

NO. RATS/LITTER 10

NO. BATS/LITTER 5

RATS EATEN/BAT 6

PLANTS EATEN/RAT 4

IS THIS A DEBUG RUN?(RETURN FOR NO)

DAY, RATS VS BATS 1	40	5
DAY, RATS VS BATS 2	110	4
DAY, RATS VS BATS 3	86	3
DAY, RATS VS BATS 4	748	12
DAY, RATS VS BATS 5	676	8
DAY, RATS VS BATS 6	6908	5
DAY, RATS VS BATS 7	6878	5
DAY, RATS VS BATS 8	75328	30
DAY, RATS VS BATS 9	75148	30
DAY, RATS VS BATS 10	742183	30

The program starts out well. Suppose we skip forward a bit and see if the system is still stable:

DAY, RATS VS BATS 50	361382800	54207419
DAY, RATS VS BATS 51	36138290	3252446
DAY, RATS VS BATS 52	182859750	19514676
DAY, RATS VS BATS 53	65771690	9865753
DAY, RATS VS BATS 54	72848892	8879177
DAY, RATS VS BATS 55	19073830	2861074
DAY, RATS VS BATS 56	20981246	15449800
DAY, RATS VS BATS 57	100	13
DAY, RATS VS BATS 58	242	13
DAY, RATS VS BATS 59	164	7
DAY, RATS VS BATS 60	1342	42

The program looks as though it can take care of itself now; indeed, if we were to follow the output for a much longer time we would see that at no time do zero or negative values appear.

As for the validity of the data, that responsibility lies with the person who formulated the model. We have seen that, especially in the present case, a computer model of natural events involves assumption, simplification, and compromise.

We have also seen how the many elements of the programmer's craft must work together in a successful debugging effort. No single technique is perfect for all applications and no method has any greater claim to fame than any other method. But used in concert with one another, and under the guidance of a logical plan of action, a few simple techniques are all that are required to debug even the most complicated of programs.

APPENDIX

DECIMAL TO BINARY/OCTAL CONVERSION TABLE*

DEC.	A_9	A_8	A_7	A_6	A_5	A_4	A_3	A_2	A_1	A_0	OCTAL
0	0	0	0	0	0	0	0	0	0	0	0 0 0 0
1	0	0	0	0	0	0	0	0	0	1	0 0 0 1
2	0	0	0	0	0	0	0	0	1	0	0 0 0 2
3	0	0	0	0	0	0	0	0	1	1	0 0 0 3
4	0	0	0	0	0	0	0	1	0	0	0 0 0 4
5	0	0	0	0	0	0	0	1	0	1	0 0 0 5
6	0	0	0	0	0	0	0	1	1	0	0 0 0 6
7	0	0	0	0	0	0	0	1	1	1	0 0 0 7
8	0	0	0	0	0	0	1	0	0	0	0 0 1 0
9	0	0	0	0	0	0	1	0	0	1	0 0 1 1
10	0	0	0	0	0	0	1	0	1	0	0 0 1 2
11	0	0	0	0	0	0	1	0	1	1	0 0 1 3
12	0	0	0	0	0	0	1	1	0	0	0 0 1 4
13	0	0	0	0	0	0	1	1	0	1	0 0 1 5
14	0	0	0	0	0	0	1	1	1	0	0 0 1 6
15	0	0	0	0	0	0	1	1	1	1	0 0 1 7
16	0	0	0	0	0	1	0	0	0	0	0 0 2 0
17	0	0	0	0	0	1	0	0	0	1	0 0 2 1
18	0	0	0	0	0	1	0	0	1	0	0 0 2 2
19	0	0	0	0	0	1	0	0	1	1	0 0 2 3
20	0	0	0	0	0	1	0	1	0	0	0 0 2 4
21	0	0	0	0	0	1	0	1	0	1	0 0 2 5
22	0	0	0	0	0	1	0	1	1	0	0 0 2 6
23	0	0	0	0	0	1	0	1	1	1	0 0 2 7
24	0	0	0	0	0	1	1	0	0	0	0 0 3 0
25	0	0	0	0	0	1	1	0	0	1	0 0 3 1
26	0	0	0	0	0	1	1	0	1	0	0 0 3 2
27	0	0	0	0	0	1	1	0	1	1	0 0 3 3
28	0	0	0	0	0	1	1	1	0	0	0 0 3 4
29	0	0	0	0	0	1	1	1	0	1	0 0 3 5
30	0	0	0	0	0	1	1	1	1	0	0 0 3 6
31	0	0	0	0	0	1	1	1	1	1	0 0 3 7

DEC.	A_9	A_8	A_7	A_6	A_5	A_4	A_3	A_2	A_1	A_0	OCTAL
32	0	0	0	0	1	0	0	0	0	0	0 0 4 0
33	0	0	0	0	1	0	0	0	0	1	0 0 4 1
34	0	0	0	0	1	0	0	0	1	0	0 0 4 2
35	0	0	0	0	1	0	0	0	1	1	0 0 4 3
36	0	0	0	0	1	0	0	1	0	0	0 0 4 4
37	0	0	0	0	1	0	0	1	0	1	0 0 4 5
38	0	0	0	0	1	0	0	1	1	0	0 0 4 6
39	0	0	0	0	1	0	0	1	1	1	0 0 4 7
40	0	0	0	0	1	0	1	0	0	0	0 0 5 0
41	0	0	0	0	1	0	1	0	0	1	0 0 5 1
42	0	0	0	0	1	0	1	0	1	0	0 0 5 2
43	0	0	0	0	1	0	1	0	1	1	0 0 5 3
44	0	0	0	0	1	0	1	1	0	0	0 0 5 4
45	0	0	0	0	1	0	1	1	0	1	0 0 5 5
46	0	0	0	0	1	0	1	1	1	0	0 0 5 6
47	0	0	0	0	1	0	1	1	1	1	0 0 5 7
48	0	0	0	0	1	1	0	0	0	0	0 0 6 0
49	0	0	0	0	1	1	0	0	0	1	0 0 6 1
50	0	0	0	0	1	1	0	0	1	0	0 0 6 2
51	0	0	0	0	1	1	0	0	1	1	0 0 6 3
52	0	0	0	0	1	1	0	1	0	0	0 0 6 4
53	0	0	0	0	1	1	0	1	0	1	0 0 6 5
54	0	0	0	0	1	1	0	1	1	0	0 0 6 6
55	0	0	0	0	1	1	0	1	1	1	0 0 6 7
56	0	0	0	0	1	1	1	0	0	0	0 0 7 0
57	0	0	0	0	1	1	1	0	0	1	0 0 7 1
58	0	0	0	0	1	1	1	0	1	0	0 0 7 2
59	0	0	0	0	1	1	1	0	1	1	0 0 7 3
60	0	0	0	0	1	1	1	1	0	0	0 0 7 4
61	0	0	0	0	1	1	1	1	0	1	0 0 7 5
62	0	0	0	0	1	1	1	1	1	0	0 0 7 6
63	0	0	0	0	1	1	1	1	1	1	0 0 7 7

* Courtesy of Fairchild Camera and Instrument Corporation

DEC.	A_9	A_8	A_7	A_6	A_5	A_4	A_3	A_2	A_1	A_0	OCTAL
64	0	0	0	1	0	0	0	0	0	0	0 1 0 0
65	0	0	0	1	0	0	0	0	0	1	0 1 0 1
66	0	0	0	1	0	0	0	0	1	0	0 1 0 2
67	0	0	0	1	0	0	0	0	1	1	0 1 0 3
68	0	0	0	1	0	0	0	1	0	0	0 1 0 4
69	0	0	0	1	0	0	0	1	0	1	0 1 0 5
70	0	0	0	1	0	0	0	1	1	0	0 1 0 6
71	0	0	0	1	0	0	0	1	1	1	0 1 0 7
72	0	0	0	1	0	0	1	0	0	0	0 1 1 0
73	0	0	0	1	0	0	1	0	0	1	0 1 1 1
74	0	0	0	1	0	0	1	0	1	0	0 1 1 2
75	0	0	0	1	0	0	1	0	1	1	0 1 1 3
76	0	0	0	1	0	0	1	1	0	0	0 1 1 4
77	0	0	0	1	0	0	1	1	0	1	0 1 1 5
78	0	0	0	1	0	0	1	1	1	0	0 1 1 6
79	0	0	0	1	0	0	1	1	1	1	0 1 1 7
80	0	0	0	1	0	1	0	0	0	0	0 1 2 0
81	0	0	0	1	0	1	0	0	0	1	0 1 2 1
82	0	0	0	1	0	1	0	0	1	0	0 1 2 2
83	0	0	0	1	0	1	0	0	1	1	0 1 2 3
84	0	0	0	1	0	1	0	1	0	0	0 1 2 4
85	0	0	0	1	0	1	0	1	0	1	0 1 2 5
86	0	0	0	1	0	1	0	1	1	0	0 1 2 6
87	0	0	0	1	0	1	0	1	1	1	0 1 2 7
88	0	0	0	1	0	1	1	0	0	0	0 1 3 0
89	0	0	0	1	0	1	1	0	0	1	0 1 3 1
90	0	0	0	1	0	1	1	0	1	0	0 1 3 2
91	0	0	0	1	0	1	1	0	1	1	0 1 3 3
92	0	0	0	1	0	1	1	1	0	0	0 1 3 4
93	0	0	0	1	0	1	1	1	0	1	0 1 3 5
94	0	0	0	1	0	1	1	1	1	0	0 1 3 6
95	0	0	0	1	0	1	1	1	1	1	0 1 3 7
96	0	0	0	1	1	0	0	0	0	0	0 1 4 0
97	0	0	0	1	1	0	0	0	0	1	0 1 4 1
98	0	0	0	1	1	0	0	0	1	0	0 1 4 2
99	0	0	0	1	1	0	0	0	1	1	0 1 4 3
100	0	0	0	1	1	0	0	1	0	0	0 1 4 4
101	0	0	0	1	1	0	0	1	0	1	0 1 4 5
102	0	0	0	1	1	0	0	1	1	0	0 1 4 6
103	0	0	0	1	1	0	0	1	1	1	0 1 4 7
104	0	0	0	1	1	0	1	0	0	0	0 1 5 0
105	0	0	0	1	1	0	1	0	0	1	0 1 5 1
106	0	0	0	1	1	0	1	0	1	0	0 1 5 2
107	0	0	0	1	1	0	1	0	1	1	0 1 5 3
108	0	0	0	1	1	0	1	1	0	0	0 1 5 4
109	0	0	0	1	1	0	1	1	0	1	0 1 5 5
110	0	0	0	1	1	0	1	1	1	0	0 1 5 6
111	0	0	0	1	1	0	1	1	1	1	0 1 5 7
112	0	0	0	1	1	1	0	0	0	0	0 1 6 0
113	0	0	0	1	1	1	0	0	0	1	0 1 6 1
114	0	0	0	1	1	1	0	0	1	0	0 1 6 2
115	0	0	0	1	1	1	0	0	1	1	0 1 6 3
116	0	0	0	1	1	1	0	1	0	0	0 1 6 4
117	0	0	0	1	1	1	0	1	0	1	0 1 6 5
118	0	0	0	1	1	1	0	1	1	0	0 1 6 6
119	0	0	0	1	1	1	0	1	1	1	0 1 6 7
120	0	0	0	1	1	1	1	0	0	0	0 1 7 0
121	0	0	0	1	1	1	1	0	0	1	0 1 7 1
122	0	0	0	1	1	1	1	0	1	0	0 1 7 2
123	0	0	0	1	1	1	1	0	1	1	0 1 7 3
124	0	0	0	1	1	1	1	1	0	0	0 1 7 4
125	0	0	0	1	1	1	1	1	0	1	0 1 7 5
126	0	0	0	1	1	1	1	1	1	0	0 1 7 6
127	0	0	0	1	1	1	1	1	1	1	0 1 7 7

DEC.	A_9	A_8	A_7	A_6	A_5	A_4	A_3	A_2	A_1	A_0	OCTAL
128	0	0	1	0	0	0	0	0	0	0	0 2 0 0
129	0	0	1	0	0	0	0	0	0	1	0 2 0 1
130	0	0	1	0	0	0	0	0	1	0	0 2 0 2
131	0	0	1	0	0	0	0	0	1	1	0 2 0 3
132	0	0	1	0	0	0	0	1	0	0	0 2 0 4
133	0	0	1	0	0	0	0	1	0	1	0 2 0 5
134	0	0	1	0	0	0	0	1	1	0	0 2 0 6
135	0	0	1	0	0	0	0	1	1	1	0 2 0 7
136	0	0	1	0	0	0	1	0	0	0	0 2 1 0
137	0	0	1	0	0	0	1	0	0	1	0 2 1 1
138	0	0	1	0	0	0	1	0	1	0	0 2 1 2
139	0	0	1	0	0	0	1	0	1	1	0 2 1 3
140	0	0	1	0	0	0	1	1	0	0	0 2 1 4
141	0	0	1	0	0	0	1	1	0	1	0 2 1 5
142	0	0	1	0	0	0	1	1	1	0	0 2 1 6
143	0	0	1	0	0	0	1	1	1	1	0 2 1 7
144	0	0	1	0	0	1	0	0	0	0	0 2 2 0
145	0	0	1	0	0	1	0	0	0	1	0 2 2 1
146	0	0	1	0	0	1	0	0	1	0	0 2 2 2
147	0	0	1	0	0	1	0	0	1	1	0 2 2 3
148	0	0	1	0	0	1	0	1	0	0	0 2 2 4
149	0	0	1	0	0	1	0	1	0	1	0 2 2 5
150	0	0	1	0	0	1	0	1	1	0	0 2 2 6
151	0	0	1	0	0	1	0	1	1	1	0 2 2 7
152	0	0	1	0	0	1	1	0	0	0	0 2 3 0
153	0	0	1	0	0	1	1	0	0	1	0 2 3 1
154	0	0	1	0	0	1	1	0	1	0	0 2 3 2
155	0	0	1	0	0	1	1	0	1	1	0 2 3 3
156	0	0	1	0	0	1	1	1	0	0	0 2 3 4
157	0	0	1	0	0	1	1	1	0	1	0 2 3 5
158	0	0	1	0	0	1	1	1	1	0	0 2 3 6
159	0	0	1	0	0	1	1	1	1	1	0 2 3 7
160	0	0	1	0	1	0	0	0	0	0	0 2 4 0
161	0	0	1	0	1	0	0	0	0	1	0 2 4 1
162	0	0	1	0	1	0	0	0	1	0	0 2 4 2
163	0	0	1	0	1	0	0	0	1	1	0 2 4 3
164	0	0	1	0	1	0	0	1	0	0	0 2 4 4
165	0	0	1	0	1	0	0	1	0	1	0 2 4 5
166	0	0	1	0	1	0	0	1	1	0	0 2 4 6
167	0	0	1	0	1	0	0	1	1	1	0 2 4 7
168	0	0	1	0	1	0	1	0	0	0	0 2 5 0
169	0	0	1	0	1	0	1	0	0	1	0 2 5 1
170	0	0	1	0	1	0	1	0	1	0	0 2 5 2
171	0	0	1	0	1	0	1	0	1	1	0 2 5 3
172	0	0	1	0	1	0	1	1	0	0	0 2 5 4
173	0	0	1	0	1	0	1	1	0	1	0 2 5 5
174	0	0	1	0	1	0	1	1	1	0	0 2 5 6
175	0	0	1	0	1	0	1	1	1	1	0 2 5 7
176	0	0	1	0	1	1	0	0	0	0	0 2 6 0
177	0	0	1	0	1	1	0	0	0	1	0 2 6 1
178	0	0	1	0	1	1	0	0	1	0	0 2 6 2
179	0	0	1	0	1	1	0	0	1	1	0 2 6 3
180	0	0	1	0	1	1	0	1	0	0	0 2 6 4
181	0	0	1	0	1	1	0	1	0	1	0 2 6 5
182	0	0	1	0	1	1	0	1	1	0	0 2 6 6
183	0	0	1	0	1	1	0	1	1	1	0 2 6 7
184	0	0	1	0	1	1	1	0	0	0	0 2 7 0
185	0	0	1	0	1	1	1	0	0	1	0 2 7 1
186	0	0	1	0	1	1	1	0	1	0	0 2 7 2
187	0	0	1	0	1	1	1	0	1	1	0 2 7 3
188	0	0	1	0	1	1	1	1	0	0	0 2 7 4
189	0	0	1	0	1	1	1	1	0	1	0 2 7 5
190	0	0	1	0	1	1	1	1	1	0	0 2 7 6
191	0	0	1	0	1	1	1	1	1	1	0 2 7 7

DEC.	A9	A8	A7	A6	A5	A4	A3	A2	A1	A0	OCTAL
192	0	0	1	1	0	0	0	0	0	0	0 3 0 0
193	0	0	1	1	0	0	0	0	0	1	0 3 0 1
194	0	0	1	1	0	0	0	0	1	0	0 3 0 2
195	0	0	1	1	0	0	0	0	1	1	0 3 0 3
196	0	0	1	1	0	0	0	1	0	0	0 3 0 4
197	0	0	1	1	0	0	0	1	0	1	0 3 0 5
198	0	0	1	1	0	0	0	1	1	0	0 3 0 6
199	0	0	1	1	0	0	0	1	1	1	0 3 0 7
200	0	0	1	1	0	0	1	0	0	0	0 3 1 0
201	0	0	1	1	0	0	1	0	0	1	0 3 1 1
202	0	0	1	1	0	0	1	0	1	0	0 3 1 2
203	0	0	1	1	0	0	1	0	1	1	0 3 1 3
204	0	0	1	1	0	0	1	1	0	0	0 3 1 4
205	0	0	1	1	0	0	1	1	0	1	0 3 1 5
206	0	0	1	1	0	0	1	1	1	0	0 3 1 6
207	0	0	1	1	0	0	1	1	1	1	0 3 1 7
208	0	0	1	1	0	1	0	0	0	0	0 3 2 0
209	0	0	1	1	0	1	0	0	0	1	0 3 2 1
210	0	0	1	1	0	1	0	0	1	0	0 3 2 2
211	0	0	1	1	0	1	0	0	1	1	0 3 2 3
212	0	0	1	1	0	1	0	1	0	0	0 3 2 4
213	0	0	1	1	0	1	0	1	0	1	0 3 2 5
214	0	0	1	1	0	1	0	1	1	0	0 3 2 6
215	0	0	1	1	0	1	0	1	1	1	0 3 2 7
216	0	0	1	1	0	1	1	0	0	0	0 3 3 0
217	0	0	1	1	0	1	1	0	0	1	0 3 3 1
218	0	0	1	1	0	1	1	0	1	0	0 3 3 2
219	0	0	1	1	0	1	1	0	1	1	0 3 3 3
220	0	0	1	1	0	1	1	1	0	0	0 3 3 4
221	0	0	1	1	0	1	1	1	0	1	0 3 3 5
222	0	0	1	1	0	1	1	1	1	0	0 3 3 6
223	0	0	1	1	0	1	1	1	1	1	0 3 3 7
224	0	0	1	1	1	0	0	0	0	0	0 3 4 0
225	0	0	1	1	1	0	0	0	0	1	0 3 4 1
226	0	0	1	1	1	0	0	0	1	0	0 3 4 2
227	0	0	1	1	1	0	0	0	1	1	0 3 4 3
228	0	0	1	1	1	0	0	1	0	0	0 3 4 4
229	0	0	1	1	1	0	0	1	0	1	0 3 4 5
230	0	0	1	1	1	0	0	1	1	0	0 3 4 6
231	0	0	1	1	1	0	0	1	1	1	0 3 4 7
232	0	0	1	1	1	0	1	0	0	0	0 3 5 0
233	0	0	1	1	1	0	1	0	0	1	0 3 5 1
234	0	0	1	1	1	0	1	0	1	0	0 3 5 2
235	0	0	1	1	1	0	1	0	1	1	0 3 5 3
236	0	0	1	1	1	0	1	1	0	0	0 3 5 4
237	0	0	1	1	1	0	1	1	0	1	0 3 5 5
238	0	0	1	1	1	0	1	1	1	0	0 3 5 6
239	0	0	1	1	1	0	1	1	1	1	0 3 5 7
240	0	0	1	1	1	1	0	0	0	0	0 3 6 0
241	0	0	1	1	1	1	0	0	0	1	0 3 6 1
242	0	0	1	1	1	1	0	0	1	0	0 3 6 2
243	0	0	1	1	1	1	0	0	1	1	0 3 6 3
244	0	0	1	1	1	1	0	1	0	0	0 3 6 4
245	0	0	1	1	1	1	0	1	0	1	0 3 6 5
246	0	0	1	1	1	1	0	1	1	0	0 3 6 6
247	0	0	1	1	1	1	0	1	1	1	0 3 6 7
248	0	0	1	1	1	1	1	0	0	0	0 3 7 0
249	0	0	1	1	1	1	1	0	0	1	0 3 7 1
250	0	0	1	1	1	1	1	0	1	0	0 3 7 2
251	0	0	1	1	1	1	1	0	1	1	0 3 7 3
252	0	0	1	1	1	1	1	1	0	0	0 3 7 4
253	0	0	1	1	1	1	1	1	0	1	0 3 7 5
254	0	0	1	1	1	1	1	1	1	0	0 3 7 6
255	0	0	1	1	1	1	1	1	1	1	0 3 7 7

DEC.	A9	A8	A7	A6	A5	A4	A3	A2	A1	A0	OCTAL
256	0	1	0	0	0	0	0	0	0	0	0 4 0 0
257	0	1	0	0	0	0	0	0	0	1	0 4 0 1
258	0	1	0	0	0	0	0	0	1	0	0 4 0 2
259	0	1	0	0	0	0	0	0	1	1	0 4 0 3
260	0	1	0	0	0	0	0	1	0	0	0 4 0 4
261	0	1	0	0	0	0	0	1	0	1	0 4 0 5
262	0	1	0	0	0	0	0	1	1	0	0 4 0 6
263	0	1	0	0	0	0	0	1	1	1	0 4 0 7
264	0	1	0	0	0	0	1	0	0	0	0 4 1 0
265	0	1	0	0	0	0	1	0	0	1	0 4 1 1
266	0	1	0	0	0	0	1	0	1	0	0 4 1 2
267	0	1	0	0	0	0	1	0	1	1	0 4 1 3
268	0	1	0	0	0	0	1	1	0	0	0 4 1 4
269	0	1	0	0	0	0	1	1	0	1	0 3 1 5
270	0	1	0	0	0	0	1	1	1	0	0 4 1 6
271	0	1	0	0	0	0	1	1	1	1	0 4 1 7
272	0	1	0	0	0	1	0	0	0	0	0 4 2 0
273	0	1	0	0	0	1	0	0	0	1	0 4 2 1
274	0	1	0	0	0	1	0	0	1	0	0 4 2 2
275	0	1	0	0	0	1	0	0	1	1	0 4 2 3
276	0	1	0	0	0	1	0	1	0	0	0 4 2 4
277	0	1	0	0	0	1	0	1	0	1	0 4 2 5
278	0	1	0	0	0	1	0	1	1	0	0 4 2 6
279	0	1	0	0	0	1	0	1	1	1	0 4 2 7
280	0	1	0	0	0	1	1	0	0	0	0 4 3 0
281	0	1	0	0	0	1	1	0	0	1	0 4 3 1
282	0	1	0	0	0	1	1	0	1	0	0 4 3 2
283	0	1	0	0	0	1	1	0	1	1	0 4 3 3
284	0	1	0	0	0	1	1	1	0	0	0 4 3 4
285	0	1	0	0	0	1	1	1	0	1	0 4 3 5
286	0	1	0	0	0	1	1	1	1	0	0 4 3 6
287	0	1	0	0	0	1	1	1	1	1	0 4 3 7
288	0	1	0	0	1	0	0	0	0	0	0 4 4 0
289	0	1	0	0	1	0	0	0	0	1	0 4 4 1
290	0	1	0	0	1	0	0	0	1	0	0 4 4 2
291	0	1	0	0	1	0	0	0	1	1	0 4 4 3
292	0	1	0	0	1	0	0	1	0	0	0 4 4 4
293	0	1	0	0	1	0	0	1	0	1	0 4 4 5
294	0	1	0	0	1	0	0	1	1	0	0 4 4 6
295	0	1	0	0	1	0	0	1	1	1	0 4 4 7
296	0	1	0	0	1	0	1	0	0	0	0 4 5 0
297	0	1	0	0	1	0	1	0	0	1	0 4 5 1
298	0	1	0	0	1	0	1	0	1	0	0 4 5 2
299	0	1	0	0	1	0	1	0	1	1	0 4 5 3
300	0	1	0	0	1	0	1	1	0	0	0 4 5 4
301	0	1	0	0	1	0	1	1	0	1	0 4 5 5
302	0	1	0	0	1	0	1	1	1	0	0 4 5 6
303	0	1	0	0	1	0	1	1	1	1	0 4 5 7
304	0	1	0	0	1	1	0	0	0	0	0 4 6 0
305	0	1	0	0	1	1	0	0	0	1	0 4 6 1
306	0	1	0	0	1	1	0	0	1	0	0 4 6 2
307	0	1	0	0	1	1	0	0	1	1	0 4 6 3
308	0	1	0	0	1	1	0	1	0	0	0 4 6 4
309	0	1	0	0	1	1	0	1	0	1	0 4 6 5
310	0	1	0	0	1	1	0	1	1	0	0 4 6 6
311	0	1	0	0	1	1	0	1	1	1	0 4 6 7
312	0	1	0	0	1	1	1	0	0	0	0 4 7 0
313	0	1	0	0	1	1	1	0	0	1	0 4 7 1
314	0	1	0	0	1	1	1	0	1	0	0 4 7 2
315	0	1	0	0	1	1	1	0	1	1	0 4 7 3
316	0	1	0	0	1	1	1	1	0	0	0 4 7 4
317	0	1	0	0	1	1	1	1	0	1	0 4 7 5
318	0	1	0	0	1	1	1	1	1	0	0 4 7 6
319	0	1	0	0	1	1	1	1	1	1	0 4 7 7

DEC.	A9	A8	A7	A6	A5	A4	A3	A2	A1	A0	OCTAL
320	0	1	0	1	0	0	0	0	0	0	0 5 0 0
321	0	1	0	1	0	0	0	0	0	1	0 5 0 1
322	0	1	0	1	0	0	0	0	1	0	0 5 0 2
323	0	1	0	1	0	0	0	0	1	1	0 5 0 3
324	0	1	0	1	0	0	0	1	0	0	0 5 0 4
325	0	1	0	1	0	0	0	1	0	1	0 5 0 5
326	0	1	0	1	0	0	0	1	1	0	0 5 0 6
327	0	1	0	1	0	0	0	1	1	1	0 5 0 7
328	0	1	0	1	0	0	1	0	0	0	0 5 1 0
329	0	1	0	1	0	0	1	0	0	1	0 5 1 1
330	0	1	0	1	0	0	1	0	1	0	0 5 1 2
331	0	1	0	1	0	0	1	0	1	1	0 5 1 3
332	0	1	0	1	0	0	1	1	0	0	0 5 1 4
333	0	1	0	1	0	0	1	1	0	1	0 5 1 5
334	0	1	0	1	0	0	1	1	1	0	0 5 1 6
335	0	1	0	1	0	0	1	1	1	1	0 5 1 7
336	0	1	0	1	0	1	0	0	0	0	0 5 2 0
337	0	1	0	1	0	1	0	0	0	1	0 5 2 1
338	0	1	0	1	0	1	0	0	1	0	0 5 2 2
339	0	1	0	1	0	1	0	0	1	1	0 5 2 3
340	0	1	0	1	0	1	0	1	0	0	0 5 2 4
341	0	1	0	1	0	1	0	1	0	1	0 5 2 5
342	0	1	0	1	0	1	0	1	1	0	0 5 2 6
343	0	1	0	1	0	1	0	1	1	1	0 5 2 7
344	0	1	0	1	0	1	1	0	0	0	0 5 3 0
345	0	1	0	1	0	1	1	0	0	1	0 5 3 1
346	0	1	0	1	0	1	1	0	1	0	0 5 3 2
347	0	1	0	1	0	1	1	0	1	1	0 5 3 3
348	0	1	0	1	0	1	1	1	0	0	0 5 3 4
349	0	1	0	1	0	1	1	1	0	1	0 5 3 5
350	0	1	0	1	0	1	1	1	1	0	0 5 3 6
351	0	1	0	1	0	1	1	1	1	1	0 5 3 7
352	0	1	0	1	1	0	0	0	0	0	0 5 4 0
353	0	1	0	1	1	0	0	0	0	1	0 5 4 1
354	0	1	0	1	1	0	0	0	1	0	0 5 4 2
355	0	1	0	1	1	0	0	0	1	1	0 5 4 3
356	0	1	0	1	1	0	0	1	0	0	0 5 4 4
357	0	1	0	1	1	0	0	1	0	1	0 5 4 5
358	0	1	0	1	1	0	0	1	1	0	0 5 4 6
359	0	1	0	1	1	0	0	1	1	1	0 5 4 7
360	0	1	0	1	1	0	1	0	0	0	0 5 5 0
361	0	1	0	1	1	0	1	0	0	1	0 5 5 1
362	0	1	0	1	1	0	1	0	1	0	0 5 5 2
363	0	1	0	1	1	0	1	0	1	1	0 5 5 3
364	0	1	0	1	1	0	1	1	0	0	0 5 5 4
365	0	1	0	1	1	0	1	1	0	1	0 5 5 5
366	0	1	0	1	1	0	1	1	1	0	0 5 5 6
367	0	1	0	1	1	0	1	1	1	1	0 5 5 7
368	0	1	0	1	1	1	0	0	0	0	0 5 6 0
369	0	1	0	1	1	1	0	0	0	1	0 5 6 1
370	0	1	0	1	1	1	0	0	1	0	0 5 6 2
371	0	1	0	1	1	1	0	0	1	1	0 5 6 3
372	0	1	0	1	1	1	0	1	0	0	0 5 6 4
373	0	1	0	1	1	1	0	1	0	1	0 5 6 5
374	0	1	0	1	1	1	0	1	1	0	0 5 6 6
375	0	1	0	1	1	1	0	1	1	1	0 5 6 7
376	0	1	0	1	1	1	1	0	0	0	0 5 7 0
377	0	1	0	1	1	1	1	0	0	1	0 5 7 1
378	0	1	0	1	1	1	1	0	1	0	0 5 7 2
379	0	1	0	1	1	1	1	0	1	1	0 5 7 3
380	0	1	0	1	1	1	1	1	0	0	0 5 7 4
381	0	1	0	1	1	1	1	1	0	1	0 5 7 5
382	0	1	0	1	1	1	1	1	1	0	0 5 7 6
383	0	1	0	1	1	1	1	1	1	1	0 5 7 7

DEC.	A9	A8	A7	A6	A5	A4	A3	A2	A1	A0	OCTAL
384	0	1	1	0	0	0	0	0	0	0	0 6 0 0
385	0	1	1	0	0	0	0	0	0	1	0 6 0 1
386	0	1	1	0	0	0	0	0	1	0	0 6 0 2
387	0	1	1	0	0	0	0	0	1	1	0 6 0 3
388	0	1	1	0	0	0	0	1	0	0	0 6 0 4
389	0	1	1	0	0	0	0	1	0	1	0 6 0 5
390	0	1	1	0	0	0	0	1	1	0	0 6 0 6
391	0	1	1	0	0	0	0	1	1	1	0 6 0 7
392	0	1	1	0	0	0	1	0	0	0	0 6 1 0
393	0	1	1	0	0	0	1	0	0	1	0 6 1 1
394	0	1	1	0	0	0	1	0	1	0	0 6 1 2
395	0	1	1	0	0	0	1	0	1	1	0 6 1 3
396	0	1	1	0	0	0	1	1	0	0	0 6 1 4
397	0	1	1	0	0	0	1	1	0	1	0 6 1 5
398	0	1	1	0	0	0	1	1	1	0	0 6 1 6
399	0	1	1	0	0	0	1	1	1	1	0 6 1 7
400	0	1	1	0	0	1	0	0	0	0	0 6 2 0
401	0	1	1	0	0	1	0	0	0	1	0 6 2 1
402	0	1	1	0	0	1	0	0	1	0	0 6 2 2
403	0	1	1	0	0	1	0	0	1	1	0 6 2 3
404	0	1	1	0	0	1	0	1	0	0	0 6 2 4
405	0	1	1	0	0	1	0	1	0	1	0 6 2 5
406	0	1	1	0	0	1	0	1	1	0	0 6 2 6
407	0	1	1	0	0	1	0	1	1	1	0 6 2 7
408	0	1	1	0	0	1	1	0	0	0	0 6 3 0
409	0	1	1	0	0	1	1	0	0	1	0 6 3 1
410	0	1	1	0	0	1	1	0	1	0	0 6 3 2
411	0	1	1	0	0	1	1	0	1	1	0 6 3 3
412	0	1	1	0	0	1	1	1	0	0	0 6 3 4
413	0	1	1	0	0	1	1	1	0	1	0 6 3 5
414	0	1	1	0	0	1	1	1	1	0	0 6 3 6
415	0	1	1	0	0	1	1	1	1	1	0 6 3 7
416	0	1	1	0	1	0	0	0	0	0	0 6 4 0
417	0	1	1	0	1	0	0	0	0	1	0 6 4 1
418	0	1	1	0	1	0	0	0	1	0	0 6 4 2
419	0	1	1	0	1	0	0	0	1	1	0 6 4 3
420	0	1	1	0	1	0	0	1	0	0	0 6 4 4
421	0	1	1	0	1	0	0	1	0	1	0 6 4 5
422	0	1	1	0	1	0	0	1	1	0	0 6 4 6
423	0	1	1	0	1	0	0	1	1	1	0 6 4 7
424	0	1	1	0	1	0	1	0	0	0	0 6 5 0
425	0	1	1	0	1	0	1	0	0	1	0 6 5 1
426	0	1	1	0	1	0	1	0	1	0	0 6 5 2
427	0	1	1	0	1	0	1	0	1	1	0 6 5 3
428	0	1	1	0	1	0	1	1	0	0	0 6 5 4
429	0	1	1	0	1	0	1	1	0	1	0 6 5 5
430	0	1	1	0	1	0	1	1	1	0	0 6 5 6
431	0	1	1	0	1	0	1	1	1	1	0 6 5 7
432	0	1	1	0	1	1	0	0	0	0	0 6 6 0
433	0	1	1	0	1	1	0	0	0	1	0 6 6 1
434	0	1	1	0	1	1	0	0	1	0	0 6 6 2
435	0	1	1	0	1	1	0	0	1	1	0 6 6 3
436	0	1	1	0	1	1	0	1	0	0	0 6 6 4
437	0	1	1	0	1	1	0	1	0	1	0 6 6 5
438	0	1	1	0	1	1	0	1	1	0	0 6 6 6
439	0	1	1	0	1	1	0	1	1	1	0 6 6 7
440	0	1	1	0	1	1	1	0	0	0	0 6 7 0
441	0	1	1	0	1	1	1	0	0	1	0 6 7 1
442	0	1	1	0	1	1	1	0	1	0	0 6 7 2
443	0	1	1	0	1	1	1	0	1	1	0 6 7 3
444	0	1	1	0	1	1	1	1	0	0	0 6 7 4
445	0	1	1	0	1	1	1	1	0	1	0 6 7 5
446	0	1	1	0	1	1	1	1	1	0	0 6 7 6
447	0	1	1	0	1	1	1	1	1	1	0 6 7 7

DEC.	A_9	A_8	A_7	A_6	A_5	A_4	A_3	A_2	A_1	A_0	OCTAL
448	0	1	1	1	0	0	0	0	0	0	0 7 0 0
449	0	1	1	1	0	0	0	0	0	1	0 7 0 1
450	0	1	1	1	0	0	0	0	1	0	0 7 0 2
451	0	1	1	1	0	0	0	0	1	1	0 7 0 3
452	0	1	1	1	0	0	0	1	0	0	0 7 0 4
453	0	1	1	1	0	0	0	1	0	1	0 7 0 5
454	0	1	1	1	0	0	0	1	1	0	0 7 0 6
455	0	1	1	1	0	0	0	1	1	1	0 7 0 7
456	0	1	1	1	0	0	1	0	0	0	0 7 1 0
457	0	1	1	1	0	0	1	0	0	1	0 7 1 1
458	0	1	1	1	0	0	1	0	1	0	0 7 1 2
459	0	1	1	1	0	0	1	0	1	1	0 7 1 3
460	0	1	1	1	0	0	1	1	0	0	0 7 1 4
461	0	1	1	1	0	0	1	1	0	1	0 7 1 5
462	0	1	1	1	0	0	1	1	1	0	0 7 1 6
463	0	1	1	1	0	0	1	1	1	1	0 7 1 7
464	0	1	1	1	0	1	0	0	0	0	0 7 2 0
465	0	1	1	1	0	1	0	0	0	1	0 7 2 1
466	0	1	1	1	0	1	0	0	1	0	0 7 2 2
467	0	1	1	1	0	1	0	0	1	1	0 7 2 3
468	0	1	1	1	0	1	0	1	0	0	0 7 2 4
469	0	1	1	1	0	1	0	1	0	1	0 7 2 5
470	0	1	1	1	0	1	0	1	1	0	0 7 2 6
471	0	1	1	1	0	1	0	1	1	1	0 7 2 7
472	0	1	1	1	0	1	1	0	0	0	0 7 3 0
473	0	1	1	1	0	1	1	0	0	1	0 7 3 1
474	0	1	1	1	0	1	1	0	1	0	0 7 3 2
475	0	1	1	1	0	1	1	0	1	1	0 7 3 3
476	0	1	1	1	0	1	1	1	0	0	0 7 3 4
477	0	1	1	1	0	1	1	1	0	1	0 7 3 5
478	0	1	1	1	0	1	1	1	1	0	0 7 3 6
479	0	1	1	1	0	1	1	1	1	1	0 7 3 7
480	0	1	1	1	1	0	0	0	0	0	0 7 4 0
481	0	1	1	1	1	0	0	0	0	1	0 7 4 1
482	0	1	1	1	1	0	0	0	1	0	0 7 4 2
483	0	1	1	1	1	0	0	0	1	1	0 7 4 3
484	0	1	1	1	1	0	0	1	0	0	0 7 4 4
485	0	1	1	1	1	0	0	1	0	1	0 7 4 5
486	0	1	1	1	1	0	0	1	1	0	0 7 4 6
487	0	1	1	1	1	0	0	1	1	1	0 7 4 7
488	0	1	1	1	1	0	1	0	0	0	0 7 5 0
489	0	1	1	1	1	0	1	0	0	1	0 7 5 1
490	0	1	1	1	1	0	1	0	1	0	0 7 5 2
491	0	1	1	1	1	0	1	0	1	1	0 7 5 3
492	0	1	1	1	1	0	1	1	0	0	0 7 5 4
493	0	1	1	1	1	0	1	1	0	1	0 7 5 5
494	0	1	1	1	1	0	1	1	1	0	0 7 5 6
495	0	1	1	1	1	0	1	1	1	1	0 7 5 7
496	0	1	1	1	1	1	0	0	0	0	0 7 6 0
497	0	1	1	1	1	1	0	0	0	1	0 7 6 1
498	0	1	1	1	1	1	0	0	1	0	0 7 6 2
499	0	1	1	1	1	1	0	0	1	1	0 7 6 3
500	0	1	1	1	1	1	0	1	0	0	0 7 6 4
501	0	1	1	1	1	1	0	1	0	1	0 7 6 5
502	0	1	1	1	1	1	0	1	1	0	0 7 6 6
503	0	1	1	1	1	1	0	1	1	1	0 7 6 7
504	0	1	1	1	1	1	1	0	0	0	0 7 7 0
505	0	1	1	1	1	1	1	0	0	1	0 7 7 1
506	0	1	1	1	1	1	1	0	1	0	0 7 7 2
507	0	1	1	1	1	1	1	0	1	1	0 7 7 3
508	0	1	1	1	1	1	1	1	0	0	0 7 7 4
509	0	1	1	1	1	1	1	1	0	1	0 7 7 5
510	0	1	1	1	1	1	1	1	1	0	0 7 7 6
511	0	1	1	1	1	1	1	1	1	1	0 7 7 7

DEC.	A_9	A_8	A_7	A_6	A_5	A_4	A_3	A_2	A_1	A_0	OCTAL
512	1	0	0	0	0	0	0	0	0	0	1 0 0 0
513	1	0	0	0	0	0	0	0	0	1	1 0 0 1
514	1	0	0	0	0	0	0	0	1	0	1 0 0 2
515	1	0	0	0	0	0	0	0	1	1	1 0 0 3
516	1	0	0	0	0	0	0	1	0	0	1 0 0 4
517	1	0	0	0	0	0	0	1	0	1	1 0 0 5
518	1	0	0	0	0	0	0	1	1	0	1 0 0 6
519	1	0	0	0	0	0	0	1	1	1	1 0 0 7
520	1	0	0	0	0	0	1	0	0	0	1 0 1 0
521	1	0	0	0	0	0	1	0	0	1	1 0 1 1
522	1	0	0	0	0	0	1	0	1	0	1 0 1 2
523	1	0	0	0	0	0	1	0	1	1	1 0 1 3
524	1	0	0	0	0	0	1	1	0	0	1 0 1 4
525	1	0	0	0	0	0	1	1	0	1	1 0 1 5
526	1	0	0	0	0	0	1	1	1	0	1 0 1 6
527	1	0	0	0	0	0	1	1	1	1	1 0 1 7
528	1	0	0	0	0	1	0	0	0	0	1 0 2 0
529	1	0	0	0	0	1	0	0	0	1	1 0 2 1
530	1	0	0	0	0	1	0	0	1	0	1 0 2 2
531	1	0	0	0	0	1	0	0	1	1	1 0 2 3
532	1	0	0	0	0	1	0	1	0	0	1 0 2 4
533	1	0	0	0	0	1	0	1	0	1	1 0 2 5
534	1	0	0	0	0	1	0	1	1	0	1 0 2 6
535	1	0	0	0	0	1	0	1	1	1	1 0 2 7
536	1	0	0	0	0	1	1	0	0	0	1 0 3 0
537	1	0	0	0	0	1	1	0	0	1	1 0 3 1
538	1	0	0	0	0	1	1	0	1	0	1 0 3 2
539	1	0	0	0	0	1	1	0	1	1	1 0 3 3
540	1	0	0	0	0	1	1	1	0	0	1 0 3 4
541	1	0	0	0	0	1	1	1	0	1	1 0 3 5
542	1	0	0	0	0	1	1	1	1	0	1 0 3 6
543	1	0	0	0	0	1	1	1	1	1	1 0 3 7
544	1	0	0	0	1	0	0	0	0	0	1 0 4 0
545	1	0	0	0	1	0	0	0	0	1	1 0 4 1
546	1	0	0	0	1	0	0	0	1	0	1 0 4 2
547	1	0	0	0	1	0	0	0	1	1	1 0 4 3
548	1	0	0	0	1	0	0	1	0	0	1 0 4 4
549	1	0	0	0	1	0	0	1	0	1	1 0 4 5
550	1	0	0	0	1	0	0	1	1	0	1 0 4 6
551	1	0	0	0	1	0	0	1	1	1	1 0 4 7
552	1	0	0	0	1	0	1	0	0	0	1 0 5 0
553	1	0	0	0	1	0	1	0	0	1	1 0 5 1
554	1	0	0	0	1	0	1	0	1	0	1 0 5 2
555	1	0	0	0	1	0	1	0	1	1	1 0 5 3
556	1	0	0	0	1	0	1	1	0	0	1 0 5 4
557	1	0	0	0	1	0	1	1	0	1	1 0 5 5
558	1	0	0	0	1	0	1	1	1	0	1 0 5 6
559	1	0	0	0	1	0	1	1	1	1	1 0 5 7
560	1	0	0	0	1	1	0	0	0	0	1 0 6 0
561	1	0	0	0	1	1	0	0	0	1	1 0 6 1
562	1	0	0	0	1	1	0	0	1	0	1 0 6 2
563	1	0	0	0	1	1	0	0	1	1	1 0 6 3
564	1	0	0	0	1	1	0	1	0	0	1 0 6 4
565	1	0	0	0	1	1	0	1	0	1	1 0 6 5
566	1	0	0	0	1	1	0	1	1	0	1 0 6 6
567	1	0	0	0	1	1	0	1	1	1	1 0 6 7
568	1	0	0	0	1	1	1	0	0	0	1 0 7 0
569	1	0	0	0	1	1	1	0	0	1	1 0 7 1
570	1	0	0	0	1	1	1	0	1	0	1 0 7 2
571	1	0	0	0	1	1	1	0	1	1	1 0 7 3
572	1	0	0	0	1	1	1	1	0	0	1 0 7 4
573	1	0	0	0	1	1	1	1	0	1	1 0 7 5
574	1	0	0	0	1	1	1	1	1	0	1 0 7 6
575	1	0	0	0	1	1	1	1	1	1	1 0 7 7

DEC.	A_9	A_8	A_7	A_6	A_5	A_4	A_3	A_2	A_1	A_0	OCTAL
576	1	0	0	1	0	0	0	0	0	0	1 1 0 0
577	1	0	0	1	0	0	0	0	0	1	1 1 0 1
578	1	0	0	1	0	0	0	0	1	0	1 1 0 2
579	1	0	0	1	0	0	0	0	1	1	1 1 0 3
580	1	0	0	1	0	0	0	1	0	0	1 1 0 4
581	1	0	0	1	0	0	0	1	0	1	1 1 0 5
582	1	0	0	1	0	0	0	1	1	0	1 1 0 6
583	1	0	0	1	0	0	0	1	1	1	1 1 0 7
584	1	0	0	1	0	0	1	0	0	0	1 1 1 0
585	1	0	0	1	0	0	1	0	0	1	1 1 1 1
586	1	0	0	1	0	0	1	0	1	0	1 1 1 2
587	1	0	0	1	0	0	1	0	1	1	1 1 1 3
588	1	0	0	1	0	0	1	1	0	0	1 1 1 4
589	1	0	0	1	0	0	1	1	0	1	1 1 1 5
590	1	0	0	1	0	0	1	1	1	0	1 1 1 6
591	1	0	0	1	0	0	1	1	1	1	1 1 1 7
592	1	0	0	1	0	1	0	0	0	0	1 1 2 0
593	1	0	0	1	0	1	0	0	0	1	1 1 2 1
594	1	0	0	1	0	1	0	0	1	0	1 1 2 2
595	1	0	0	1	0	1	0	0	1	1	1 1 2 3
596	1	0	0	1	0	1	0	1	0	0	1 1 2 4
597	1	0	0	1	0	1	0	1	0	1	1 1 2 5
598	1	0	0	1	0	1	0	1	1	0	1 1 2 6
599	1	0	0	1	0	1	0	1	1	1	1 1 2 7
600	1	0	0	1	0	1	1	0	0	0	1 1 3 0
601	1	0	0	1	0	1	1	0	0	1	1 1 3 1
602	1	0	0	1	0	1	1	0	1	0	1 1 3 2
603	1	0	0	1	0	1	1	0	1	1	1 1 3 3
604	1	0	0	1	0	1	1	1	0	0	1 1 3 4
605	1	0	0	1	0	1	1	1	0	1	1 1 3 5
606	1	0	0	1	0	1	1	1	1	0	1 1 3 6
607	1	0	0	1	0	1	1	1	1	1	1 1 3 7
608	1	0	0	1	1	0	0	0	0	0	1 1 4 0
609	1	0	0	1	1	0	0	0	0	1	1 1 4 1
610	1	0	0	1	1	0	0	0	1	0	1 1 4 2
611	1	0	0	1	1	0	0	0	1	1	1 1 4 3
612	1	0	0	1	1	0	0	1	0	0	1 1 4 4
613	1	0	0	1	1	0	0	1	0	1	1 1 4 5
614	1	0	0	1	1	0	0	1	1	0	1 1 4 6
615	1	0	0	1	1	0	0	1	1	1	1 1 4 7
616	1	0	0	1	1	0	1	0	0	0	1 1 5 0
617	1	0	0	1	1	0	1	0	0	1	1 1 5 1
618	1	0	0	1	1	0	1	0	1	0	1 1 5 2
619	1	0	0	1	1	0	1	0	1	1	1 1 5 3
620	1	0	0	1	1	0	1	1	0	0	1 1 5 4
621	1	0	0	1	1	0	1	1	0	1	1 1 5 5
622	1	0	0	1	1	0	1	1	1	0	1 1 5 6
623	1	0	0	1	1	0	1	1	1	1	1 1 5 7
624	1	0	0	1	1	1	0	0	0	0	1 1 6 0
625	1	0	0	1	1	1	0	0	0	1	1 1 6 1
626	1	0	0	1	1	1	0	0	1	0	1 1 6 2
627	1	0	0	1	1	1	0	0	1	1	1 1 6 3
628	1	0	0	1	1	1	0	1	0	0	1 1 6 4
629	1	0	0	1	1	1	0	1	0	1	1 1 6 5
630	1	0	0	1	1	1	0	1	1	0	1 1 6 6
631	1	0	0	1	1	1	0	1	1	1	1 1 6 7
632	1	0	0	1	1	1	1	0	0	0	1 1 7 0
633	1	0	0	1	1	1	1	0	0	1	1 1 7 1
634	1	0	0	1	1	1	1	0	1	0	1 1 7 2
635	1	0	0	1	1	1	1	0	1	1	1 1 7 3
636	1	0	0	1	1	1	1	1	0	0	1 1 7 4
637	1	0	0	1	1	1	1	1	0	1	1 1 7 5
638	1	0	0	1	1	1	1	1	1	0	1 1 7 6
639	1	0	0	1	1	1	1	1	1	1	1 1 7 7

DEC.	A_9	A_8	A_7	A_6	A_5	A_4	A_3	A_2	A_1	A_0	OCTAL
640	1	0	1	0	0	0	0	0	0	0	1 2 0 0
641	1	0	1	0	0	0	0	0	0	1	1 2 0 1
642	1	0	1	0	0	0	0	0	1	0	1 2 0 2
643	1	0	1	0	0	0	0	0	1	1	1 2 0 3
644	1	0	1	0	0	0	0	1	0	0	1 2 0 4
645	1	0	1	0	0	0	0	1	0	1	1 2 0 5
646	1	0	1	0	0	0	0	1	1	0	1 2 0 6
647	1	0	1	0	0	0	0	1	1	1	1 2 0 7
648	1	0	1	0	0	0	1	0	0	0	1 2 1 0
649	1	0	1	0	0	0	1	0	0	1	1 2 1 1
650	1	0	1	0	0	0	1	0	1	0	1 2 1 2
651	1	0	1	0	0	0	1	0	1	1	1 2 1 3
652	1	0	1	0	0	0	1	1	0	0	1 2 1 4
653	1	0	1	0	0	0	1	1	0	1	1 2 1 5
654	1	0	1	0	0	0	1	1	1	0	1 2 1 6
655	1	0	1	0	0	0	1	1	1	1	1 2 1 7
656	1	0	1	0	0	1	0	0	0	0	1 2 2 0
657	1	0	1	0	0	1	0	0	0	1	1 2 2 1
658	1	0	1	0	0	1	0	0	1	0	1 2 2 2
659	1	0	1	0	0	1	0	0	1	1	1 2 2 3
660	1	0	1	0	0	1	0	1	0	0	1 2 2 4
661	1	0	1	0	0	1	0	1	0	1	1 2 2 5
662	1	0	1	0	0	1	0	1	1	0	1 2 2 6
663	1	0	1	0	0	1	0	1	1	1	1 2 2 7
664	1	0	1	0	0	1	1	0	0	0	1 2 3 0
665	1	0	1	0	0	1	1	0	0	1	1 2 3 1
666	1	0	1	0	0	1	1	0	1	0	1 2 3 2
667	1	0	1	0	0	1	1	0	1	1	1 2 3 3
668	1	0	1	0	0	1	1	1	0	0	1 2 3 4
669	1	0	1	0	0	1	1	1	0	1	1 2 3 5
670	1	0	1	0	0	1	1	1	1	0	1 2 3 6
671	1	0	1	0	0	1	1	1	1	1	1 2 3 7
672	1	0	1	0	1	0	0	0	0	0	1 2 4 0
673	1	0	1	0	1	0	0	0	0	1	1 2 4 1
674	1	0	1	0	1	0	0	0	1	0	1 2 4 2
675	1	0	1	0	1	0	0	0	1	1	1 2 4 3
676	1	0	1	0	1	0	0	1	0	0	1 2 4 4
677	1	0	1	0	1	0	0	1	0	1	1 2 4 5
678	1	0	1	0	1	0	0	1	1	0	1 2 4 6
679	1	0	1	0	1	0	0	1	1	1	1 2 4 7
680	1	0	1	0	1	0	1	0	0	0	1 2 5 0
681	1	0	1	0	1	0	1	0	0	1	1 2 5 1
682	1	0	1	0	1	0	1	0	1	0	1 2 5 2
683	1	0	1	0	1	0	1	0	1	1	1 2 5 3
684	1	0	1	0	1	0	1	1	0	0	1 2 5 4
685	1	0	1	0	1	0	1	1	0	1	1 2 5 5
686	1	0	1	0	1	0	1	1	1	0	1 2 5 6
687	1	0	1	0	1	0	1	1	1	1	1 2 5 7
688	1	0	1	0	1	1	0	0	0	0	1 2 6 0
689	1	0	1	0	1	1	0	0	0	1	1 2 6 1
690	1	0	1	0	1	1	0	0	1	0	1 2 6 2
691	1	0	1	0	1	1	0	0	1	1	1 2 6 3
692	1	0	1	0	1	1	0	1	0	0	1 2 6 4
693	1	0	1	0	1	1	0	1	0	1	1 2 6 5
694	1	0	1	0	1	1	0	1	1	0	1 2 6 6
695	1	0	1	0	1	1	0	1	1	1	1 2 6 7
696	1	0	1	0	1	1	1	0	0	0	1 2 7 0
697	1	0	1	0	1	1	1	0	0	1	1 2 7 1
698	1	0	1	0	1	1	1	0	1	0	1 2 7 2
699	1	0	1	0	1	1	1	0	1	1	1 2 7 3
700	1	0	1	0	1	1	1	1	0	0	1 2 7 4
701	1	0	1	0	1	1	1	1	0	1	1 2 7 5
702	1	0	1	0	1	1	1	1	1	0	1 2 7 6
703	1	0	1	0	1	1	1	1	1	1	1 2 7 7

DEC.	A_9	A_8	A_7	A_6	A_5	A_4	A_3	A_2	A_1	A_0	OCTAL
704	1	0	1	1	0	0	0	0	0	0	1 3 0 0
705	1	0	1	1	0	0	0	0	0	1	1 3 0 1
706	1	0	1	1	0	0	0	0	1	0	1 3 0 2
707	1	0	1	1	0	0	0	0	1	1	1 3 0 3
708	1	0	1	1	0	0	0	1	0	0	1 3 0 4
709	1	0	1	1	0	0	0	1	0	1	1 3 0 5
710	1	0	1	1	0	0	0	1	1	0	1 3 0 6
711	1	0	1	1	0	0	0	1	1	1	1 3 0 7
712	1	0	1	1	0	0	1	0	0	0	1 3 1 0
713	1	0	1	1	0	0	1	0	0	1	1 3 1 1
714	1	0	1	1	0	0	1	0	1	0	1 3 1 2
715	1	0	1	1	0	0	1	0	1	1	1 3 1 3
716	1	0	1	1	0	0	1	1	0	0	1 3 1 4
717	1	0	1	1	0	0	1	1	0	1	1 3 1 5
718	1	0	1	1	0	0	1	1	1	0	1 3 1 6
719	1	0	1	1	0	0	1	1	1	1	1 3 1 7
720	1	0	1	1	0	1	0	0	0	0	1 3 2 0
721	1	0	1	1	0	1	0	0	0	1	1 3 2 1
722	1	0	1	1	0	1	0	0	1	0	1 3 2 2
723	1	0	1	1	0	1	0	0	1	1	1 3 2 3
724	1	0	1	1	0	1	0	1	0	0	1 3 2 4
725	1	0	1	1	0	1	0	1	0	1	1 3 2 5
726	1	0	1	1	0	1	0	1	1	0	1 3 2 6
727	1	0	1	1	0	1	0	1	1	1	1 3 2 7
728	1	0	1	1	0	1	1	0	0	0	1 3 3 0
729	1	0	1	1	0	1	1	0	0	1	1 3 3 1
730	1	0	1	1	0	1	1	0	1	0	1 3 3 2
731	1	0	1	1	0	1	1	0	1	1	1 3 3 3
732	1	0	1	1	0	1	1	1	0	0	1 3 3 4
733	1	0	1	1	0	1	1	1	0	1	1 3 3 5
734	1	0	1	1	0	1	1	1	1	0	1 3 3 6
735	1	0	1	1	0	1	1	1	1	1	1 3 3 7
736	1	0	1	1	1	0	0	0	0	0	1 3 4 0
737	1	0	1	1	1	0	0	0	0	1	1 3 4 1
738	1	0	1	1	1	0	0	0	1	0	1 3 4 2
739	1	0	1	1	1	0	0	0	1	1	1 3 4 3
740	1	0	1	1	1	0	0	1	0	0	1 3 4 4
741	1	0	1	1	1	0	0	1	0	1	1 3 4 5
742	1	0	1	1	1	0	0	1	1	0	1 3 4 6
743	1	0	1	1	1	0	0	1	1	1	1 3 4 7
744	1	0	1	1	1	0	1	0	0	0	1 3 5 0
745	1	0	1	1	1	0	1	0	0	1	1 3 5 1
746	1	0	1	1	1	0	1	0	1	0	1 3 5 2
747	1	0	1	1	1	0	1	0	1	1	1 3 5 3
748	1	0	1	1	1	0	1	1	0	0	1 3 5 4
749	1	0	1	1	1	0	1	1	0	1	1 3 5 5
750	1	0	1	1	1	0	1	1	1	0	1 3 5 6
751	1	0	1	1	1	0	1	1	1	1	1 3 5 7
752	1	0	1	1	1	1	0	0	0	0	1 3 6 0
753	1	0	1	1	1	1	0	0	0	1	1 3 6 1
754	1	0	1	1	1	1	0	0	1	0	1 3 6 2
755	1	0	1	1	1	1	0	0	1	1	1 3 6 3
756	1	0	1	1	1	1	0	1	0	0	1 3 6 4
757	1	0	1	1	1	1	0	1	0	1	1 3 6 5
758	1	0	1	1	1	1	0	1	1	0	1 3 6 6
759	1	0	1	1	1	1	0	1	1	1	1 3 6 7
760	1	0	1	1	1	1	1	0	0	0	1 3 7 0
761	1	0	1	1	1	1	1	0	0	1	1 3 7 1
762	1	0	1	1	1	1	1	0	1	0	1 3 7 2
763	1	0	1	1	1	1	1	0	1	1	1 3 7 3
764	1	0	1	1	1	1	1	1	0	0	1 3 7 4
765	1	0	1	1	1	1	1	1	0	1	1 3 7 5
766	1	0	1	1	1	1	1	1	1	0	1 3 7 6
767	1	0	1	1	1	1	1	1	1	1	1 3 7 7

DEC.	A_9	A_8	A_7	A_6	A_5	A_4	A_3	A_2	A_1	A_0	OCTAL
768	1	1	0	0	0	0	0	0	0	0	1 4 0 0
769	1	1	0	0	0	0	0	0	0	1	1 4 0 1
770	1	1	0	0	0	0	0	0	1	0	1 4 0 2
771	1	1	0	0	0	0	0	0	1	1	1 4 0 3
772	1	1	0	0	0	0	0	1	0	0	1 4 0 4
773	1	1	0	0	0	0	0	1	0	1	1 4 0 5
774	1	1	0	0	0	0	0	1	1	0	1 4 0 6
775	1	1	0	0	0	0	0	1	1	1	1 4 0 7
776	1	1	0	0	0	0	1	0	0	0	1 4 1 0
777	1	1	0	0	0	0	1	0	0	1	1 4 1 1
778	1	1	0	0	0	0	1	0	1	0	1 4 1 2
779	1	1	0	0	0	0	1	0	1	1	1 4 1 3
780	1	1	0	0	0	0	1	1	0	0	1 4 1 4
781	1	1	0	0	0	0	1	1	0	1	1 4 1 5
782	1	1	0	0	0	0	1	1	1	0	1 4 1 6
783	1	1	0	0	0	0	1	1	1	1	1 4 1 7
784	1	1	0	0	0	1	0	0	0	0	1 4 2 0
785	1	1	0	0	0	1	0	0	0	1	1 4 2 1
786	1	1	0	0	0	1	0	0	1	0	1 4 2 2
787	1	1	0	0	0	1	0	0	1	1	1 4 2 3
788	1	1	0	0	0	1	0	1	0	0	1 4 2 4
789	1	1	0	0	0	1	0	1	0	1	1 4 2 5
790	1	1	0	0	0	1	0	1	1	0	1 4 2 6
791	1	1	0	0	0	1	0	1	1	1	1 4 2 7
792	1	1	0	0	0	1	1	0	0	0	1 4 3 0
793	1	1	0	0	0	1	1	0	0	1	1 4 3 1
794	1	1	0	0	0	1	1	0	1	0	1 4 3 2
795	1	1	0	0	0	1	1	0	1	1	1 4 3 3
796	1	1	0	0	0	1	1	1	0	0	1 4 3 4
797	1	1	0	0	0	1	1	1	0	1	1 4 3 5
798	1	1	0	0	0	1	1	1	1	0	1 4 3 6
799	1	1	0	0	0	1	1	1	1	1	1 4 3 7
800	1	1	0	0	1	0	0	0	0	0	1 4 4 0
801	1	1	0	0	1	0	0	0	0	1	1 4 4 1
802	1	1	0	0	1	0	0	0	1	0	1 4 4 2
803	1	1	0	0	1	0	0	0	1	1	1 4 4 3
804	1	1	0	0	1	0	0	1	0	0	1 4 4 4
805	1	1	0	0	1	0	0	1	0	1	1 4 4 5
806	1	1	0	0	1	0	0	1	1	0	1 4 4 6
807	1	1	0	0	1	0	0	1	1	1	1 4 4 7
808	1	1	0	0	1	0	1	0	0	0	1 4 5 0
809	1	1	0	0	1	0	1	0	0	1	1 4 5 1
810	1	1	0	0	1	0	1	0	1	0	1 4 5 2
811	1	1	0	0	1	0	1	0	1	1	1 4 5 3
812	1	1	0	0	1	0	1	1	0	0	1 4 5 4
813	1	1	0	0	1	0	1	1	0	1	1 4 5 5
814	1	1	0	0	1	0	1	1	1	0	1 4 5 6
815	1	1	0	0	1	0	1	1	1	1	1 4 5 7
816	1	1	0	0	1	1	0	0	0	0	1 4 6 0
817	1	1	0	0	1	1	0	0	0	1	1 4 6 1
818	1	1	0	0	1	1	0	0	1	0	1 4 6 2
819	1	1	0	0	1	1	0	0	1	1	1 4 6 3
820	1	1	0	0	1	1	0	1	0	0	1 4 6 4
821	1	1	0	0	1	1	0	1	0	1	1 4 6 5
822	1	1	0	0	1	1	0	1	1	0	1 4 6 6
823	1	1	0	0	1	1	0	1	1	1	1 4 6 7
824	1	1	0	0	1	1	1	0	0	0	1 4 7 0
825	1	1	0	0	1	1	1	0	0	1	1 4 7 1
826	1	1	0	0	1	1	1	0	1	0	1 4 7 2
827	1	1	0	0	1	1	1	0	1	1	1 4 7 3
828	1	1	0	0	1	1	1	1	0	0	1 4 7 4
829	1	1	0	0	1	1	1	1	0	1	1 4 7 5
830	1	1	0	0	1	1	1	1	1	0	1 4 7 6
831	1	1	0	0	1	1	1	1	1	1	1 4 7 7

DEC.	A9	A8	A7	A6	A5	A4	A3	A2	A1	A0	OCTAL
832	1	1	0	1	0	0	0	0	0	0	1 5 0 0
833	1	1	0	1	0	0	0	0	0	1	1 5 0 1
834	1	1	0	1	0	0	0	0	1	0	1 5 0 2
835	1	1	0	1	0	0	0	0	1	1	1 5 0 3
836	1	1	0	1	0	0	0	1	0	0	1 5 0 4
837	1	1	0	1	0	0	0	1	0	1	1 5 0 5
838	1	1	0	1	0	0	0	1	1	0	1 5 0 6
839	1	1	0	1	0	0	0	1	1	1	1 5 0 7
840	1	1	0	1	0	0	1	0	0	0	1 5 1 0
841	1	1	0	1	0	0	1	0	0	1	1 5 1 1
842	1	1	0	1	0	0	1	0	1	0	1 5 1 2
843	1	1	0	1	0	0	1	0	1	1	1 5 1 3
844	1	1	0	1	0	0	1	1	0	0	1 5 1 4
845	1	1	0	1	0	0	1	1	0	1	1 5 1 5
846	1	1	0	1	0	0	1	1	1	0	1 5 1 6
847	1	1	0	1	0	0	1	1	1	1	1 5 1 7
848	1	1	0	1	0	1	0	0	0	0	1 5 2 0
849	1	1	0	1	0	1	0	0	0	1	1 5 2 1
850	1	1	0	1	0	1	0	0	1	0	1 5 2 2
851	1	1	0	1	0	1	0	0	1	1	1 5 2 3
852	1	1	0	1	0	1	0	1	0	0	1 5 2 4
853	1	1	0	1	0	1	0	1	0	1	1 5 2 5
854	1	1	0	1	0	1	0	1	1	0	1 5 2 6
855	1	1	0	1	0	1	0	1	1	1	1 5 2 7
856	1	1	0	1	0	1	1	0	0	0	1 5 3 0
857	1	1	0	1	0	1	1	0	0	1	1 5 3 1
858	1	1	0	1	0	1	1	0	1	0	1 5 3 2
859	1	1	0	1	0	1	1	0	1	1	1 5 3 3
860	1	1	0	1	0	1	1	1	0	0	1 5 3 4
861	1	1	0	1	0	1	1	1	0	1	1 5 3 5
862	1	1	0	1	0	1	1	1	1	0	1 5 3 6
863	1	1	0	1	0	1	1	1	1	1	1 5 3 7
864	1	1	0	1	1	0	0	0	0	0	1 5 4 0
865	1	1	0	1	1	0	0	0	0	1	1 5 4 1
866	1	1	0	1	1	0	0	0	1	0	1 5 4 2
867	1	1	0	1	1	0	0	0	1	1	1 5 4 3
868	1	1	0	1	1	0	0	1	0	0	1 5 4 4
869	1	1	0	1	1	0	0	1	0	1	1 5 4 5
870	1	1	0	1	1	0	0	1	1	0	1 5 4 6
871	1	1	0	1	1	0	0	1	1	1	1 5 4 7
872	1	1	0	1	1	0	1	0	0	0	1 5 5 0
873	1	1	0	1	1	0	1	0	0	1	1 5 5 1
874	1	1	0	1	1	0	1	0	1	0	1 5 5 2
875	1	1	0	1	1	0	1	0	1	1	1 5 5 3
876	1	1	0	1	1	0	1	1	0	0	1 5 5 4
877	1	1	0	1	1	0	1	1	0	1	1 5 5 5
878	1	1	0	1	1	0	1	1	1	0	1 5 5 6
879	1	1	0	1	1	0	1	1	1	1	1 5 5 7
880	1	1	0	1	1	1	0	0	0	0	1 5 6 0
881	1	1	0	1	1	1	0	0	0	1	1 5 6 1
882	1	1	0	1	1	1	0	0	1	0	1 5 6 2
883	1	1	0	1	1	1	0	0	1	1	1 5 6 3
884	1	1	0	1	1	1	0	1	0	0	1 5 6 4
885	1	1	0	1	1	1	0	1	0	1	1 5 6 5
886	1	1	0	1	1	1	0	1	1	0	1 5 6 6
887	1	1	0	1	1	1	0	1	1	1	1 5 6 7
888	1	1	0	1	1	1	1	0	0	0	1 5 7 0
889	1	1	0	1	1	1	1	0	0	1	1 5 7 1
890	1	1	0	1	1	1	1	0	1	0	1 5 7 2
891	1	1	0	1	1	1	1	0	1	1	1 5 7 3
892	1	1	0	1	1	1	1	1	0	0	1 5 7 4
893	1	1	0	1	1	1	1	1	0	1	1 5 7 5
894	1	1	0	1	1	1	1	1	1	0	1 5 7 6
895	1	1	0	1	1	1	1	1	1	1	1 5 7 7

DEC.	A9	A8	A7	A6	A5	A4	A3	A2	A1	A0	OCTAL
896	1	1	1	0	0	0	0	0	0	0	1 6 0 0
897	1	1	1	0	0	0	0	0	0	1	1 6 0 1
898	1	1	1	0	0	0	0	0	1	0	1 6 0 2
899	1	1	1	0	0	0	0	0	1	1	1 6 0 3
900	1	1	1	0	0	0	0	1	0	0	1 6 0 4
901	1	1	1	0	0	0	0	1	0	1	1 6 0 5
902	1	1	1	0	0	0	0	1	1	0	1 6 0 6
903	1	1	1	0	0	0	0	1	1	1	1 6 0 7
904	1	1	1	0	0	0	1	0	0	0	1 6 1 0
905	1	1	1	0	0	0	1	0	0	1	1 6 1 1
906	1	1	1	0	0	0	1	0	1	0	1 6 1 2
907	1	1	1	0	0	0	1	0	1	1	1 6 1 3
908	1	1	1	0	0	0	1	1	0	0	1 5 1 4
909	1	1	1	0	0	0	1	1	0	1	1 6 1 5
910	1	1	1	0	0	0	1	1	1	0	1 6 1 6
911	1	1	1	0	0	0	1	1	1	1	1 6 1 7
912	1	1	1	0	0	1	0	0	0	0	1 6 2 0
913	1	1	1	0	0	1	0	0	0	1	1 6 2 1
914	1	1	1	0	0	1	0	0	1	0	1 6 2 2
915	1	1	1	0	0	1	0	0	1	1	1 6 2 3
916	1	1	1	0	0	1	0	1	0	0	1 6 2 4
917	1	1	1	0	0	1	0	1	0	1	1 6 2 5
918	1	1	1	0	0	1	0	1	1	0	1 6 2 6
919	1	1	1	0	0	1	0	1	1	1	1 6 2 7
920	1	1	1	0	0	1	1	0	0	0	1 6 3 0
921	1	1	1	0	0	1	1	0	0	1	1 6 3 1
922	1	1	1	0	0	1	1	0	1	0	1 6 3 2
923	1	1	1	0	0	1	1	0	1	1	1 6 3 3
924	1	1	1	0	0	1	1	1	0	0	1 6 3 4
925	1	1	1	0	0	1	1	1	0	1	1 6 3 5
926	1	1	1	0	0	1	1	1	1	0	1 6 3 6
927	1	1	1	0	0	1	1	1	1	1	1 6 3 7
928	1	1	1	0	1	0	0	0	0	0	1 6 4 0
929	1	1	1	0	1	0	0	0	0	1	1 6 4 1
930	1	1	1	0	1	0	0	0	1	0	1 6 4 2
931	1	1	1	0	1	0	0	0	1	1	1 6 4 3
932	1	1	1	0	1	0	0	1	0	0	1 6 4 4
933	1	1	1	0	1	0	0	1	0	1	1 6 4 5
934	1	1	1	0	1	0	0	1	1	0	1 6 4 6
935	1	1	1	0	1	0	0	1	1	1	1 6 4 7
936	1	1	1	0	1	0	1	0	0	0	1 6 5 0
937	1	1	1	0	1	0	1	0	0	1	1 6 5 1
938	1	1	1	0	1	0	1	0	1	0	1 6 5 2
939	1	1	1	0	1	0	1	0	1	1	1 6 5 3
940	1	1	1	0	1	0	1	1	0	0	1 6 5 4
941	1	1	1	0	1	0	1	1	0	1	1 6 5 5
942	1	1	1	0	1	0	1	1	1	0	1 6 5 6
943	1	1	1	0	1	0	1	1	1	1	1 6 5 7
944	1	1	1	0	1	1	0	0	0	0	1 6 6 0
945	1	1	1	0	1	1	0	0	0	1	1 6 6 1
946	1	1	1	0	1	1	0	0	1	0	1 6 6 2
947	1	1	1	0	1	1	0	0	1	1	1 6 6 3
948	1	1	1	0	1	1	0	1	0	0	1 6 6 4
949	1	1	1	0	1	1	0	1	0	1	1 6 6 5
950	1	1	1	0	1	1	0	1	1	0	1 6 6 6
951	1	1	1	0	1	1	0	1	1	1	1 6 6 7
952	1	1	1	0	1	1	1	0	0	0	1 6 7 0
953	1	1	1	0	1	1	1	0	0	1	1 6 7 1
954	1	1	1	0	1	1	1	0	1	0	1 6 7 2
955	1	1	1	0	1	1	1	0	1	1	1 6 7 3
956	1	1	1	0	1	1	1	1	0	0	1 6 7 4
957	1	1	1	0	1	1	1	1	0	1	1 6 7 5
958	1	1	1	0	1	1	1	1	1	0	1 6 7 6
959	1	1	1	0	1	1	1	1	1	1	1 6 7 7

DEC.	A_9	A_8	A_7	A_6	A_5	A_4	A_3	A_2	A_1	A_0	OCTAL
960	1	1	1	1	0	0	0	0	0	0	1 7 0 0
961	1	1	1	1	0	0	0	0	0	1	1 7 0 1
962	1	1	1	1	0	0	0	0	1	0	1 7 0 2
963	1	1	1	1	0	0	0	0	1	1	1 7 0 3
964	1	1	1	1	0	0	0	1	0	0	1 7 0 4
965	1	1	1	1	0	0	0	1	0	1	1 7 0 5
966	1	1	1	1	0	0	0	1	1	0	1 7 0 6
967	1	1	1	1	0	0	0	1	1	1	1 7 0 7
968	1	1	1	1	0	0	1	0	0	0	1 7 1 0
969	1	1	1	1	0	0	1	0	0	1	1 7 1 1
970	1	1	1	1	0	0	1	0	1	0	1 7 1 2
971	1	1	1	1	0	0	1	0	1	1	1 7 1 3
972	1	1	1	1	0	0	1	1	0	0	1 7 1 4
973	1	1	1	1	0	0	1	1	0	1	1 7 1 5
974	1	1	1	1	0	0	1	1	1	0	1 7 1 6
975	1	1	1	1	0	0	1	1	1	1	1 7 1 7
976	1	1	1	1	0	1	0	0	0	0	1 7 2 0
977	1	1	1	1	0	1	0	0	0	1	1 7 2 1
978	1	1	1	1	0	1	0	0	1	0	1 7 2 2
979	1	1	1	1	0	1	0	0	1	1	1 7 2 3
980	1	1	1	1	0	1	0	1	0	0	1 7 2 4
981	1	1	1	1	0	1	0	1	0	1	1 7 2 5
982	1	1	1	1	0	1	0	1	1	0	1 7 2 6
983	1	1	1	1	0	1	0	1	1	1	1 7 2 7
984	1	1	1	1	0	1	1	0	0	0	1 7 3 0
985	1	1	1	1	0	1	1	0	0	1	1 7 3 1
986	1	1	1	1	0	1	1	0	1	0	1 7 3 2
987	1	1	1	1	0	1	1	0	1	1	1 7 3 3
988	1	1	1	1	0	1	1	1	0	0	1 7 3 4
989	1	1	1	1	0	1	1	1	0	1	1 7 3 5
990	1	1	1	1	0	1	1	1	1	0	1 7 3 6
991	1	1	1	1	0	1	1	1	1	1	1 7 3 7

DEC.	A_9	A_8	A_7	A_6	A_5	A_4	A_3	A_2	A_1	A_0	OCTAL
992	1	1	1	1	1	0	0	0	0	0	1 7 4 0
993	1	1	1	1	1	0	0	0	0	1	1 7 4 1
994	1	1	1	1	1	0	0	0	1	0	1 7 4 2
995	1	1	1	1	1	0	0	0	1	1	1 7 4 3
996	1	1	1	1	1	0	0	1	0	0	1 7 4 4
997	1	1	1	1	1	0	0	1	0	1	1 7 4 5
998	1	1	1	1	1	0	0	1	1	0	1 7 4 6
999	1	1	1	1	1	0	0	1	1	1	1 7 4 7
1000	1	1	1	1	1	0	1	0	0	0	1 7 5 0
1001	1	1	1	1	1	0	1	0	0	1	1 7 5 1
1002	1	1	1	1	1	0	1	0	1	0	1 7 5 2
1003	1	1	1	1	1	0	1	0	1	1	1 7 5 3
1004	1	1	1	1	1	0	1	1	0	0	1 7 5 4
1005	1	1	1	1	1	0	1	1	0	1	1 7 5 5
1006	1	1	1	1	1	0	1	1	1	0	1 7 5 6
1007	1	1	1	1	1	0	1	1	1	1	1 7 5 7
1008	1	1	1	1	1	1	0	0	0	0	1 7 6 0
1009	1	1	1	1	1	1	0	0	0	1	1 7 6 1
1010	1	1	1	1	1	1	0	0	1	0	1 7 6 2
1011	1	1	1	1	1	1	0	0	1	1	1 7 6 3
1012	1	1	1	1	1	1	0	1	0	0	1 7 6 4
1013	1	1	1	1	1	1	0	1	0	1	1 7 6 5
1014	1	1	1	1	1	1	0	1	1	0	1 7 6 6
1015	1	1	1	1	1	1	0	1	1	1	1 7 6 7
1016	1	1	1	1	1	1	1	0	0	0	1 7 7 0
1017	1	1	1	1	1	1	1	0	0	1	1 7 7 1
1018	1	1	1	1	1	1	1	0	1	0	1 7 7 2
1019	1	1	1	1	1	1	1	0	1	1	1 7 7 3
1020	1	1	1	1	1	1	1	1	0	0	1 7 7 4
1021	1	1	1	1	1	1	1	1	0	1	1 7 7 5
1022	1	1	1	1	1	1	1	1	1	0	1 7 7 6
1023	1	1	1	1	1	1	1	1	1	1	1 7 7 7

INDEX